Ivan Kondov, Gevorg Poghosyan, Ole Kirner, Olaf Schneider and Frank Schmitz (eds.)

Workshop
„Computational Methods in Science and Engineering" (SimLabs@KIT 2010)
Proceedings, Karlsruhe, Germany, November 29 – 30, 2010

Workshop
Computational Methods in Science and Engineering (SimLabs@KIT 2010)

Proceedings, Karlsruhe, Germany, November 29 – 30, 2010

edited by
Ivan Kondov, Gevorg Poghosyan, Ole Kirner,
Olaf Schneider and Frank Schmitz

Impressum

Karlsruher Institut für Technologie (KIT)
KIT Scientific Publishing
Straße am Forum 2
D-76131 Karlsruhe
www.ksp.kit.edu

KIT – Universität des Landes Baden-Württemberg und nationales
Forschungszentrum in der Helmholtz-Gemeinschaft

KIT Scientific Publishing 2011
Print on Demand

ISBN 978-3-86644-693-9

Contents

Preface

Computer simulation complements experiment and theory and has become essentially the third pillar in scientific research. Especially in natural sciences and engineering it is often indispensable for fundamental research and modern technological development.

The simulation laboratories (SimLabs) have been recently established at the Karlsruhe Institute of Technology (KIT) and the Research Center Jülich (FZJ) as an integrated part of the Helmholtz program "Supercomputing". The mission of the SimLabs is community-oriented research and support in specific scientific fields involving computer simulations and to act as links between the scientific communities and providers of computing and storage resources. Particularly, the SimLabs provide assistance in performing simulations on upcoming exaflop computers and on novel computer architectures, such as GPUs, and perform own research in close cooperation with scientific institutes through joint projects. The SimLabs located at the Steinbuch Centre for Computing (SCC) at KIT are named after the existing KIT Centers (Energy, NanoMikro, Elementary Particle and Astroparticle Physics, Climate and Environment) due to the thematic focus of the corresponding communities.

The workshop SimLabs@KIT in November 2011 gathered scientific communities using computer simulations in their research. In particular, users of high performance computing (HPC) and data intensive computing (DIC), as well as groups developing numerical methods participated at the workshop. The participants reviewed the advancements in the respective scientific areas, collected new ideas, shared experience in the application area of HPC and also addressed their requirements to the SimLabs regarding HPC resources and support. In addition, the workshop was an opportunity to introduce the SimLabs at KIT to the broader public.

In this volume we provide a compilation of the major contributions at the workshop equally covering applications from different research fields and ranging from capacity up to capability computing. Besides classical computing aspects such as parallelization, the focus of these proceedings is on multiscale approaches and methods for tackling algorithm and data complexity. Also practical aspects regarding the usage of the HPC infrastructure and available tools and software at the SCC are presented.

We cordially thank all workshop participants and the authors for their presentations at the meeting and the preparing of the camera-ready proceeding papers. We hope that with this workshop we have established a series of continuous events to bring together the research and computing communities to review the progress in the respective scientific fields.

Karlsruhe, May 2011

Ivan Kondov
Gevorg Poghosyan
Ole Kirner
Olaf Schneider
Frank Schmitz

Multiscale materials and biomolecular simulations at Simulation Lab NanoMikro

Ivan Kondov[1], Robert Maul, Konstantin Klenin, Martin Brieg, Angela Poschlad,

Alexej Bagrets, Velimir Meded, Stefan Bozic

Steinbuch Centre for Computing, Karlsruhe Institute of Technology
Hermann-von-Helmholtz-Platz 1, 76344 Eggenstein-Leopoldshafen, Germany
[1]E-mail: ivan.kondov@kit.edu

Abstract

Recently, the Simulation Lab NanoMikro at Steinbuch Centre for Computing (SCC) has been established as a connecting link between computing centers and the communities of computational materials science and nanoscience. By pooling expertise in high performance computing as well as providing high-level services and support, the Simulation Lab has assisted scientific groups in these communities in development and deployment of scientific simulation codes. In this proceeding we provide an introduction to Simulation Lab NanoMikro and an overview of our topics of research.

1 The nanoscience community at KIT: Center NanoMikro

Two major structures from the Karlsruhe Institute of Technology (KIT) research environment have governed the thematic orientation of Simulation Lab NanoMikro. On the one hand side this is the DFG Center for Functional Nanostructures (CFN) [1] at the former University of Karlsruhe, on the other the Helmholtz program "NanoMikro" [2]. Today, these two communities together form the KIT Nano- and Microscale research and technology center (Center NanoMikro).

As the other Simulation Labs at SCC and at Jülich Supercomputing Centre (JSC), our Simulation Lab is part of the current program "Supercomputing" of the Helmholtz association. Nevertheless, the Lab has emerged earlier from numerous cooperations with this community during the predecessor program, particularly within the CampusGrid project in which two user workshops (in 2007 and 2009) took place and yielded very positive feedback. The Simulation Lab is now an essential part of this cooperation network at KIT and participates actively in the scientific research process of the community.

2 R&D activities

Our activities were not limited to classical computing center support. Rather we are involved in specific research topics and commit substantial resources in joint R&D projects. The R&D activities consist of three major areas: high performance computing, methods development and integration of simulation software and services. It will be shown in the following that these three areas are interrelated and have common aspects.

2.1 High performance computing

The HPC activities include mostly classical tasks of a computing center – porting to new architectures, performance optimization and parallelization of currently deployed code in the community. Recently, our efforts are focused on porting of developed codes (e.g. POEM, TURBOMOLE) to GPU and hybrid CPU/GPU architectures. In various consultations and workshops we help the groups to find suitable resources (at KIT or elsewhere) for their specific applications and get access at optimal conditions.

2.2 Method development

The team of the Simulation Lab works closely together with their partner groups, mainly from KIT, to develop and implement novel methods and thus to add new features in existing software. In the following we will outline some of them.

2.2.1 Methods for protein simulation

In the field of protein folding and structure prediction we develop biophysical methods based on a transferable protein force field PFF02 and efficient folding algorithms for distributed computer architectures. These methods are implemented in the code POEM++. A challenge that we currently address is the development of high-throughput approaches of high prediction quality for proteins with low sequence similarity compared to already resolved proteins. Recently, extension of the methodology has been performed combining the physics-based model with techniques from bioinformatics [3]. The code POEM++ has been recently supplemented with routines to treat disulfide bridges in proteins [4, 5].

If only the native structure of a protein is of interest the simulation of the folding process using e.g. molecular dynamics is too computationally demanding. The approach adopted in POEM++ identifies these structures by searching the minimum of the free energy landscape of a given protein, which according to the thermodynamic hypothesis [6] corresponds to the native structure. Our involvement in this project focuses on the development of new models for the PFF02 force field [7], which maps protein structures to their free energy. Of particular interest are solvent and electrostatic interactions, since they are the most computationally demanding. Another aspect of our work is porting these coded models to GPU architectures to fully use the resources which are provided by the distributed computing project POEM@HOME [8].

The computational effort of biomolecular simulations can be significantly reduced by means of implicit solvent models in which the energy generally contains a correction depending on the surface area and/or the volume of the molecule. We derived exact, easy-to-use analytical formulas for the latter quantities and their derivatives with respect to atomic coordinates. In addition, we developed an efficient, linear-scaling algorithm for the construction of the power diagram required for practical implementation of these formulas [9]. Recently, our approach was implemented for practical application in a C++ header-only template library. This library is used in the POEM++ program package. This method is particularly suitable for special architectures with low memory bandwidth like GPUs.

2.2.2 Global optimization methods

Many fields of scientific simulation need efficient methods for global optimization, i.e. the search for the global minimum or maximum of an objective function. For example, in protein structure prediction (see Section 2.2.1) the objective function is the free energy of the protein as a function of the atomic coordinates (all-atom protein force field). The computational complexity of global optimization is non-polynomial, i.e. the effort for solution increases dramatically with the dimension of the objective function. This is why, rigorous direct methods, e.g. such using interval arithmetic or branch-and-bound algorithms are limited to relatively small problems and, to solve problems with hundreds or thousands degrees of freedom, approximate stochastic and meta-heuristic methods have to be employed (see Ref. 10 for a recent review of all methods). To this end, we have recently implemented the particle swarm method [11] and tested it for applications from the field of protein structure prediction. The method is parallelized with MPI and now available in the C++ library ArFlock.

2.2.3 Methods for morphology simulation

Modeling of extended molecular morphologies of organic materials requires simulation methods which cover processes at long time scales and overcome the limitations of molecular dynamics. In the past period we have implemented new features into our Metropolis Monte Carlo implementation DEPOSIT for molecular deposition simulation of organic thin films [12]. To take intra-molecular rearrangement of the molecular constituents into account, we have integrated internal rotational degrees of freedom of the molecules using classical dihedral potentials. In addition, we have implemented a local relaxation scheme to take structural relaxation in the surrounding of the attached molecule into account. This method was recently integrated into a workflow and employed in simulations of OLEDs (see Sections 3 and 5).

2.2.4 Density functional theory

In the field of first-principles electronic structure calculations, an accurate and efficient modeling of the dispersion van der Waals (vdW) interactions remained so far a challenging computational problem. Our recent initiative aims towards an implementation, as a post-processing tool to the existing density functional codes, of the non-local vdW density functional (vdW-DF) [13] which has been applied recently to several vdW systems with encouraging success. The promising method is based on the formally exact adiabatic-connection fluctuation-dissipation theorem and expresses the non-local correlation energy, as a double spatial integral, which evaluation, however, is computationally demanding.

We are following an efficient approach [14] exploiting a factorization of the integration kernel with a subsequent use of the fast Fourier transform, which reduces a computational cost from $O(N^2)$ to $O(N \log N)$ operations, where N is a number of grid points to represent the electron density. We expect that the developed tool enables rigorous modeling, e.g., of the structure and transport properties of metal/organic interfaces, which is in the focus of the developing field of molecular electronics.

2.3 Integration of simulation software and high-level services

Most recently, the team got involved in the challenging area of simulation software integration and developing high-level e-infrastructures-based services in order to enable the faster uptake of existing productive e-infrastructures, such as EGI, DEISA and PRACE, by diverse and demanding applications of the community. The services that we will establish will tackle the quickly increasing complexity of simulation protocols. This increased complexity is due to the fact that modern materials require modeling comprising several individual methods and codes used in a certain sequence (workflow). On the other hand the data exchanged between these different codes has to be handled "on the fly" using automated pre-, postprocessors and wrappers, or standard data formats. In Section 5, we will give more insight into this R&D area.

3 Application areas

Our applications and areas of cooperation are thematically related to highly prioritized topics in the program NanoMikro, KIT Center NanoMikro, CFN and European research agenda.

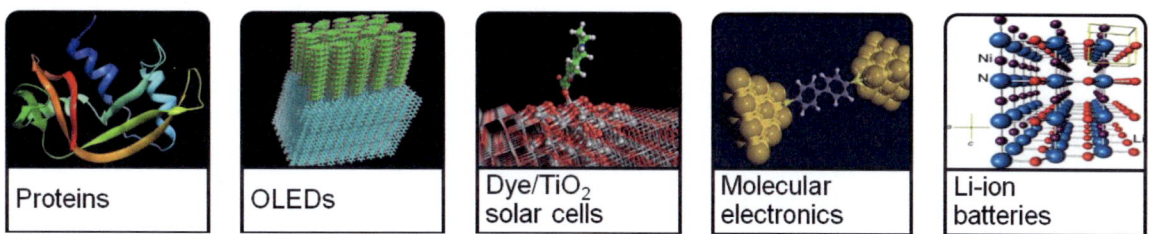

Figure 1: Examples of application of interest.

3.1 Protein folding and structure prediction

Since knowing the three dimensional structure of a protein is one of the key requirements for understanding its function, the folding process and the prediction of the folded structure are subject to intense research. Besides methods from bioinformatics, that require knowledge of structures of similar proteins, physics-based methods have gained a lot of attention. For studying dynamical processes like protein folding, molecular dynamics simulations are commonly employed. By using a classical force field, which is modeled to capture the relevant physical interactions while remaining computationally feasible, the dynamics of proteins can be studied at atomic detail. Only recently, all-atom molecular dynamics was used to successfully fold proteins, such as FiP35 and villin, from completely extended conformations in all-atom molecular dynamics simulations on the millisecond time scale conducted on a special-purpose computer [15].

However, the stochastic and meta-heuristic search techniques combined with the transferable all-atom protein force field PFF02 implemented in the code POEM (see Section 2.2.1) are still the methods of choice for protein structure prediction, i.e. to find the native structure starting with knowledge of the amino-acid sequence and bypassing the actual folding process. A series of proteins could be simulated starting from extended conformations obtaining their native conformations [16] and, using the IBM Glue Gene, larger proteins could be simulated within a single day [17]. In particular beta-sheet proteins as well as proteins with mixed alpha-helix and beta-sheet secondary structures [18] or disulfide bridges could be simulated with success [4, 5]. Recent studies employed GPUs to perform simulations and made the methods affordable for very large proteins [19].

3.2 Systems for charge storage, charge transport and energy conversion

3.2.1 Li-ion batteries

Lithium (Li)-ion batteries are a type of rechargeable battery, currently a very popular technological choice because of their high energy-to-weight ratios and slow self-discharge when not in use. Some work has already been reported on the calculation of the electrode materials properties, based on first principles calculations, e.g. employing density functional theory (DFT). Until now, there is a lack of up-scaling of these atomistic data into elementary kinetic models that would allow predicting the batteries' electrochemical behavior. Together with our international partners [20] we evaluate the physicochemical properties (e.g. Li-ion activation barriers) using DFT simulations of relevant electrode materials for Li-ion batteries, which are to be used as illustrative examples of our multi-scale modeling methodology. Furthermore, we propose a physical methodology to scale up the atomistic data from the DFT step into elementary kinetic models; physical and mathematical description of the electrochemical double layer as well as electrochemical elementary steps far from thermodynamic equilibrium conditions, including Li-ion intercalation mechanisms and solid electrolyte interface (SEI) degradation.

3.2.2 Molecular wires / molecular electronics

Switchable nanojunctions based on functional molecules or nanowires are interesting for the development of novel electronic devices in alternative to the conventional silicon-based micro-electronics. In cooperation with an experimental group from the CFN we have investigated the influence of thermally activated single-atom fluctuations in silver nanojunctions [21]. In this project we made use of recently implemented features in our code DEPOSIT (see Section 2.2.3). Moreover, our multiscale approach for the description of the electrolyte surrounding of the nanojunction gave new insights into the electrochemical properties of the device.

3.2.3 Organic Light Emitting Diodes (OLEDs)

Organic materials have promising features for application in novel field effect transistors, light emitting diodes, and solar cells. These devices consist of a large number of different organic layers (typically 5-20). Here we investigate the interface morphologies of so called SMOLEDs (small molecule OLEDs) which have huge influence on energetic activation barriers and charge carrier mobility in the device. To capture the statistics of the system it is necessary to take a sufficiently large simulation box into account containing about $2 \cdot 10^4$ atoms. Our results serve as input data for electrostatics and quantum chemistry calculations of our partners in the European project 'MINOTOR' [22].

3.2.4 Dye–semiconductor interfaces

Photoinduced electron transfer (ET) at dye–semiconductor interfaces is the key step of photonic energy conversion in solar cells (photovoltaics). Photoinduced ET is an ultrafast process on the femtosecond scale and hence the electronic population dynamics, the role of surface states as well as effects of electronic-vibrational couplings are of particular interest. In a recent study [23] we investigated the system alizarin–TiO_2 using first-principles (DFT) electronic structure calculations on atomistic finite and infinite cluster models to characterize the system and to parameterize a model Hamiltonian including electronic-vibrational coupling. On the basis of this modeling procedure, accurate quantum dynamical simulations were performed employing the multilayer multi-configurational time-dependent Hartree method.

The results of the simulations have shown that the electron injection process takes place on an ultrafast femtosecond timescale and is accompanied by significant electronic coherence effects. A detailed analysis has revealed that the electron-transfer process proceeds via a two-step mechanism involving an intermediate state localized at the dye–substrate interface [23].

4 Support

Besides research and development the Simulation Lab NanoMikro provides support on different program codes that are employed widely in many groups at KIT. Due to providing support for both users and code developers we can accelerate the transfer of new codes or functionalities to the user communities and convey feedback to developers efficiently. In order to provide a single point for access we employ the Service Desk of SCC [24] to gather and process support requests.

5 Integration of simulation software and higher-level services

Computational materials science plays an essential role for development of products with novel properties (examples: catalysis, semiconductors, alloys etc.). Nevertheless, next generation materials exhibit increasing complexity and multiscale structure. Also "classical" systems like the biological cell and its building blocks include structures on many length scales. Thus the physical models and the simulation protocols employ many different well established methods and different codes to treat the steps in these protocols. However, the lack of integration of these individual codes, the increasing complexity of models and need of distributed HPC resources reduces industrial usability of the methods. In addition, joint effort of groups providing expertise for all different methods is needed. These aspects are treated within the project MMM@HPC [20] in which we bring together scientists from industry and academia into a unified community which is able to use the e-infrastructure to solve modern real-life problems. The main requirements of (nano)material scientists for the developed infrastructure and our solution approaches will be summarized in the following.

5.1 Reusable interfaces and workflows

For implementation of application interfaces we adopted GridBeans [25] which is a modern technology for seamless integration taking advantage of modern grid middleware, such as UNICORE or Globus. On the other hand, the application protocols are mapped onto scientific workflows containing individual application interfaces (GridBeans). Every GridBean provides a graphical user interface and can be readily included into different workflows without further modifications. Moreover, the workflows created for one specific task can be reused in other simulations with minor parametric modifications.

5.2 Robust tools and standards for data exchange between individual codes

In the field of materials modeling a variety of data formats are used and virtually every individual code has its own non-standard input and output formats. Thus, we aim to enhance data interoperability of individual GridBeans employing the Chemical Markup Language (CML) standard and work together with experienced developers from other projects, such as UNICORE and Open-MolGRID.

OpenMolGRID is an extendable framework for the collaboration of individual codes originally used in molecular science. For each supported code a specific adaptor translates the input/output data into CML. With GridBeans based on OpenMolGRID it's easy to define workflows because the framework handles automatically the translation to the individual data formats. Additionally GridBeans based on the framework has a graphical user interface that is common in look and feel.

5.3 Solutions for licensing issues

Unfortunately, many of the simulation codes used in the community are provided under non-free (proprietary) licenses. Hence there must be a mechanism that controls access to commercial software in a multi user environment. With UNICORE Virtual Organizations Systems (UVOS) and Security Assertion Markup Language (SAML) techniques exist to handle this requirement. The concept of virtual organization (VO) is used to group all persons which are authorized to use a licensed code. The VOs are managed on a server which is able to issue assertion tokens to the restricted software. These authorization tokens will be checked to allow access to the restricted codes.

All requirements outlined above pose a great challenge for both code developers and providers of e-infrastructures and are therefore a subject of active development. In addition, the following properties are of great importance, however, implemented in state-of-the-art e-infrastructures: (1) Security and reliability: Industrial applications need secure handling (communication, storage) of simulation data. Additionally, the storage, the connection and the processes must be error-tolerant and thus reliable. All these are implemented properties of the underlying generic e-infrastructures and they are reused in our approach. (2) Capacity (high throughput) and capability (high performance): Applications addressed in the community are particularly demanding with regard to computing and storage resources. This is why, the scalable deployment of the application services requires linking to HPC and distributed resources, e.g. such as those provided in the projects EGI and PRACE.

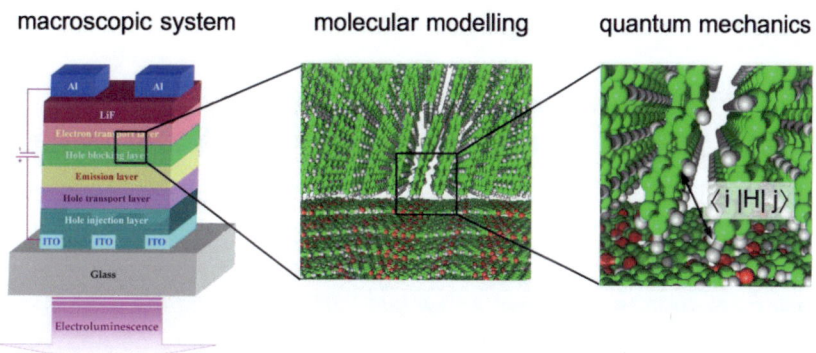

Figure 2: Multiscale modeling of an OLED.

At the end of the paper, we present in Figure 2 a model of an Organic Light Emitting Diode (OLED) in order to illustrate the concept of multiscale modeling. This OLED model requires treatment on different size scales using different code types – quantum mechanics, molecular mechanics, kinetic Monte Carlo (coarse-grained method) and finite element analysis (continuous method). Two of the interfaces are shown on the figure. We aim genericity of the developed workflow so that we consider several different codes that can perform one specific step in the simulation protocol. Some of the codes employed for the different scales are summarized in the table. Our code selection criteria are maturity, open accessibility, high parallel performance, and availability of expertise by partners.

Acknowledgement

We thank the SCC directorial board and F. Schmitz for continuously supporting us, our project partners G. Schön (CFN), W. Wenzel (INT), F. Evers (TKM), F. Weigend (ICP), K.-P. Bohnen and R. Heid (IFP) from KIT, O. Zimmermann (JSC, Jülich), M. Thoss (U. Erlangen) and the Helmholtz Association for basic funding within Program "Supercomputing".

References

[1]   DFG Center for Functional Nanostructures, URL: http://cfn.kit.edu.

[2]   HGF Program NanoMikro, URL: http://www.nmp.kit.edu.

[3]   P. Anand, T. Strunk, I. Meliciani, M. Brieg, M. Wolf, K. Klenin and W. Wenzel, Performance of an All-Atom Free-Energy Approach for Protein Structure Prediction, CASP 9 Abstract Book p. 195, URL: http://predictioncenter.org/casp9/doc/Abstracts.pdf.

[4]   Kondov, I.; Verma, A. & Wenzel, Folding and Structure Prediction of Proteins Containing Disulfide Bridges, In: *NIC Series: From Computational Biophysics to Systems Biology (CBSB07)*, W. Hansmann, U. H. E.; Meinke, J.; Mohanty, S. & Zimmermann, O. (ed.) , John von Neumann Institute for Computing, Vol. 36, 185 (2007).

[5]   Kondov, I.; Verma, A. & Wenzel, W., Folding Path and Funnel Scenarios for Two Small Disulfide-Bridged Proteins, Biochem. 48, 8195-8205 (2009).

[6]   Christian B. Anfinsen, Principles that Govern the Folding of Protein Chains, Science 181, 223-230 (1973).

[7]   A. Verma and W. Wenzel, A free-energy approach for all-atom protein simulation, Biophys. J. 96, 3483-3494 (2009).

[8]   POEM@HOME, URL: http://boinc.fzk.de/poem/.

[9]   K. Klenin, F. Tristram, T. Strunk, W. Wenzel, Derivatives of molecular surface area and volume: Simple and exact analytical formulas (submitted to J. Comp. Chem.).

[10] Floudas, C. and Gounaris, C., A review of recent advances in global optimization, J. Glob. Opt. 45, 3-38 (2009).

[11] Kennedy, J. and Eberhart, R., Particle swarm optimization, In Proceedings of IEEE International Conference on Neural Networks, 1995, p. 1942 (1995).

[12] F.-Q. Xie, R. Maul, A. Augenstein, Ch. Obermair, E.B. Starikov, W. Wenzel, G. Schön, and Th. Schimmel, Independently switchable atomic transistors with predefined quantum conductance by reversible contact reconstruction, Nano Lett. 8, 4493 (2008).

[13] M. Dion, H. Rydberg, E. Schröder, D. C. Langreth, and B. I. Lundqvist, Van der Waals Density Functional for General Geometries, Phys. Rev. Lett. 92, 246401 (2004).

[14] Guillermo Román-Pérez and José M. Soler, Efficient Implementation of a van derWaals Density Functional: Application to Double-Wall Carbon Nanotubes, Phys. Rev. Lett. 103, 096102 (2009).

[15] Shaw, D. E.; Maragakis, P.; Lindorff-Larsen, K.; Piana, S.; Dror, R. O.; Eastwood, M. P.; Bank, J. A.; Jumper, J. M.; Salmon, J. K.; Shan, Y. & Wriggers, W., Atomic-Level Characterization of the Structural Dynamics of Proteins, Science 330, 341-346 (2010).

[16] Verma, A. & Wenzel, W. Protein structure prediction by all-atom free-energy refinement, BMC Struct. Biol. 7, 12 (2007).

[17] Verma, A.; Gopal, S. M.; Schug, A.; Oh, J. S.; Klenin, K. V.; Lee, K. H. and Wenzel W., Massively Parallel All Atom Protein Folding in a Single Day, In: Parallel Computing: Architectures, Algorithms and Applications, W. Bischof, C.; B¨ucker, M.; Gibbon, P.; Joubert, G.; Lippert, T.; Mohr, B. & Peters, F. (ed.), Vol. 38, p. 527-534 (2007).

[18] Strunk, T.; Verma, A.; Gopal, S. M.; Schug, A.; Klenin, K. and Wenzel W., De Novo Protein Folding with Distributed Computational Resources, In: *Multiscale Simulation Methods in Molecular Sciences (Lecture notes)*, W. Grotendorst, J.; Attig, N.; Blügel, S. & Marx, D. (ed.), Vol. 42, 397-420 (2009).

[19] T. Strunk, M. Wolf, and W. Wenzel, Development and evaluation of a GPU-optimized N-body term for the simulation of biomolecules, *ibid*.

[20] Project MMM@HPC: Multiscale Materials Modelling on High Performance Computer Architectures, URL: http://www.multiscale-modelling.eu.

[21] R. Maul, F.-Q. Xie, Ch. Obermair, I. Bâldea, H. Köppel, G. Schön, Th. Schimmel, and W. Wenzel, Direct in-situ observation of single atom processes in reconstructions of metallic point contacts (submitted to Advanced Materials).

[22] Project MINOTOR: Modelling of electronic processes at interfaces in organic-based electronic devices, URL: http://www.materianova.be/minotor/.

[23] J. Li, I. Kondov, H. Wang, and M. Thoss., Theoretical Study of Photoinduced Electron-Transfer Processes in the Dye−Semiconductor System Alizarin-TiO_2, J. Phys. Chem. C 114, 18481 (2010).

[24] SCC Service Desk, URL: http://www.scc.kit.edu/hotline.

[25] R. Ratering, A. Lukichev, M. Riedel, D. Mallmann, A. Vanni, C. Cacciari, S. Lanzarini, K. Benedyczak, M. Borcz, R. Kluszcynski, P. Bala, G. Ohme, GridBeans: Support e-Science and Grid Applications, Proceedings of the Second IEEE International Conference on e-Science and Grid Computing (e-Science'06), p. 45, IEEE 2006.

Trends in HPC Biomolecular Simulations of Proteins and RNA

Alexander Schug

Department of Chemistry, University of Umeå, Linnaeus väg 10, 90187 Umeå, Sweden
E-mail: alexander.schug@chem.umu.se

Abstract

Proteins and RNA form the biomolecular machinery in a cell. Valuable insight into the relationship between their structure and function has been gained from computer simulations using techniques like molecular dynamics (MD), which have established themselves as a complementary tool to experimental observations. Many interesting biological processes like protein folding occur on the millisecond to second timescales while the feasible timescales even on large supercomputers are often limited to, at most, a few microseconds of simulation time. This limit is being steadily pushed by the exploration of novel computing platforms like GPU computing or ANTON, advanced sampling techniques, the use of distributed computing, or coarse-graining the simulations and adjusting the level of detail to the biological question at hand. Specific recent examples range from the huge Ribosome to protein complexes like two-component signal transduction systems to RNA-systems like riboswitches and illustrate how simulations of different complexity explain biomolecular behavior.

1   Introduction

Proteins and RNAs are the molecular workhorses in cells, responsible for a wide range of biological tasks as diverse as genetic regulation, oxygen transport, signal transduction, and muscle function. Computer simulations act as a valuable tool in investigating and understanding these biomolecules, as they can access regimes outside the experimental resolution complementing existing data. Also, biomolecules are far from the static, idealized visualization suggested by, for example, rendered protein pictures but are in constant motion. Also, it is important to note that not only the actual biomolecules but also the surrounding solvent (in general water) must be treated. The challenge in simulations is modeling the system realistically yet sufficiently simplified to make simulating biologically relevant timescales computationally tractable.

Two main families of simulation techniques are Molecular Dynamics (MD, for recent reviews see [1, 2]) and Monte Carlo (MC, some exemplary techniques [3-8]). MC neglects the time evolution of the biomolecular system and aims at an efficient sampling of the underlying energy landscape to calculate thermodynamic properties. Sophisticated sampling schemes have been devised to rapidly explore the conformational space and characterize its free-energy landscape [9]. For example in *in-silico* drug design, one can forego the dynamics of the system, i.e. the development of the system over time, entirely, to identify the energetically most stable conformation and gain a static description of the pharmaceutically relevant complex. In contrast MD simulates the time development by integrating over many short time intervals (usually on the order of femtoseconds) and results in a trajectory. A major challenge in MD is reaching biologically relevant timescales, as current simulations are typically limited to a few microseconds, well below the timescale where conformational transitions associated with function occur.

By adjusting the level of detail in the simulations, one can reduce computational demands. In general, one condenses the quantum-mechanical effects dominating molecular interactions into so-called classical force fields. The range of choices includes, on the highly detailed side, mixed quantum-mechanical/molecular-mechanical approaches, all-atom resolved force-fields and, on the coarse-grained side, groups of atoms or parts of molecules (for example amino-acids for proteins) collapsed into single beads. Another factor is the simulation technique. To simulate the dynamics of the entire docking process or large-scale conformational change, one has to integrate the equations of motion. Even simulations covering only a few microseconds, a time well below typical biologically relevant timescales, require for small-sized proteins the use of very large HPC resources. Several approaches attempt to overcome these challenges: Baring hardware improvements, better software implementations reduce the amount of inter-processor communication and increase the number of CPUs which can be efficiently utilized. Advanced simulation schemes concentrate the simulations on (rare) events of interest by applying an external bias on the simulation or simulating the system in parallel at different temperatures. In distributed computing schemes, one combines information from an arbitrary number of simulations into a single trajectory. Both simulation methods and the exploration of novel HPC computing architectures have made significant progress in recent years. A particular notable example is ANTON, a novel specialized supercomputer which has recently enabled the first MD simulation on the millisecond timescale [10].

2 Reaching the Millisecond Timescale in Molecular Dynamics: Parallel Computing, Distributed Computing, and Novel Hardware Architectures

Given the ongoing astonishing growth of computational resources, one would assume that computer simulations of biomolecular systems should be easily able to reach on HPC arbitrarily long timescales by simply using a sufficient number of cores and partitioning the system accordingly. There are, however, limits to the number of subunits efficiently contributing to a simulation. The main reasons for this lack of scalability are ubiquitous long-range interactions, in particular electrostatics, which result in high amounts of network communication. Elaborate schemes focus on more efficient methods of calculation of such long-range interactions. Frequently used techniques like Particle Mesh Ewald [11] are based on the Ewald summation and split the calculation into a short-ranged sum in real-space and a long-range sum in Fourier-space. Improved parallelization protocols reduce network traffic and enable many cores to efficiently contribute to the simulation [12, 13]. It was found, that better organization of MPI calls (Message Passing Interface) avoids bottlenecks of network communication and can result in up to tenfold faster simulations [14].

Instead of using centralized HPC resources, *distributed computing* approaches like FOLD-ING@HOME [15, 16] or POEM@HOME use heterogeneous computers connected by the Internet. Instead of partitioning the system itself into spatial subunits which results in high amounts of network communication at each time step, they aim at partitioning the entire simulation into small "sub simulations" which can be quickly calculated on a single computer, requiring communication just before and after the calculations. Participants donate unused computing time on their home computers and acquire via screensavers computing packages from a central server, calculate their task and return the results to the server. In MD the individual simulations are short and need to be re-assembled into larger trajectories. Similar approaches have been shown to be highly effective in MC minimization scaling up to thousands of cores [17].

Novel computing hardware offers another avenue of speeding up simulations. Graphic Processing Units (GPUs) and Cell cores [18, 19] are examples for specialized hardware, which have been adopted from entertainment electronics for use in scientific computations. While they are faster than traditional CPUs (for example a NVIDIA Tesla C2050 GPU offers 1 TFLOPS, Intel Core i7 980 XE 100 GFLOPS), they are challenging to program due to limited memory and slow-downs on conditional jumps. In 2008 the combination of CPUs with GPUs in a hybrid approach, lead to the HPC Roadrunner (Los Alamos National Laboratory) which was first on the TOP500 list of supercomputers and has been used for simulations of the Ribosome with explicit water (3.2 Mio atoms) [20], which is so far the largest MD simulation. So far the longest simulation with 1 millisecond has been performed on ANTON, a specialized computing platform for MD simulations [10].

3 Empirical and Coarse-Grained Force Field Development

Developing force fields for molecular simulations is a challenging task as atomic quantum-mechanical interactions are condensed into the terms of a classical force field and balance a detailed accurate description of the system against computational feasibility. A typical empirical force field is based on the Born-Oppenheimer approximation and sums over terms associated with chemical bonds, angles, dihedrals, the van-der-Waals interaction and an electrostatic potential [21, 22]. An important question is the treatment of solvent and both explicit and implicit water models are used [23, 24]. While the former describe the surrounding solvent in higher detail, the latter can reduce computational demands significantly and have been found sufficient for many requirements.

Of special interest is the transferability of force fields between different systems [25, 26]. Particular parameterizations often possess a bias towards specific secondary structure elements like helices or beta-sheets. While at the beginning of this decade force fields showed transferability between different similar proteins [27-29], they typically had a bias towards helical content [30]. It is therefore encouraging, that recent force fields report progress of incorporating different secondary structure elements for the same parameterization [10, 29]. Still, these empirical force fields are computationally demanding. Improvements in accelerated sampling techniques allow to effectively increase the sampled time by introducing biasing potentials to focus on rare events as conformational transitions and mathematically adjusting for the bias [31, 32].

Another venue of research aims at lowering computational demands by the use of simplified coarse-grained (CG) models to study biomolecular systems [33-38]. Many interesting systems are large (several Mio atoms) and undergo processes on the timescale of milliseconds or slower. CG models aim at identifying the essential and minimal set of variables required to describe such systems realistically. For example in protein folding, typical models based on energy landscape theory [39-41] treat each amino acid as a single bead and have proven to be in good agreement with experimental measurements [42-48]. It is possible to increase the resolution and add multiple beads for each amino acid [49, 50]. For other biomolecular systems like DNA [51-53] or RNA [54, 55] equivalent models have been developed. CG can routinely investigate large-scale conformational transitions associated with function [56] and made predictions in agreement with experimental data like for Adenylate Kinase [57, 58], the folding of Riboswitches [59-61], knotted proteins [62] or the Rop dimer [63-65]. Recent research also explores multi-scale models, in which parts of the system are described in higher accuracy than other CG parts to reduce computational effort [66-70].

4   Complementing Limited Structural Information by Integrating genomic Information into Molecular Simulation

The starting point for biomolecular simulations are experimentally resolved three-dimensional structures. The common techniques NMR and X-ray crystallography have been invaluable in providing these structures but some systems, for example membrane-bound proteins or protein complexes, are very difficult to crystallize and too large for NMR. Theoretical approaches to predict these structures have met mixed success. Structural templates, a necessity for homology modeling, are not always available and physics/chemistry-based approaches struggle with the accuracy of their force fields or computationally prohibitive costs for larger systems.

Recent work took advantage of the ongoing growth of sequential information by searching for patterns of statistically correlated patterns of mutations in co-evolving proteins [71, 72]. The evolutionary necessity to maintain biomolecular function limits the mutational space for interacting amino acids and links spatially close amino acids in their mutational patterns. A sufficiently large set of sequences allows identifying the interface of co-evolving proteins. The inclusion of this information in molecular simulations can predict the complex structure. The blind prediction of a protein complex in two-component signal transduction shows high agreement between the predicted structure [73, 74] and a concurrently published crystal structure [75]. This research might pave the way to investigate a whole range of systems, for which little structural data exists.

5 Summary and Outlook

Biomolecular systems are successfully complementing experimental biochemical results. Current force fields are sufficiently sophisticated to accommodate different secondary structures for the same parameterization. Novel developments in HPC hardware have recently allowed the first millisecond simulations, which is the timescale of (un)folding and conformational transitions for many proteins, and simulations of huge biomolecular systems as of the Ribosome with millions of atoms. Mixed-theory approaches promise to provide structures, which are experimentally difficult to resolve. Future work of HPC-biomolecular simulation promises therefore increasingly detailed insight into biomolecular processes on biologically relevant timescales.

Acknowledgements

This research was conducted using the resources of High Performance Computing Center North (HPC2N) grant SNIC001-10-193.

References

1. Adcock, S.A. and J.A. McCammon, *Molecular dynamics: Survey of methods for simulating the activity of proteins.* Chem Rev, 2006. **106**(5): p. 1589-1615.

2. Scheraga, H.A., M. Khalili, and A. Liwo, *Protein-folding dynamics: Overview of molecular simulation techniques.* Ann Rev Phys Chem, 2007. **58**: p. 57-83.

3. Hansmann, U.H. and Y. Okamoto, *New Monte Carlo algorithms for protein folding.* Curr Opin Struct Biol, 1999. **9**(2): p. 177-83.

4. Hansmann, U.H.E. and Y. Okamoto, *Prediction of Peptide Conformations by Multicanonical Algorithm-New Approach to the Multiple-Minima Problem.* J Comp Chem, 1993. **14**(11): p. 1333-1338.

5. Kirkpatrick, S., C.D. Gelatt, Jr., and M.P. Vecchi, *Optimization by Simulated Annealing.* Science, 1983. **220**(4598): p. 671-680.

6. Mitsutake, A. and Y. Okamoto, *Multidimensional generalized-ensemble algorithms for complex systems.* J Chem Phys, 2009. **130**(21): p. 214105.

7. Schug, A., et al., *Comparison of Stochastic optimization methods for all-atom folding of the Trp-cage protein.* Chemphyschem, 2005. **6**(12): p. 2640-2646.

8. Schug, A. and W. Wenzel, *An evolutionary strategy for all-atom folding of the 60-amino-acid bacterial ribosomal protein L20.* Biophys J, 2006. **90**(12): p. 4273-4280.

9. Benedix, A., et al., *Predicting free energy changes using structural ensembles.* Nat Meth, 2009. **6**(1): p. 3-4.

10. Shaw, D.E., et al., *Atomic-level characterization of the structural dynamics of proteins.* Science, 2010. **330**(6002): p. 341-6.

11. Essmann, U., et al., *A smooth particle Eswald method.* J Chem Phys, 1995. **103**: p. 8577-8593.

12. Hess, B., et al., *GROMACS 4: Algorithms for Highly Efficient, Load-Balanced, and Scalable Molecular Dynamics.* J Chem Theory Comp, 2008. **4**: p. 435-447.

13. Phillips, J.C., et al., *Scalable molecular dynamics with NAMD.* J Comp Chem, 2005. **26**(16): p. 1781-1802.

14. Kutzner, C., et al., *Speeding up parallel GROMACS on high-latency networks.* J Comp Chem, 2007. **28**(12): p. 2075-84.

15. Pande, V.S., et al., *Atomistic protein folding simulations on the submillisecond time scale using worldwide distributed computing.* Biopol, 2003. **68**(1): p. 91-109.

16. Shirts, M. and V.S. Pande, *COMPUTING: Screen Savers of the World Unite!* Science, 2000. **290**(5498): p. 1903-4.

17. Verma, A., et al., *Massively parallel protein folding in a single day.* Parallel Computing: Archtitectures, Algorithms and Applications, 2007. **38**: p. 527-534.

18. Luttmann, E., et al., *Accelerating molecular dynamic simulation on the cell processor and Playstation 3.* J Comp Chem, 2009. **30**(2): p. 268-74.

19. Olivier, S., et al. *Porting the GROMACS Molecular Dynamics Code to the Cell Processor.* in *IEEE International Parallel and Distributed Processing Symposium.* 2007. IPDPS.

20. Whitford, P.C., J.N. Onuchic, and K.Y. Sanbonmatsu, *Connecting energy landscapes with experimental rates for aminoacyl-tRNA accommodation in the ribosome.* J Am Chem Soc, 2010. **132**(38): p. 13170-1.

21. Brooks, B.R., et al., *Charmm - a Program for Macromolecular Energy, Minimization, and Dynamics Calculations.* J Comp Chem, 1983. **4**(2): p. 187-217.

22. Case, D.A., et al., *The Amber biomolecular simulation programs.* J Comp Chem, 2005. **26**(16): p. 1668-88.

23. Chen, J., C.L. Brooks, 3rd, and J. Khandogin, *Recent advances in implicit solvent-based methods for biomolecular simulations.* Curr Opin Struct Biol, 2008. **18**(2): p. 140-8.

24. Mobley, D.L., K.A. Dill, and J.D. Chodera, *Treating entropy and conformational changes in implicit solvent simulations of small molecules.* J Phys Chem B, 2008. **112**(3): p. 938-46.

25. Fujitsuka, Y., et al., *Optimizing physical energy functions for protein folding.* Proteins, 2004. **54**(1): p. 88-103.

26. Ponder, J.W. and D.A. Case, *Force fields for protein simulations,* in *Protein Simulations*2003. p. 27-+.

27. Herges, T., A. Schug, and W. Wenzel, *Protein structure prediction with Stochastic optimization methods: Folding and misfolding the villin headpiece.* Computational Science and Its Applications - Iccsa 2004, Pt 3, 2004. **3045**: p. 454-464.

28. Herges, T. and W. Wenzel, *An all-atom force field for tertiary structure prediction of helical proteins.* Biophys J, 2004. **87**(5): p. 3100-3109.

29. Wenzel, W., *Predictive folding of a beta-hairpin protein in an all-atom free-energy model.* Europhys Lett, 2006. **76**(1): p. 156-162.

30. Best, R.B., N.V. Buchete, and G. Hummer, *Are current molecular dynamics force fields too helical?* Biophys J, 2008. **95**(1): p. 07-9.

31. Grant, B.J., A.A. Gorfe, and J.A. McCammon, *Ras conformational switching: simulating nucleotide-dependant conformational transitions with accelerated molecular dynamics.* PLOS Comput Bio, 2009. **5**(3): p. 1000325.

32. Grant, B.J., A.A. Gorfe, and J.A. McCammon, *Large conformational changes in proteins: signaling and other functions.* Curr Opin Struct Biol, 2010. **20**(2): p. 142-7.

33. Liwo, A., et al., *Modification and optimization of the united-residue (UNRES) potential energy function for canonical simulations. I. Temperature dependence of the effective energy function and tests of the optimization method with single training proteins.* J Phys Chem B, 2007. **111**(1): p. 260-85.

34. Marrink, S.J., et al., *The MARTINI force field: coarse grained model for biomolecular simulations.* J Phys Chem B, 2007. **111**(27): p. 7812-24.

35. Neri, M., et al., *Coarse-grained model of proteins incorporating atomistic detail of the active site.* Phys Rev Lett, 2005. **95**(21): p. 218102.

36. Rader, A.J., *Coarse-grained models: getting more with less.* Curr Opin Pharmacol, 2010. **10**(6): p. 753-9.

37. Schug, A., C. Hyeon, and J. Onuchic, *Coarse-Grained Structure-Based Simulations of Proteins and RNA*, in *Coarse-Graining of Condensed Phase and Biomolecular Systems*, V.G. A., Editor 2009. p. 123-140.

38. Voth, G.A., *Coarse-Graining of Condensed Phase and Biomolecular Systems*2009: CRC Press.

39. Bryngelson, J.D., et al., *Funnels, Pathways, and the Energy Landscape of Protein-Folding - a Synthesis.* Proteins-Struct Funct and Gen, 1995. **21**(3): p. 167-195.

40. Onuchic, J.N. and P.G. Wolynes, *Theory of protein folding.* Curr Opin Struct Bio, 2004. **14**(1): p. 70-75.

41. Schug, A. and J.N. Onuchic, *From protein folding to protein function and biomolecular binding by energy landscape theory.* Curr Opin Pharmacol, 2010. **10**(6): p. 709-14.

42. Chavez, L.L., J.N. Onuchic, and C. Clementi, *Quantifying the roughness on the free energy landscape: Entropic bottlenecks and protein folding rates.* J Am Chem Soc, 2004. **126**(27): p. 8426-8432.

43. Cheung, M.S., A.E. Garcia, and J.N. Onuchic, *Protein folding mediated by solvation: Water expulsion and formation of the hydrophobic core occur after the structural collapse.* Proc Nat Acad Sci U S A, 2002. **99**(2): p. 685-690.

44. Clementi, C., P.A. Jennings, and J.N. Onuchic, *Prediction of folding mechanism for circular-permuted proteins.* J Mol Biol, 2001. **311**(4): p. 879-890.

45. Dill, K.A., et al., *The protein folding problem.* Annu Rev Biophys, 2008. **37**: p. 289-316.

46. Levy, Y. and J.N. Onuchic, *Mechanisms of protein assembly: lessons from minimalist models.* Acc Chem Res, 2006. **39**(2): p. 135-42.

47. Ratje, A.H., et al., *Head swivel on the ribosome facilitates translocation by means of intra-subunit tRNA hybrid sites.* Nature, 2010. **468**(7324): p. 713-6.

48. Wales, D.J., *Energy landscapes: some new horizons.* Curr Op Struct Biol, 2010. **20**: p. 3-10.

49. Oliveira, L.C., A. Schug, and J.N. Onuchic, *Geometrical features of the protein folding mechanism are a robust property of the energy landscape: a detailed investigation of several reduced models.* J Phys Chem B, 2008. **112**(19): p. 6131-6.

50. Lammert, H., A. Schug, and J.N. Onuchic, *Robustness and generalization of structure-based models for protein folding and function.* Prot: Struct, Funct and Bioinf, 2009. **77**(4): p. 881-891.

51. Levy, Y., J.N. Onuchic, and P.G. Wolynes, *Fly-casting in protein-DNA binding: frustration between protein folding and electrostatics facilitates target recognition.* J Am Chem Soc, 2007. **129**(4): p. 738-9.

52. Thomas, A.K., et al., *A coarse grain model for DNA.* J Chem Phys, 2007. **126**(8): p. 084901.

53. Savelyev, A. and G.A. Papoian, *Chemically accurate coarse graining of double-stranded DNA.* Proc Natl Acad Sci U S A, 2010. **107**(47): p. 20340-5.

54. Hyeon, C., R.I. Dima, and D. Thirumalai, *Size, shape, and flexibility of RNA structures.* J Chem Phys, 2006. **125**(19): p. 194905.

55. Thirumalai, D. and C. Hyeon, *RNA and protein folding: common themes and variations.* Biochem, 2005. **44**(13): p. 4957-70.

56. Best, R.B., Y.G. Chen, and G. Hummer, *Slow protein conformational dynamics from multiple experimental structures: The helix/sheet transition of arc repressor.* Structure, 2005. **13**(12): p. 1755-1763.

57. Whitford, P.C., et al., *Conformational transitions of adenylate kinase: Switching by cracking.* J Mol Biol, 2007. **366**(5): p. 1661-1671.

58. Olsson, U. and M. Wolf-Watz, *Overlap between folding and functional energy landscapes for adenylate kinase conformational change.* Nat Comm, 2010. **1**(8): p. 111.

59. Blount, K.F. and R.R. Breaker, *Riboswitches as antibacterial drug targets.* Nat Biotech, 2006. **24**(12): p. 1558-64.

60. Breaker, R.R., *Complex riboswitches.* Science, 2008. **319**(5871): p. 1795-7.

61. Whitford, P.C., et al., *Nonlocal helix formation is key to understanding S-adenosylmethionine-1 riboswitch function.* Biophys J, 2009. **96**(2): p. L7-9.

62. Bolinger, D., et al., *A Stevedore's Protein Knot.* PLOS Comput Bio, 2010. **6**(4): p. e1000731.

63. Gambin, Y., et al., *Direct single-molecule observation of a protein living in two opposed native structures.* Proc Natl Acad Sci U S A, 2009. **106**(25): p. 10153-8.

64. Levy, Y., et al., *Symmetry and frustration in protein energy landscapes: A near degeneracy resolves the Rop dimer-folding mystery.* Proc Natl Acad Sci U S A, 2005. **102**(7): p. 2373-2378.

65. Schug, A., et al., *Mutations as trapdoors to two competing native conformations of the Rop-dimer.* Proc Natl Acad Sci USA, 2007. **104**: p. 17674-17679.

66. Christen, M. and W.F. van Gunsteren, *Multigraining: an algorithm for simultaneous fine-grained and coarse-grained simulation of molecular systems.* J Chem Phys, 2006. **124**(15): p. 154106.

67. Heath, A.P., L.E. Kavraki, and C. Clementi, *From coarse-grain to all-atom: toward multiscale analysis of protein landscapes.* Proteins, 2007. **68**(3): p. 646-61.

68. Liu, P., et al., *Reconstructing atomistic detail for coarse-grained models with resolution exchange.* J Chem Phys, 2008. **129**(11): p. 114103.

69. Kwak, W. and U.H. Hansmann, *Efficient sampling of protein structures by model hopping.* Phys Rev Lett, 2005. **95**(13): p. 138102.

70. Lyman, E., F.M. Ytreberg, and D.M. Zuckerman, *Resolution exchange simulation.* Phys Rev Lett, 2006. **96**(2): p. 028105.

71. Weigt, M., et al., *Identification of direct residue contacts in protein-protein interaction by message passing.* Proc Natl Acad Sci U S A, 2009. **106**(1): p. 67-72.

72. White, R.A., et al., *Features of protein-protein interactions in two-component signaling deduced from genomic libraries.* Meth Enzymol, 2007. **422**: p. 75-101.

73. Schug, A., et al., *Computational modeling of phosphotransfer complexes in two-component signaling.* Meth Enzymol, 2010. **471**: p. 43-58.

74. Schug, A., et al., *High resolution complexes from integrating genomic information with molecular simulation.* Proc Natl Acad Sci U S A, 2009. **106**(52): p. 22124-22129.

75. Casino, P., V. Rubio, and A. Marina, *Structural insight into partner specificity and phosphoryl transfer in two-component signal transduction.* Cell, 2009. **139**(2): p. 325-36.

Realistic Simulations of Strongly Correlated Systems

Andreas Dolfen and Erik Koch

German Research School for Simulation Sciences,
FZ-Jülich and RWTH Aachen University, 52425 Jülich, Germany
E-mail: {a.dolfen, e.koch}@grs-sim.de

Abstract

The physics of strongly correlated materials poses one of the most challenging problems in condensed-matter sciences. Standard approximations applicable to wide classes of materials such as the local density approximation fail, due to the importance of the Coulomb repulsion between localized electrons. Instead, we resort to non-perturbative many-body methods. The calculations are, however, only feasible for rather small model systems. The full Hamiltonian of a real material is approximated by a model Hamiltonian comprising only the most important electronic degrees of freedom, while the effect of all other electrons is included in an average way by renormalizing the parameters. Realistic calculations of strongly correlated materials need to include sufficiently many of these electronic degrees of freedom. The new generation of massively parallel supercomputers allows for these realistic calculations. However, exploiting their computational power requires newly devised algorithms. As a solver we use the Lanczos method, which needs the full many-body state of the correlated system. It is thus limited by the available main memory. The foremost problem for a distributed-memory implementation is that the multiplication of the Hamiltonian to the many-body state leads to highly non-local memory access patterns. Our solution to this problem relies on the efficient implementation of MPI collective communication on these systems. We show that the new algorithm scales extremely well on JUGENE, Jülich's Blue Gene/P. The concept underlying this massively parallel implementation is not restricted to correlated electrons but can also be used in simulating quantum spin systems. Moreover, it can also be extended to exploit further levels of parallelization as provided, for instance, by non-conventional processing units such as the Cell Broadband Engine.

1 Motivation

For a long time it has been a dream of solid state physicists to understand and predict properties of materials. The fundamental laws describing our world between the nuclear and astronomical scales are well-known. In principle, all we need to do is solve the time-dependent many-body Schrödinger equation. Neglecting relativistic effects it takes the form

$$i\frac{\partial}{\partial t}|\Psi\rangle = \mathscr{H}|\Psi\rangle \, ,$$

where $|\Psi\rangle$ is the many-body wavefunction and

$$\mathscr{H} = \sum_{\alpha=1}^{N_n} \frac{\vec{P}_\alpha^2}{2M_\alpha} + \sum_{j=1}^{N_e} \frac{\vec{p}_j^2}{2m} - \sum_{j=1}^{N_e} \sum_{\alpha=1}^{N_n} \frac{Z_\alpha}{|\vec{r}_j - \vec{R}_\alpha|} + \sum_{j<k}^{N_e} \frac{1}{|\vec{r}_j - \vec{r}_k|} + \sum_{\alpha<\beta}^{N_n} \frac{Z_\alpha Z_\beta}{|\vec{R}_\alpha - \vec{R}_\beta|}$$

denotes the many-body Hamiltonian of the system in atomic units. Z_α is the atomic number, M_α the mass, $\vec{R}_\alpha$ the position, and $\vec{P}_\alpha$ the momentum of nucleus α. $\vec{p}_j$ and $\vec{r}_j$ denote the jth electron's momentum and position. N_e, N_n are the number of electrons and nuclei, respectively. This equation does not only describe essentially all everyday phenomena but also unusual quantum effects, such as superconductivity, superfluidity, or the entanglement of states that lies at the heart of quantum computing.

However, Dirac realized that this "Theory of almost Everything" comes with a catch. It leads "to equations which are too complicated to be soluble". The complexity, Dirac refers to, arises from the quantum many-body nature of the problem. As illustration let us consider a simplified iron atom. With its $N_e = 26$ electrons the total electronic wavefunction depends on 26 times 3 coordinates. Choosing a very crude approximation by specifying the wavefunction on a grid with 10 points per coordinate yields 10^{78} numbers to store – let alone process. This huge amount of data cannot even be stored on a hard drive as large as our home galaxy, the milky way.

Still, the quantitative description of solids is not an entirely hopeless enterprise. There are successful approximations that work surprisingly well for wide classes of materials. The most prominent examples are approximations to density functional theory [1]. They effectively map the hard many-body problem to an effective single-particle problem that can be efficiently solved numerically. Essential to these approximations is that the Coulomb repulsion is described on a mean-field level. However, for many materials of scientific as well as technological interest, density-functional theory fails to give even qualitative insights. In these strongly correlated materials the electronic interaction is so strong that the phenomena produced cannot be predicted by studying the electrons individually — instead, we need to describe them collectively. Therefore, we have to solve the many-electron problem exactly. Clearly we cannot do this for the full Hamiltonian. Instead, we consider a simplified model Hamiltonian, which describes only those electrons that are essential to the correlation effects [2]. We illustrate this for the example of TTF-TCNQ, a quasi one-dimensional organic metal.

Figure 1 introduces the basic constituents of this metal-free metal, the two stable molecules TTF and TCNQ. Since the highest molecular orbital (HOMO) of TTF is significantly higher

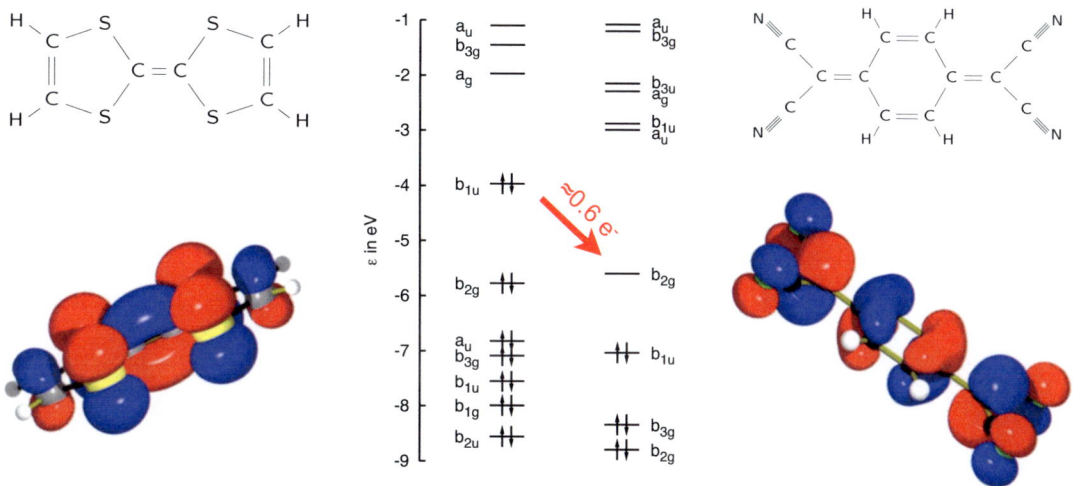

Figure 1: The molecular metal TTF-TCNQ. Center: molecular levels of the isolated molecules; left: TTF molecule with the highest occupied molecular orbital (HOMO); right: TCNQ with the lowest unoccupied molecular orbital (LUMO). The red arrow denotes the charge transfer of 0.6 electrons from the TTF-HOMO to the TCNQ-LUMO.

in energy than the lowest unoccupied molecular orbital (LUMO) of TCNQ, a charge transfer of on average 0.6 electrons takes place when assembling the crystal. Its structure is dominated by stacks of like molecules. There is a sizeable overlap between the molecular orbitals of π-character between adjacent molecules. Perpendicular to the stacks the overlap is three orders of magnitude smaller – thus, negligible. This in tandem with the charge transfer and relatively strong Coulomb repulsion within the molecular orbitals makes TTF-TCNQ a one-dimensional metal with striking many-body effects.

As shown above, we cannot treat all the electrons in the molecular solid explicitly. Instead, we focus our efforts on the most important electronic states: the partially filled TTF-HOMO and TCNQ-LUMO. The effects of the other electrons are included by considering their screening effects [3]. The simplest model Hamiltonian which captures both effects, the motion of the electrons as well as the strong Coulomb interaction is the Hubbard model

$$H = - \sum_{\sigma, i \neq j} t_{ij} c_{i\sigma}^\dagger c_{j\sigma} + U \sum_i n_{i\uparrow} n_{i\downarrow}, \qquad [1]$$

where the first term describes the kinetic energy with t_{ij} being the amplitude for an electron to hop from the molecule at site i to lattice site j. Note that hopping does not change the spin σ. The second term represents the Coulomb repulsion between two electrons in the same molecular orbital. Both terms are illustrated in Figure 2. The value of U is a parameter which

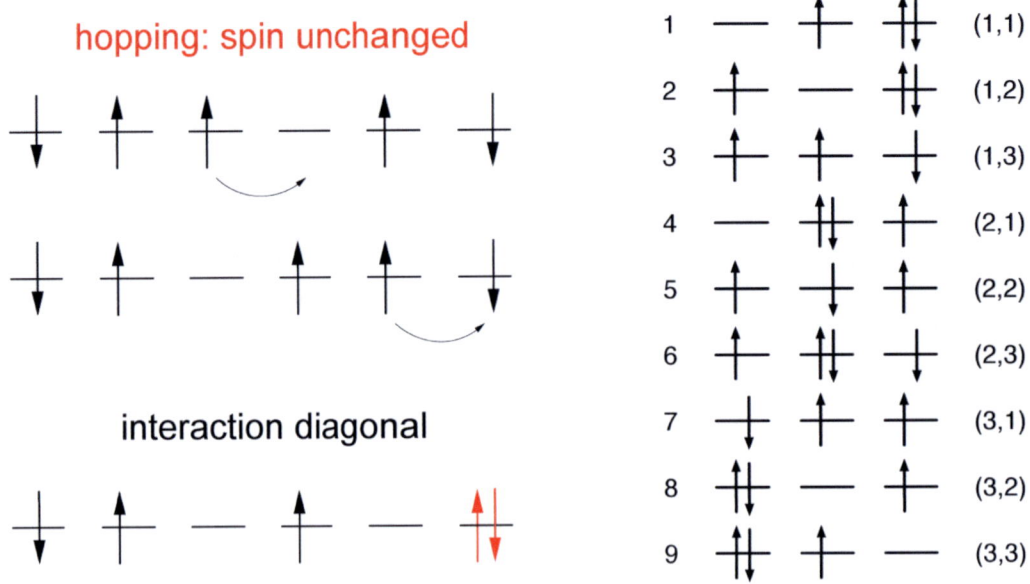

Figure 2: Illustration of the Hubbard model and the configuration basis of the Hilbert space. Upper left: next neighbor hopping (kinetic term); lower left: Coulomb repulsion U; right: basis for a three site system with two up and one down spin electron. The left label denotes the index of the configuration. Equivalently, a state is also unambiguously labeled by a tuple of up- and down-configuration index.

characterizes the strength of the local Coulomb interaction in the molecular orbitals and thus is different for HOMOs and LUMOs. $n_{i\uparrow}n_{i\downarrow}$ is one if the orbital is doubly occupied and zero otherwise. Both processes are sketched in the left part of the figure.

The Hamiltonian conserves the number of electrons of either spin. Hence, we only need to consider [1] on Hilbert spaces $\mathscr{H}$ with a fixed number of spin-up $N_\uparrow$ and spin-down $N_\downarrow$ electrons. For a finite system of L orbitals the dimension is $\binom{L}{N_\uparrow} \cdot \binom{L}{N_\downarrow}$. For an example of three orbitals and two up- and one down-spin electron, there are therefore 9 different configurations. They are sketched in Figure 2. Even though we significantly simplified the problem, we still have to face the many-body problem. A system with 20 orbitals and 10 electrons of either spin already contains more than 34 billion (34 134 779 536) different configurations. Storing a single many-body state for this system in double precision requires about 254 GB.

2 Lanczos Method

Even for small systems the full Hamiltonian easily becomes too large to be completely stored in any computers memory. Fortunately, in its real-space configuration basis representation the matrix is very sparse. Each configuration is only connected to few others by hopping and the Coulomb repulsion part of the Hamiltonian is diagonal.

For the partial diagonalization of huge sparse matrices the iterative Lanczos method is the method of choice. It provides the ground-state eigenvalue as well as the ground-state vector and eventually also gives efficient access to dynamical correlation functions.

It starts from a random vector $|\phi_0\rangle$, leading to a first energy value $E_0 = E[\phi_0] = \langle\phi_0|H|\phi_0\rangle$. In analogy to the gradient descent method, the method goes in the direction of steepest descent in the energy functional, which is given by $H|\phi_0\rangle$. The resulting vector is orthogonalized with respect to the starting vector, i.e.

$$\langle\phi_1|H|\phi_0\rangle\,|\phi_1\rangle = H|\phi_0\rangle - \langle\phi_0|H|\phi_0\rangle\,|\phi_0\rangle \ .$$

Now the same step is done with $|\phi_1\rangle$ leading to

$$\langle\phi_2|H|\phi_1\rangle\,|\phi_2\rangle = H|\phi_1\rangle - \langle\phi_1|H|\phi_1\rangle\,|\phi_1\rangle - \langle\phi_1|H|\phi_0\rangle\,|\phi_0\rangle \ ,$$

or in general,

$$\beta_{n+1}|\phi_{n+1}\rangle = H|\phi_n\rangle - \alpha_n|\phi_n\rangle - \beta_n|\phi_{n-1}\rangle \ ,$$

where $n \in 2,\dots,m$ and

$$\alpha_n = \langle\phi_n|H|\phi_n\rangle, \quad \beta_{n+1} = \langle\phi_{n+1}|H|\phi_n\rangle.$$

From this equation we see that the Hamiltonian H is tridiagonal in the basis of the Lanczos vectors. In practice we only need of the order of $\mathcal{O}(100) \ll \dim(\mathcal{H})$ iterations to converge to the ground-state. If we are after the ground-state energy this method only needs to keep two vectors of the size of the Hilbert space in memory. For the ground-state vector, a third vector is required. As discussed above the dimension grows swiftly and thus the applicability of the method is limited by the maximum available main memory.

3 Computational Aspects

The sparse matrix-vector multiplication is at the core of the Lanczos method. It is the most time-consuming function and easily dominates the others already for small systems.

On shared memory systems an efficient implementation of this matrix-vector multiplication is embarrassingly simple: The vector elements of the new vector $|\phi_{n+1}\rangle$ can be calculated independently. Hence, different processes can work on different chunks of the result vector. The vector $|\phi_n\rangle$ as well as the matrix elements are only read, so that there is no need for locking. An OpenMP parallelization thus needs only a single pragma. Similarly, parallelizing the scalar

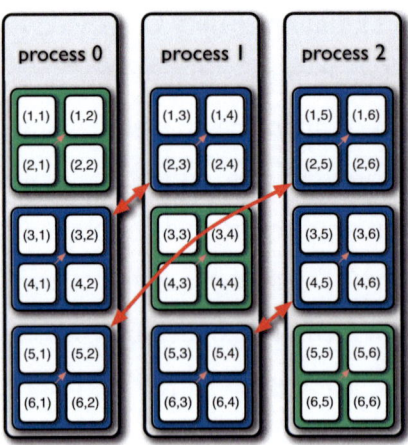

Figure 3: Transpose operation that makes memory access process-local when calculating the operation of the Hamiltonian on the state-vector. The communication (red arrows) is realized by a call to `MPI_Alltoall`, which usually is very efficient on modern supercomputers due to its general applicability. The small arrows indicate the local operations needed to complete the matrix-transpose.

products and norms we obtain almost ideal speed-up on an IBM p690 frame of JUMP at the Forschungszentrum Jülich. Using this implementation we are, however, restricted to a single node with 128 GB of memory.

New generations of massively parallel supercomputers have much larger aggregated main memories and possess a significantly higher computational performance. To leverage their power we port our Lanczos solver to MPI. The kinetic energy term of the Hamiltonian (1) has non-diagonal terms and therefore leads to non-local memory access patterns. A naive distributed memory parallelization is to emulate a shared memory by direct remote memory access via MPI one-sided communication. This approach leads, however, to a severe speed-down, i.e. the more processors we use, the longer we have to wait for the result. This sad state of affairs is shown in the left plot of Figure 4.

A simple albeit important observation leads to an efficient distributed memory implementation. The Hamiltonian contains no spin-flip processes. Thus, hopping of up-spin electrons only connects configurations with changed up-spin electrons. The down-spin electron configuration remains untouched. Hence, if we manage to store all up-spin configurations for a fixed down-spin configuration in the memory of a single process, this part of the kinetic energy can be performed locally. Figure 2 illustrates this: for a fixed index $i_\downarrow$, all $i_\uparrow$ configurations follow and can be stored in the memory of a single process. Obviously, this basis can naturally be indexed by a tuple $(i_\downarrow, i_\uparrow)$ (right labels in Figure 2) instead of the global index (left labels). We can therefore equivalently regard the vectors as matrices $v(i_\downarrow, i_\uparrow)$ with indices $i_\downarrow$ and $i_\uparrow$. Now it is easy to see that a matrix transpose reshuffles the data elements such that the down configurations are sequentially in memory and local to the thread. Hence, their part of the kinetic energy can be carried out without further communication.

The performance of the sparse matrix-vector multiplication rests on the efficiency of the matrix-transpose operation. We use the `MPI_Alltoall` function. It expects the data packages which will be sent to a given process to be stored contiguously in memory. This is, however, not true in our case, since we would like to store the spin-down electron configurations sequentially in memory, i.e. the matrix is stored column wise. For `MPI_Alltoall` to work properly, we would have to bring the data elements in row-major order. A local matrix-transpose would do this. However, the involved matrices are in general rectangular, leading to expensive local-copy and reordering operations. By calling `MPI_Alltoall` for each column separately this can be avoided (red arrows in Figure 3). Afterwards, only a local strided transposition has to be performed (small pink arrows) to obtain the fully transposed matrix or Lanczos vector [4, 5].

Target for the development of the BlueGene architecture was high performance/price and performance/power consumption ratios. The main idea is to build the system out of a very large number of nodes, which taken for themselves have only a relatively modest clock rate and performance, leading to lower power consumption and low cost. Using relatively slow processors also implies a better balance between CPU speed and the usually considerably slower memory and network access. That this goal was achieved is evident in main plot of Figure 4, which shows the speed-up for a calculation where in each iteration a state vector (up to 254 GB) is "transposed" twice. The implementation described so far uses `MPI_Alltoall` which assumes that the matrix to be transposed is a square matrix and that the dimension $dim_\uparrow = dim_\downarrow$ is divisible by the number of MPI processes. To overcome these restrictions we generalized the algorithm to `MPI_Alltoallv` [4].

At first glance this method seems to be tailor-made for exactly this problem – which is true. The idea is, however, easily generalized to other quantum models such as Heisenberg-like models [6].

4 Non-Conventional Computing Units – The Cell Broadband Engine

Some of the latest generation supercomputers are hybrid systems being equipped with additional non-conventional computing units. One example is QPACE, a supercomputer based solely on the Cell Broadband Engine (CBE). We can think of these Cell ships as small clusters, or in Cell language synergistic processing elements (SPEs), on a chip. In addition there is a conventional

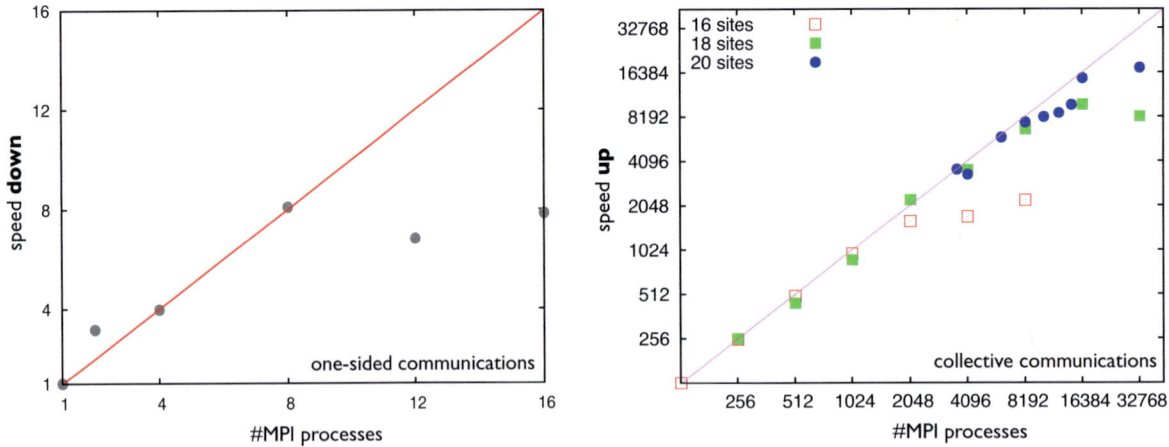

Figure 4: Performance of the Lanczos code for different system sizes: The left plot shows the speed-down for the one-sided communications implementation on JUMP (p690) for a half-filled cluster of 14 sites. The right plot provides the speed-up using MPI collectives for 16, 18, and 20 sites at half-filling performed on Jülich's IBM Blue Gene/P JuGene in virtual node mode (VN). We observe almost linear scaling until the speed-up levels off due to too small problem size. It becomes linear again for larger systems.

PowerPC core, called the PPE. To make use of the offered computational power we add a further level of parallelization to our Lanczos solver.

First we focus on the diagonal part of the Hamiltonian, the Coulomb interaction. In our implementation a single configuration is bit-encoded in two integers, one for the up-spin configuration and one for the down-spin configuration. The local Hubbard term requires the evaluation of the number of doubly occupied sites, i.e. $\sum_i n_{i\uparrow} n_{i\downarrow}$. This can be achieved by using a bit-wise and operation on the two integers followed by a sideways addition. This yields the number of doubly occupied sites in this particular configuration.

Conceptually, there are two approaches to evaluate the interaction energy. We can either calculate the number of doubly occupied sites for each configuration on the PPEs and store the result in main memory. When now performing the interaction part of the matrix-vector multiplication we need to stream the vector and the precalculated diagonal elements to the SPEs. This results in three DMA operations (2 get and a single put operation) per chunk. We call this approach precalculation. Alternatively we could calculate the diagonal elements on-the-fly within the SPEs, saving one DMA-get per chunk. Depending on the memory bandwidth/computation ratio either pre- or on-the-fly calculation is superior. On ordinary architectures like our Blue-Gene implementation precalculation performs better when we can afford to store the diagonal elements.

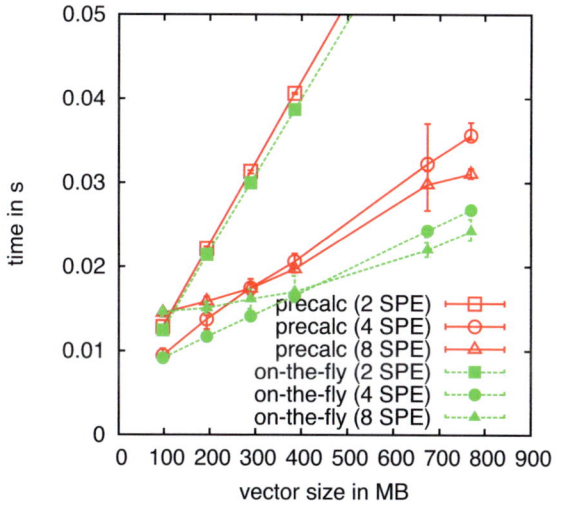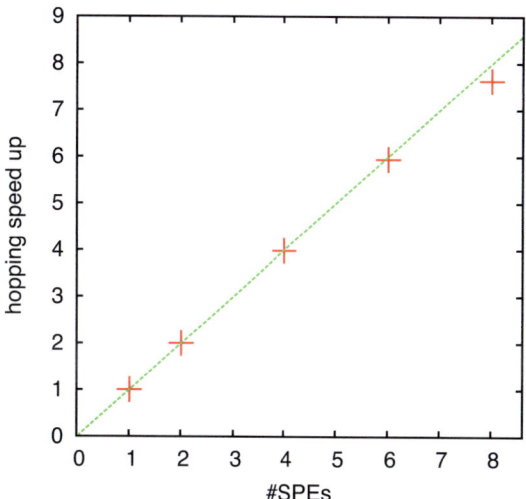

Figure 5: Left: Comparison of the runtime for pre- and on-the-fly calculation of the Hubbard term for different numbers of SPEs. For two SPEs both methods are almost equally fast. From four SPEs on, the on-the-fly calculation becomes significantly faster. This is because the bandwidth is bounded and the precalculation-code is transfer-wise more expensive. For four SPEs it is almost fully saturated and thus on-the-fly calculation becomes more efficient. Right: Speed-up of scalar hopping code with slices being small enough that no inter-SPE communication is needed.

On the CBE we can exploit the SPE parallelization with their SIMD capabilities. The SPEs provide three (SIMDized) intrinsics `spu_and`, `spu_cntb` and `spu_sumb` which cover all operations needed. Using double-buffering we can overlap the on-the-fly calculation with the communication. The left plot of Figure 5 shows the timings for pre- (red solid lines) vs. on-the-fly calculation (green dashed lines) for different numbers of SPEs. We observe the expected linear increase of runtime with respect to vector size. For a single SPE (not shown) and two SPEs both implementations are essentially equally fast. Using four SPEs or more the on-the-fly calculation is significantly more efficient: The memory bandwidth from main memory to the SPEs on a CBE is exhausted while utilizing more and more SPEs increases computing power.

The off-diagonal multiplication is considerably harder to implement. Again we face the problem of non-local memory accesses. On this level of parallelization a slice is distributed over local stores of different SPEs. If a slice fits into a single local store and thus all computations can be done SPE-locally a scalar implementation yields an essentially ideal speed-up (c.f. right plot of Figure 5). This is however only the case for rather small test cases. The idea to tackle the problem of non-local memory access is as follows: In all implementations two slices are needed anyway. One is updated while the other one is read. Both are initially distributed in the same way over the SPEs. In the first step all SPEs perform all hopping operations which can be satisfied by their local piece of the second slice. After this operation is completed, the second slice is rotated along the bus connecting the SPEs. Hence, the SPEs have now access to other vector elements. Once a full rotation is completed each SPE has had the opportunity to read each element and therefore to carry out all hopping operations. Thus, giving an efficient implementation on the CBE.

References

[1] W. Kohn, *Nobel Lecture: Electronic structure of matter: wave functions and density functionals*, Rev. Mod. Phys. **71**, 1253, 1999.

[2] E. Koch and E. Pavarini, *Multiple Scales in Solid State Physics*, Proceedings of the Summer School on Multiscale Modeling and Simulations in Science 2007, Springer.

[3] L. Cano-Cortés, A. Dolfen, J. Merino, J. Behler, B. Delley, K. Reuter, and E. Koch, *Coulomb parameters and photoemission for the molecular metal TTF-TCNQ*, Eur. Phys. J. B **56**, 173, 2007.

[4] A. Dolfen, *Massively parallel exact diagonalization of strongly correlated systems*, Diploma Thesis, RWTH Aachen, 2006.

[5] A. Dolfen, E. Pavarini, and E. Koch, *New Horizons for the Realistic Description of Materials with Strong Correlations*, Innovatives Supercomputing in Deutschland **4**, 16, Spring 2006.

[6] A. Dolfen, Y. Luo, and E. Koch, *Simulating materials with strong correlations on Blue Gene/L*, Proceedings of the International Conference ParCo, 2007, 601.

Development and evaluation of a GPU-optimized N-body term for the simulation of biomolecules

Timo Strunk, Moritz Wolf, and Wolfgang Wenzel

Institute of Nanotechnology, Karlsruhe Institute of Technology

Hermann-von-Helmholtz-Platz 1, 76344 Eggenstein-Leopoldshafen, Germany

Abstract

Advancements in massively parallel sampling of the conformational space of biomolecules enables, for example, protein structure prediction, *in-silico* drug development and cell signaling. Despite the existence of highly distributed protein simulation architectures like POEM@HOME, there was no abundant computational resource both strong in serial strength and in parallel sampling.

In this study we investigate the optimization of our N-body Lennard Jones force field for the efficient Monte-Carlo sampling of small to medium-size biomolecules on massively parallel architectures, like modern GPUs. We benchmark both NVIDIA and AMD GPU chipsets in the OpenCL framework in comparison to CPU architectures. The N-body interactions are broken down into small local grids, which fit into the local GPU caches to permit simultaneous evaluation.

Using the N-body term we accelerate the Lennard-Jones and Clash-Potential of the complete free-energy PFF02 [1] shown to fold a multitude of different protein-folds and implement a modified structure-based Lennard Jones force field. We proof the applicability of our novel force field by reversible folding-simulations of a three-helix protein using this Go-potential from completely unfolded structures.

1 Introduction

Recent developments in the field of High Performance Computing enabled the availability of cheap highly-parallel multicore architectures in the form of commodity GPUs. Although high maximum performance in the multi-teraflop range could be achieved [12], the maximum throughput always comes at the price of limited interconnection between the cores and almost no branching in the processed code. The presented code solves this by parallel filling of local caches, which can then be accessed randomly without a performance penalty and is based on a work by Elsen et al. [4].

In our endeavor to accelerate general N-body force fields we ported the SMOG-Potential [2] to the OpenCL [9] architecture.

The computational demand of this force field is primarily contained in the sum of all non-bonded interactions, which grows with O (N^2). For regular protein conformations the number of neighbors is approximately O $(N \log N)$ and the number of dihedral and angle terms can be estimated with O (N), as each amino acid has a specific amount of angles.

Although there are many ways to define cutoff potentials for Lennard-Jones type force fields [3]. Our primary concern lies in the efficient execution of the full N^2 sum, as the developed force field code will further be used in electrostatic calculations, where the long-range Coulomb interaction hinders the introduction of a cutoff.

2   Methods

2.1 SMOG-Potential

We chose the complete SMOG (**S**tructure-based **MO**dels in **G**romacs) potential (Eq. 1) as our simulation potential as it incorporates a regular N-body term for repulsive interactions among other terms maintaining proper physical covalent bond order. In addition the N-body term is similar to the one of PFF02 [1], where our implementation will replace Lennard-Jones, Clash-check and electrostatics potentials.

$$V = \sum_{bonds} \varepsilon_r (r - r_0)^2 + \sum_{angles} \varepsilon_\theta (\theta - \theta_0)^2 + \sum_{impropers / planar} \varepsilon_\chi (\chi - \chi_0)^2$$

$$+ \sum_{backbone} \varepsilon_{BB} F_D(\phi) + \sum_{sidechain} \varepsilon_{SC} F_D(\phi)$$

$$+ \sum_{contacts} \varepsilon_C \left[\left(\frac{\sigma_{ij}}{r} \right)^{12} - 2 \left(\frac{\sigma_{ij}}{r} \right)^6 \right] + \sum_{non-contacts} \varepsilon_{NC} \left(\frac{\sigma_{ij}}{r} \right)^{12}$$

where,

$$F_D(\phi) = [1 - \cos(\phi - \phi_0)] + \frac{1}{2}[1 - \cos(3(\phi - \phi_0))]$$

Equation 1: The SMOG-Potential is a Go-Potential of the shown form. The bond-, angle-, improper and planar terms maintain backbone geometry. Flexible dihedral angles are given cosine terms. Non-local native interactions are given attractive 6-12 interactions and non-native interactions are given repulsive terms. The parameters ε are scaling factors to scale the covalent bond, angle, dihedral, all atom contact and all atom non-contact force field terms in relation to each other. The symbols r, θ, χ and φ are the covalent bond distance, angle and dihedral angle variables; the respective parameters with the subscript 0 are the values in the native conformation. The σ_{ij} are the Lennard Jones parameters for atoms i and j. The ported N-body term is the sum over all non-contact atoms i and j. Numerical values for all parameters can be found in [2].

By encoding the native three-dimensional structure of the analyzed protein into the potential energy explicitly, the rough physical potential energy of the protein is smoothed out leading to fast sampling of near-native states in comparison to the full physical free energy. This guided sampling allows for the simulation of multiple folding events in finite time. By definition, the force field models the native conformation at the global minimum of the employed force field.

2.2 Sampling strategy

We sample the protein's free-energy landscape using random Monte-Carlo side- and main-chain dihedral perturbations. This keeps the bond-lengths and -angles of the studied protein intact and permits larger motions per step than molecular dynamics techniques at the cost of an explicit time-resolution. This step size will be called "move step" from now on.

2.3 Parallelization strategy

The OpenCL programming model maps a general workgroup scheme to the underlying hardware. The hardware cores are divided into workgroups, which are themselves divided into work items. One kernel (which is basically a C-function) is then executed by one workgroup for all work items in parallel. Work items of a workgroup share a local shared memory cache, which can be accessed without memory access conflicts either coalesced or in a broadcast (which means all work items read the same memory). The global device memory can only be quickly read from or written to in an aligned (coalesced) fashion, meaning that work items i and $i+1$ have to read memory addresses j and $j+1$. Register memory is local to the work item and severely limited.

One Lennard-Jones force field evaluation requires the availability of all atom positions of the given protein conformation as well as the availability of one parameter per coordinate. The matrix of N-body interactions is broken down into local segments fitting into the local shared memory caches as seen in Figure 1.

Algorithm

1. Each work item loads its assigned coordinate into its registers (work item j retrieves coordinate j).

2. The number of bodies is partitioned into intervals of size #atoms / #group_size. Each workgroup loads all coordinates of interval 1 into shared memory. As this is done in parallel, the algorithm stops until all copy operations are finished. In contrast to step number 1 this operation can cause bank conflicts as different workgroups access the same memory bank.

3. The work items of one workgroup iterate synchronously over the coordinates of the interval and calculate the interaction between the assigned coordinate and the coordinate of the interval. If the assigned coordinate and the coordinate of the interval match, one work item branches and skips the loop.

4. Once the loop over the interval finished, the algorithm waits until all work items of a workgroup arrive at this point and continues with the next interval at 2.

5. After all intervals are handled, each work item writes its result in a result vector.

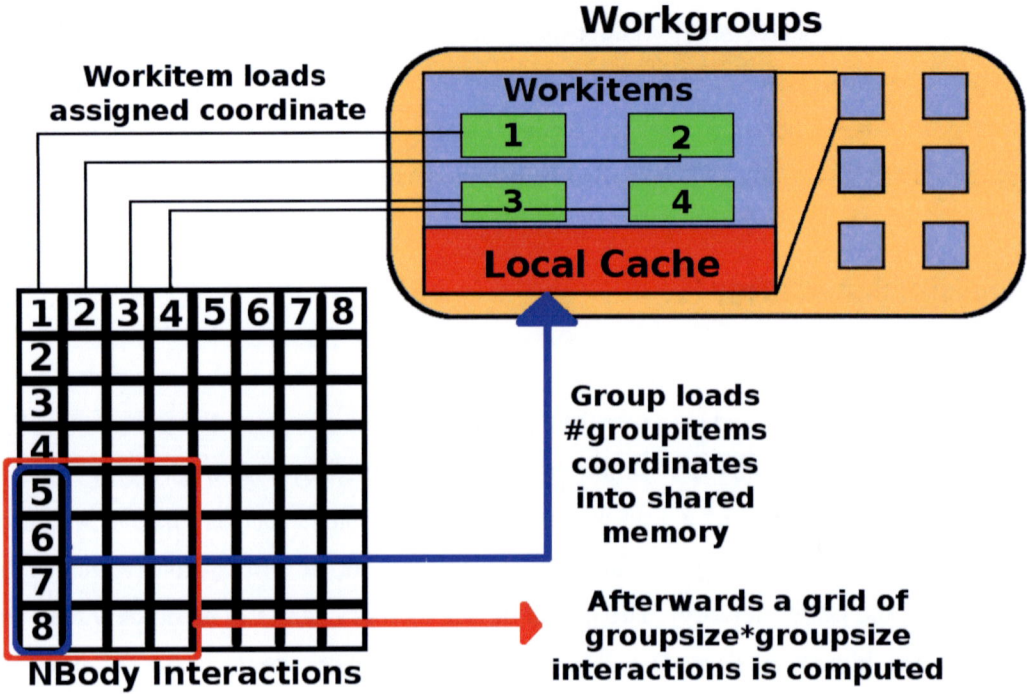

Figure 1: Functionality of the N-body code used for the Lennard-Jones interaction between all simulated atoms. Every column of the N×N matrix is assigned to a workgroup that computes one block simultaneously with all its work items.

Algorithm in pseudo-code

```
lj_kernel ( float4_vector pos, float_vector params, float_vector output,
int number_of_atoms, (shared memory) float4_vector local_pos,
(shared memory) float_vector local_params )
{
    # Abbrevations:
    lid = local id in workgroup, gid = global id, localSize = size of workgroup;
    sum = 0.0f;
    # Each core loads one coordinate into fast register memory in parallel:
    (register) float4 const my_pos = pos[gid];
    (register) float const my_param = params[gid];
    # For each group, we load all atom positions of the group (localSize) into
    # the shared memory segment local_pos
```

```
# memory is shared only inside the workgroup
for ( i = 0; i < number_of_groups; i = i+1 )
{
    # global_index is the index of the atom to be loaded by this workitem
    global_index = i * localSize + lid;
    # Positions and parameters for this workgroup
    # are loaded into shared memory
    local_pos[lid] = pos[global_index];
    local_params[lid] = params[global_index];
    # Barrier waits until the local memory is initialized by all members
    # of the workgroup
    Local-Barrier;
    for ( j = 0; j < localSize; j = j + 1 )
    {
        partner_index = i*localSize+j;
        # Avoid singularity, 1/r with r = 0
        if ( gid == partner_index ) continue;
        # Avoid Access of memory beyond array border at number_of_atoms
        if ( partner_index >= number_of_atoms ) continue;
        # compute distance vector between partner and workitem's coordinate
        float4 distv = local_pos[j] - my_pos;
        distv.w = 0.0f;
        # compute distance to the power of 12
        float rq = dot(distv, distv);
        rq*=rq;
        rq*=rq*rq;
        sum += my_param*local_params[j] / rq;
    }
    # We wait until all n^2 interactions are evaluated inside of the interval:
    Local-Barrier;
}
# In case we have a valid workitem, we write our result to global memory:
if ( gid < number_of_atoms )
{
    output[gid] = sum / 2.0f;
}
else
{
    output[gid] = 0.0f;
}
}
```

2.4 OpenCL framework

Computations are run atop the OpenCL implementations of both the ATI Stream SDK 2.2 for AMD-GPUs and general x86 CPU cores and the NVIDIA CUDA (Compute Unified Device Architecture) toolkit 3.1 for NVIDIA-GPUs. The code was written in single precision using floating-point accuracy in the OpenCL 1.0 standard without use of any extensions. The maximum workgroup size is a constraint of the OpenCL framework and limited at 1024 currently. Depending on the kernel complexity only smaller workgroup size limits are allowed. The exact upper limit can be queried from inside the framework. For our kernel the limits were 256, 512 and 1024 for the AMD-GPU, NVIDIA-GPU and CPU architectures.

2.5 Hardware

Simulations were performed on NVIDIA-GPU and AMD-GPU and CPU hardware, specifically:

1. AMD Radeon 5870 GPU [10]
    a. 20 compute units a 16 stream cores clocked at 850 MHz (320 = maximum number of possible concurrently running work items)
    b. 1024 MB RAM peak bandwidth: 153GB/s

2. NVIDIA GTX 285 [11]
    a. 30 compute units a 8 CUDA cores = 240 CUDA cores clocked at 1.48GHz (240 = maximum number of concurrently running work items)
    b. 1024 MB RAM peak bandwidth: 159GB/s

3. 2-socket AMD Opteron Processor 2435 (referred to as AMD-CPU)
    a. Per socket: 6 CPU cores, 6 MB L3 cache (shared)
    b. Per core: 512 KB L2 cache
    c. RAM: 64 GB

4. Reference run: 1 CPU core of the system outlined in 3, no OpenCL scheduling

Workgroup sizes during the runs were varied from a workgroup size of 16 to the maximum workgroup size of the device.

3   Simulations

Validating the force field was possible using energy comparisons of simulations using the Gromacs package, which implements the force field on CPU cores. The correct working of our program package was then verified by simulating a complete unfolding and refolding event of the three-helix bundle protein 1F4I, a small UV excision repair protein homolog (Figure 2).

To test and benchmark our code we conducted simulations with three proteins:

1. 1F4I − a UV excision repair protein homolog [5]
    a. 365 atoms
    b. 10 000 move steps

2. 2PAJ − a putative cytosine-guanine deaminase [6]

a. 3194 atoms

b. 10 000 move steps

3. 2VZ8 – The crystal structure of a mammalian fatty acid synthase [7]

a. 30 281 atoms

b. 10 000 move steps for GPU, 200 move steps for CPU

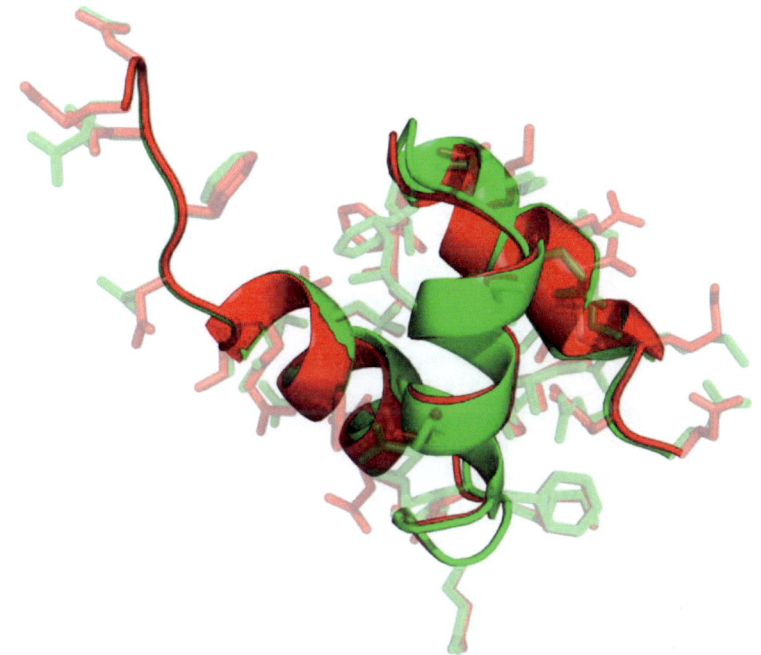

Figure 2: Alignment between native structure of 1F4I (red) and the best found conformation (green). Starting from an entirely stretched conformation, the system ended up in its native state. This annealing simulation from 5000 K to 10 K was computed on a GTX285 NVIDIA-GPU. It took about 5 minutes to evaluate 90 000 energies.

4 Results

4.1 1F4I folding – proof of principle

The simulations started from a completely stretched conformation for a total step count of 90 000 steps. The maximum RMSD in the stretched conformation was 37.5 Å. The dihedral moves were biased towards physical beta- and alpha regions of the Ramachandran-plot to avoid unphysical states. During the search for the global optimum, the temperature was scaled geometrically from 5000 K to 10 K ending at a RMSD of 1.5 Å (Figure 3). This folding simulation took about 5 minutes on the GTX285 architecture.

After showing the validity of our approach, benchmarks using various workgroup and system sizes of the three architectures were performed.

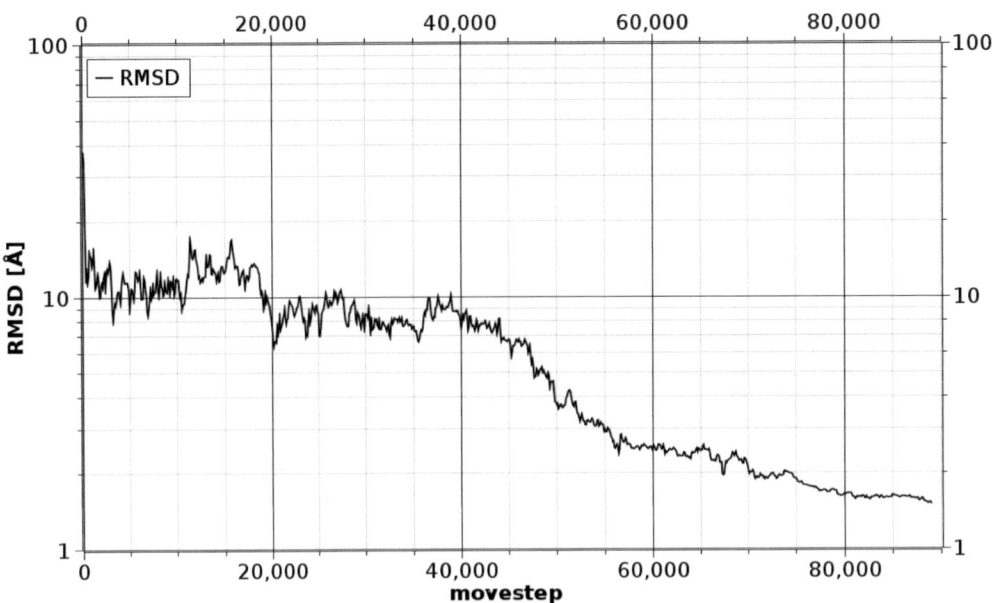

Figure 3: RMSD vs. move step for the folding simulation of 1F4I. Starting from 37.5 Å the system found its native conformation in about 10^5 move steps.

4.2 Workgroup scaling

1F4I

The folding simulations of 1F4I present the smallest system that we sampled using our parallelized code. With 365 atoms this amounts to 133 225 N-body interactions to be calculated. As the chosen workgroup size is either near the number of atoms or approaching the number of cores in one SIMT (Single Instruction, Multiple Thread) group (the number of work items which have to execute the same code path without branches), this presents the worst case scenario for the GPUs. The CPU cores benefit from a system this small, because the whole conformation fits inside the local caches. The scaling behavior can be observed in Figure 4: All three architectures struggle. The AMD-GPU comes out slowest with optimum workgroup size of 128 at 50s and longer runtimes for lower and higher workgroup sizes. As long as the number of CUDA- or Stream-cores (GTX: 240, ATI 5870: 320) is smaller than the number of atoms, all cores could in theory be running at the same time. This assumes however that the number of atoms is a multiple of the workgroup size; something which is usually not present in real-world proteins. Workgroups are always computed completely, which means that for a bigger workgroup size there will usually be a bigger overhead to be computed. This overhead of work items, which will be computed in addition to the real work items, can be estimated by workgroup size − number of atoms modulo workgroup size. We can see that in case of a workgroup size of 128, this formula only gives an overhead of 19 work items.

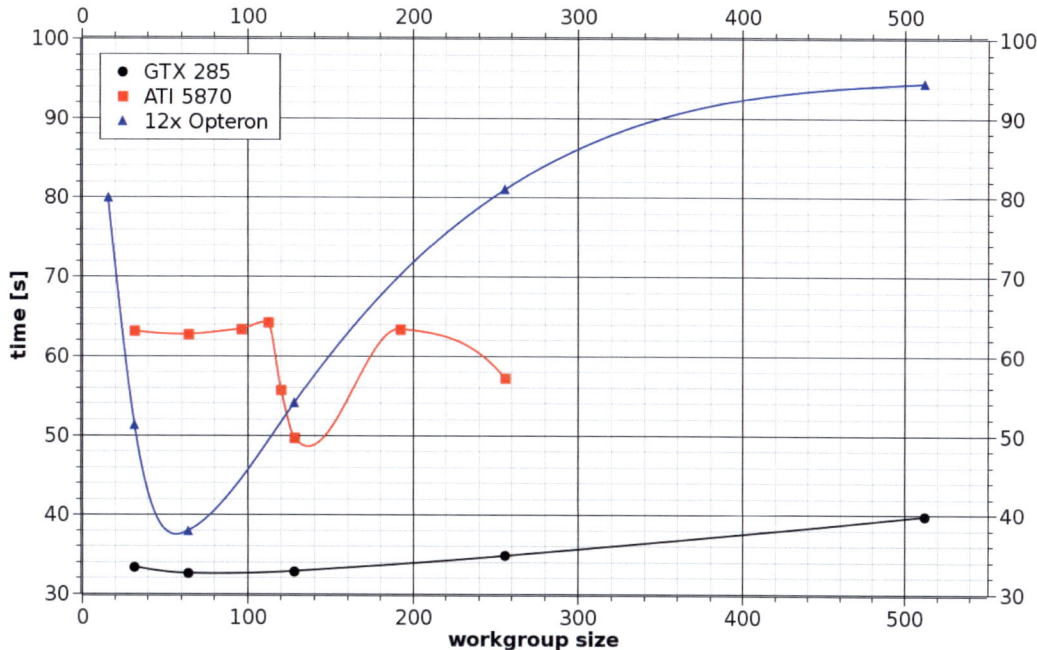

Figure 4: This figure shows the influence of the workgroup size for a small amount of simulated atoms on different platforms. The simulated Protein 1F4I consists of 365 atoms. At this small dimension the CPU cores can beat the performance of our ATI 5870.

For the AMD-GPU this relates to one 'unused' compute cores (with 16 compute units each), for the NVIDIA-GPU, two compute cores handle 'unused' work.

So in general going to smaller workgroup sizes increases the number of global to local memory accesses, while a bigger workgroup size means more additional work at the end of the run. Additionally for the CPU architecture a high workgroup size means a high number of concurrent threads, which puts stress on the scheduler.

The GTX shows no such scaling behavior and attains the first place with a runtime of 32 seconds at a workgroup size of 64. Due to the much higher clock frequency of the CUDA cores it seems to be memory bound in this scenario. Only at big workgroup sizes of 512, which correspond to only 1 running workgroup does the performance degrade noticeable, which can be accounted to the divergence of the workgroups, as work items with ids bigger than the number of atoms are branching.

The 2x6 core CPU system achieves second place also at a workgroup size of 64, which translates roughly into 5 threads per Core. However, looking at the CPU usage in this case shows that only 2 cores are processing at the same time. This is easily accounted to the memory overhead of copying from global to local memory for the CPU. As everything is done serially, the CPU cores are ready with their iterations before a new workgroup can start with new data. It is interesting to note that when going to large workgroup sizes the OpenCL implementation and the legacy CPU implementation converge to the same runtime, as also the OpenCL implementation can only run with one thread then, because of the scheduler overhead.

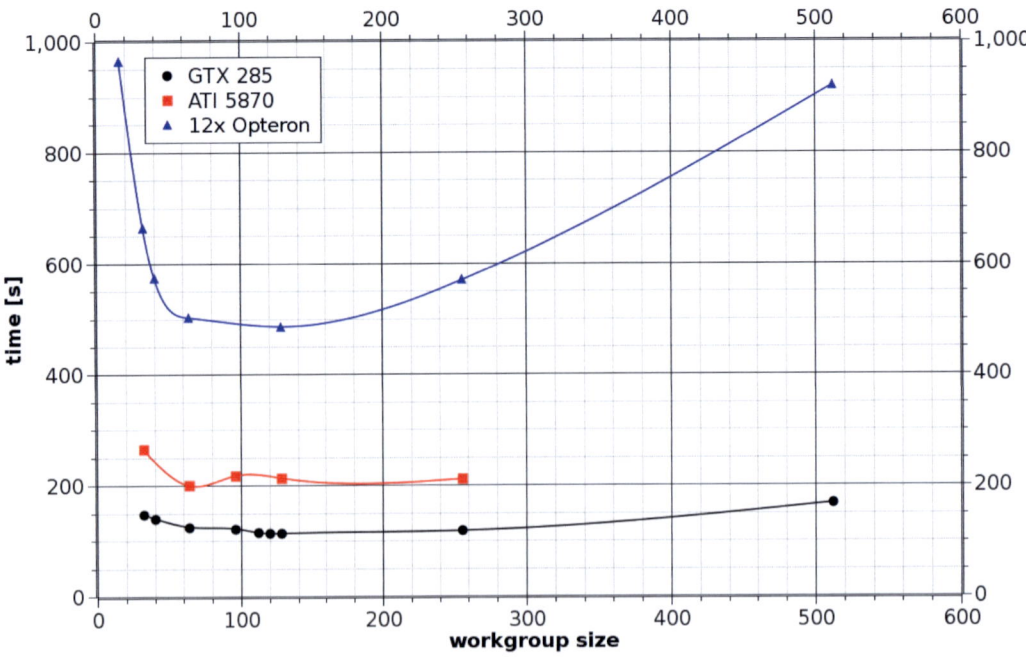

Figure 5: For a medium sized protein 2PAJ with 3194 atoms, both GPUs are 2-3 times faster than the 12 CPU cores together.

2PAJ

With 3194 atoms this protein fills all the graphics cards processors completely for the small work group sizes. The graphics cards are 2-3 times faster than the 12 core CPU, giving about a speedup of 25 compared to a single core CPU (Figure 5). The AMD-GPU peaks at a workgroup size of 64, which corresponds to 50 total workgroups for the 20 cores. NVIDIA peaks at a workgroup size of 128, which corresponds to 25 workgroups for the 30 cores.

2VZ8

The mammalian fatty acid synthase is the biggest protein we simulated. It consists of 3966 amino acids and contains more than 30 000 atoms. In this dimension, the biggest workgroup always lead to faster results. While the GTX285 could perform the 10 000 simulation steps in 44.5 minutes the AMD-GPU needed approximately the double runtime with 87.5 minutes. Figure 6 shows the relation between the count of simulated atoms and the duration of such a simulation. The 12-core CPU finished after roughly 10 minutes for 200 steps, which extrapolates to roughly 500 minutes for the total runtime. Estimating a twelvefold runtime for a single-core CPU, a single threaded simulation of this system would take 4 days.

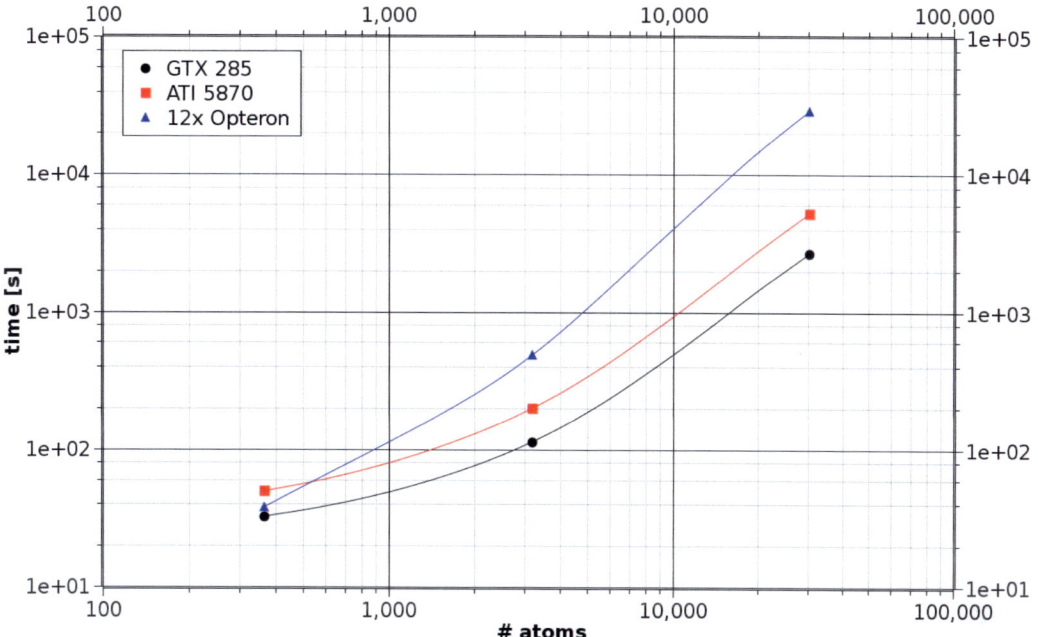

Figure 6: Duration of a 10 000 steps simulation versus number of atoms in the three proteins. The CPU measuring point for the 2VZ8 protein was estimated by simulating the first 200 steps.

5   Conclusion

In this paper we have presented a very successful port of the SMOG potential to GPU architectures. Comparison of the simulation times of the biggest simulated protein shows that a simulation, which previously ran for 4 days on a single core machine, now finishes after 44 minutes on a GPU with a speedup of 130 compared to a single CPU. This not only enables to finish more work in the same time, but actually extends the domain of proteins, which can be simulated in finite time.

We could further show that a single OpenCL N-body code base allows for optimized code on multiple architectures; a major porting benefit compared to similarly implemented CUDA codebases.

System size was a major issue in our investigation as the GPUs were only in use completely in our simulation of the biggest protein 2VZ8. Still, even at the smallest system size a speedup of 2 compared to a 12 core Opteron could be achieved on the GPU.

The complete folding event of 1F4I in a runtime of five minutes demonstrates the applicability of such a GPU system as a virtual laboratory for protein-protein interactions and protein-ligand docking.

Acknowledgement

We thank the Simulation Lab NanoMikro at SCC for providing access to GPU systems, support and for helpful discussions, and AMD for providing the Radeon 5870 GPU. Further we acknowledge the Carl-Zeiss Stiftung for funding of this forcefield development.

References

[1] A. Verma and W. Wenzel, "A Free-Energy Approach for All-Atom Protein Simulation," *Biophysical journal* 96, no. 9 (May 6, 2009): 3483-3494.

[2] P. C. Whitford et al., "An all-atom structure-based potential for proteins: Bridging minimal models with all-atom empirical forcefields," *Proteins: Structure, Function, and Bioinformatics* 75, no. 2 (2009): 430-441.

[3] J. Barnes and P. Hut, "A hierarchical O (N log N) force-calculation algorithm," *Nature* 324, no. 6096 (December 4, 1986): 446-449.

[4] E. Elsen et al., "N-body simulation on GPUs," in *Proceedings of the 2006 ACM/IEEE conference on Supercomputing* (Tampa, Florida: ACM, 2006), 188.

[5] E. S. Withers-Ward et al., "Biochemical and Structural Analysis of the Interaction between the UBA(2) Domain of the DNA Repair Protein HHR23A and HIV-1 Vpr†," *Biochemistry* 39, no. 46 (November 1, 2000): 14103-14112.

[6] R. S. Hall et al., "Discovery and Structure Determination of the Orphan Enzyme Isoxanthopterin Deaminase," *Biochemistry* 49, no. 20 (May 25, 2010): 4374-4382.

[7] T. Maier, M. Leibundgut, and N. Ban, "The Crystal Structure of a Mammalian Fatty Acid Synthase," *Science* 321, no. 5894 (2008): 1315-1322.

[8] D. van der Spoel, E. Lindahl, B. Hess, C Kutzner, A. R. van Buuren, E. Apol, P. J. Meulenhoff, D. P. Tieleman, A. L.T.M. Sijbers, K. A. Feenstra, R. van Drunen, H. J. C. Berendsen, "Version 4 of the Gromacs manual" 2006.

[9] OpenCL 1.0 Specification – The OpenGL Specification and the OpenGL Shading Language Specification. URL: http://www.opengl.org/registry/.

[10] AMD Stream SDK 2.2 OpenCL Programming Guide. URL: http://developer.amd.com/gpu /ATIStreamSDK/assets/ATI_Stream_SDK_OpenCL_Programming_Guide.pdf.

[11] NVIDIA CUDA 3.0 OpenCL Programming Guide. URL: http://developer.download.nvidia.com /compute/cuda/3_0/toolkit/docs/NVIDIA_OpenCL_ProgrammingGuide.pdf.

[12] T. Hamada et al., "42 TFlops hierarchical N-body simulations on GPUs with applications in both astrophysics and turbulence," in *Proceedings of the Conference on High Performance Computing Networking, Storage and Analysis* (Portland, Oregon: ACM, 2009), 1-12.

Highly efficient numerical implementation of the Chalker–Coddington network model and applications

Soumya Bera[1,2], Ferdinand Evers[1,2], Ivan Kondov[3]

[1] Institut für Theorie der Kondensierten Materie, [2] Institute of Nanotechnology,

[3] Steinbuch Centre for Computing, Karlsruhe Institute of Technology

[1] P.O.Box 6980, 76049 Karlsruhe, [2,3] P.O.Box 3640, 76021 Karlsruhe, Germany

E-mail: {soumya.bera, ferdinand.evers, ivan.kondov}@kit.edu

Abstract

A formulation of quantum dynamics at the Anderson transition in terms of a network model was introduced by Chalker and Coddington in 1988 to describe the integer quantum Hall effect. Such network models have been systematically exploited in both analytical studies and numerical simulations and played a key role in advancing our understanding of quantum Hall critical points, including not only the conventional integer quantum Hall effect but also systems with unconventional symmetries. On the other hand, highly efficient numerical routines for diagonalizing sparse matrices that have been developed over the last decade. Combined with the increase in computer power and an improved understanding of finite-size effects, this development has recently paved the way for highly accurate numerical studies of critical behavior for a variety of Anderson critical points.

Recently, we have developed a highly optimized numerical implementation of the Chalker–Coddington network model (CCNM) with intensive use of sparse matrix libraries ARPACK and MUMPS for diagonalization and solving linear equations, respectively. In particular, we have performed detailed profiling of the serial code and subsequently employed multi-layer strategies for parallelization. The dimension of the matrices computed is of the order of 10 million x 10 million and 10^6 disorder realizations have been done. For the computations the parallel machine HP XC3000 (HC3) at KIT has been used. The favorable scaling of the implementation allowed to investigate the interaction effect at the integer quantum Hall transition (IQHT) as well as relations between point contact conductance and multifractality in the numerical framework using the CCNM.

1 Introduction

A great many aspects of the integer quantum Hall transition (IQHT) are well understood in the framework of the non-interacting single-particle picture. At the same time, the role of the electron–electron interaction at the criticality is still not well comprehended. Although a screened interaction is irrelevant in the sense of renormalization group (RG) theory, it gives rise to dissipation and determines the nature of temperature and frequency scaling near the critical point. We have carried out a large-scale numerical simulation using the CCNM for calculating different disorder wavefunction correlations that appear at different orders of perturbation series to calculate the different critical exponents.

The Point Contact Conductance (PCC) at the integer quantum Hall transition is experimental way of probing the "multifractality" at the IQHT. Here, we investigate different relations between PCC and wavefunction statistics i.e, multifractality in the numerical framework using CCNM at the integer quantum Hall transition.

Aiming to address these challenging questions we have implemented the CCNM in efficient program code. In this paper, we will first introduce the model, our implementation approach, as well as the pursued parallelization strategies. Then, we will focus on the computing performance of the program code, particularly for treatment of large CCN Models and with extensive disorder averaging.

2 Methods

2.1 Model description

The Chalker–Coddington network model [1] is a random network model that describes aspect of the motion of electrons in two spatial dimensions in a strong perpendicular magnetic field and a smooth random potential. A typical representation of the model is shown in Fig. 1. The general idea behind the model is that electrons follow equipotential lines on the potential landscape [2]. They move in a square lattice in one direction only such that the time reversal symmetry is broken. Every crossing in the lattice is a scattering node where electrons, coming from a specific direction, can move left or right with certain probabilities. The probability is the same at every node in this model and equal to 1/2 at criticality. A scattering matrix (S_j) describes each of the node of the lattice where every unidirectional incoming (k,l) and outgoing (m,n) links represent the wavefunction amplitudes ψ_m, ψ_n, ψ_k, and ψ_l

$$\begin{pmatrix} \psi_m \\ \psi_n \end{pmatrix} = S_j \begin{pmatrix} \psi_k \\ \psi_l \end{pmatrix}; \qquad S_j = \begin{pmatrix} t_{mk} & t_{ml} \\ t_{nk} & t_{nl} \end{pmatrix} \tag{1}$$

where t_{mk}, t_{ml}, t_{nk}, and t_{nl} are the complex scattering coefficients and $R_j = |t_{ml}|^2 = |t_{nk}|^2$ and $T_j = 1 - R_j = |t_{mk}|^2 = |t_{nl}|^2$ define the reflection and transmission amplitudes at the node j respectively. The wavefunction Ψ on the network consists of complex amplitudes that were defined above for each node j of the lattice. The time evolution of such a state is given by

$$|\Psi(t+1)\rangle = U_E|\Psi(t)\rangle \tag{2}$$

where U_E is the energy dependent unitary "network" operator. The stationary solution of such a state is

$$|\Psi(t)\rangle = e^{-i\phi}|\Psi(t+1)\rangle \tag{3}$$

where $\phi \in \mathbb{R}$. Combining Eqs. (2) and (3) we get the eigenvalue equation [3] as

$$U_E|\Psi\rangle = e^{i\phi}|\Psi\rangle \ . \tag{4}$$

The solution of the eigenvalue problem, i.e. the set of the quasi-energies (ϕ) and eigenvectors (Ψ), constitute the basic quantities that enter the calculation of almost any physical observable.

2.2 Matrix Elements and Observables

Specifically, to address the statistical properties of the interaction matrix elements we calculate the first and second order interaction correction (SOC) to the imaginary part of the self-energy [4]. The function

$$\mathscr{K}_1(E) = \frac{\Delta^2}{2}\left\langle \sum_{\alpha,\beta} |\mathscr{B}_{\alpha,\beta}(\mathbf{r}_1,\mathbf{r}_2)|^2 \delta(E+\omega-\varepsilon_\alpha)\delta(E-\varepsilon_\beta) \right\rangle \tag{5}$$

describes the correlation between two non-interacting wavefunctions. It enters the interaction matrix elements, where $\mathscr{B}_{\alpha,\beta}(\mathbf{r}_1,\mathbf{r}_2) = \Psi_\alpha(\mathbf{r}_1)\Psi_\beta(\mathbf{r}_2) - \Psi_\alpha(\mathbf{r}_2)\Psi_\beta(\mathbf{r}_1)$ with $\Psi_\alpha(\mathbf{r}_1)$ being the wavefunction amplitude at spatial point $\mathbf{r}_1$. The ε_α and ε_β are the eigenenergies and ω is the frequency that is comparable to the mean level spacing Δ in our regime of interest. The brackets $\langle\rangle$ denote the averaging over different disorder realizations. Similarly, one can also express the higher order correlation function, appearing in higher order perturbation theory as a combination with eight wavefunctions,

$$\mathscr{K}_2(E) = \frac{\Delta^4}{8}\left\langle \sum_{\alpha,\beta,\gamma,\delta} \mathscr{B}^*_{\alpha,\beta}(\mathbf{r}_1,\mathbf{r}_2)\mathscr{B}_{\delta,\gamma}(\mathbf{r}_1,\mathbf{r}_2)\mathscr{B}^*_{\gamma,\delta}(\mathbf{r}_3,\mathbf{r}_4)\mathscr{B}_{\beta,\alpha}(\mathbf{r}_3,\mathbf{r}_4) \right.$$
$$\left. \times\delta(E-\varepsilon_\alpha)\delta(\varepsilon'+\Omega-\varepsilon_\beta)\delta(\varepsilon+\Omega-\varepsilon_\delta) \right\rangle. \tag{6}$$

Here, we consider the situation at criticality where wavefunctions fluctuate strongly, thus to minimize the statistical error we need to average over many disorder realizations, typically $10^4 - 10^6$. Moreover, an important contribution to the correlation function at criticality comes from rare events, so that extremely good statistics is needed and parallelization becomes necessary.

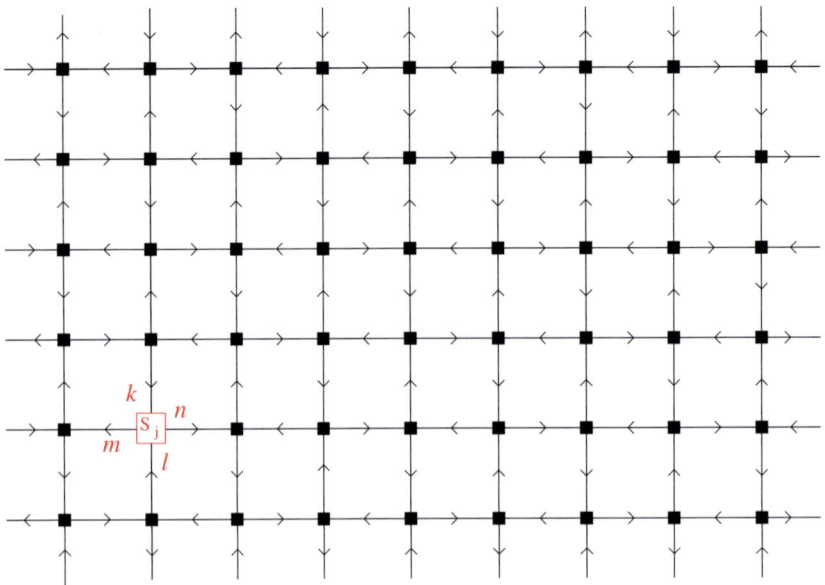

Figure 1: A section of the Chalker–Coddington network model in the quantum Hall regime with directed links and scattering centers at each crossing. Each saddle point is represented by the scattering matrix S_j with two incoming (k,l) and two outgoing links (m,n) with corresponding scattering coefficients t_{mk}, t_{ml}, t_{nk}, and t_{nl}, as represented in the figure. We employ periodic boundary conditions in both directions of the square lattice.

Similarly, the calculation of the PCC proceeds via the solution of the time evolution of the wavefunction in the following way [5]

$$|\Psi(t+1)\rangle = U(|\Psi(t)\rangle + a|c\rangle + b|c'\rangle) \tag{7}$$

here $|c\rangle, |c'\rangle$ denote the basis states with unit amplitude at current injection links c, c' respectively, where a, b are the amplitudes of current fed into the links. To implement the draining action we define a projection operator P_C by $P_C|\Psi\rangle = \Psi(C)|C\rangle$, where $C = c, c'$. Now after including the draining action, Eq. (7) becomes

$$|\Psi(t+1)\rangle = U[(1 - P_c)(1 - P_{c'})|\Psi(t)\rangle + a|c\rangle + b|c'\rangle]. \tag{8}$$

The stationary condition for the current carrying states implies $|\Psi_\infty\rangle = \lim_{t\to\infty}|\Psi(t)\rangle$ with which we deduce the system of linear equations as

$$(1 - U_P)|\Psi_\infty\rangle = U(a|c\rangle + b|c'\rangle) \tag{9}$$

where we define $U_P = U(1 - P_c - P_{c'})$. According to Landauer–Büttiker formula, the PCC is given by the transmission probability, T. The transmission probability is defined by feeding one unit of current at link c and zero at c' and computing the amplitude of Ψ_∞ at link c'. Thus we set $a = 1$ and $b = 0$ in Eq. (9) to measure the conductance as $T = |\langle c'|\Psi_\infty\rangle|^2$.

For each disorder configuration we solve the system of linear equations (9) and get only one conductance value for a specific system size, L. This is an expensive task as to get a good statistical measure of the conductance we need to solve the system of linear equation for $10^4 - 10^6$ disorder realizations. As solving the system of linear equations takes most of the time in the program, we use two level of parallelism to deal with the problem which will be discussed in detail in the following sections.

2.3 Code optimization and parallelization

The CCNM described in the previous section has been implemented in Fortran 90 in previous work. In order to efficiently tackle numerics with sparse matrices the program makes intensive use of the high performance libraries ARPACK and MUMPS. In particular, the Implicitly Restarted Arnoldi Iteration from the ARPACK package [6] was employed to compute approximations to eigenvalues from Eq. (4). Typically, the first 6 or 8 eigenvalues are computed. To solve the system of linear equations (9) the Multi-frontal Massively Parallel sparse direct Solver (MUMPS) [7–9] and PORD reordering [10] were used.

Recently, we performed numerous optimizations to improve the serial performance of the code and to identify and to reduce the number of bottlenecks. Reducing the number of bottlenecks was important for efficient parallelization of the overall code with minor programming and tuning effort due to the law of diminishing returns. It turned out that for all models (first-order correction, SOC and PCC) the call to the linear solver (here the MUMPS library) was the most expensive part. However, we measured that only 65-70% and 85% of the run time was used by MUMPS in the PCC and SOC models, respectively. The rest of the time is used by several other parts of the code. For example the driver subroutine including the calls to MUMPS and the subroutine defining the network operator (U) take together up to 15%, and in the SOC model the subroutine, that calculates the correlation function as defined in Eq. (6), takes up to 15% of the run time for a specific choice of the system size L.

In the next subsections we describe our strategies to parallelization.

2.3.1 Parallelization of the disorder averaging

With the original version of the code the calculations had been carried out in many very long running serial jobs (they have taken time of the order of months) to compute several thousands up to million of disorder realizations. This is why we first considered parallelization of the disorder averaging. We implemented it using reduction global communications of MPI such as `mpi_reduce`. Because a job over million disorder realizations cannot be finished within a single week even with very high MPI task numbers we implemented in addition means to checkpoint the calculation and to continue later in a new job restarting from the last checkpoint.

2.3.2 Parallelization of the linear solver

The two major advantages to perform parallelization at this level are memory reduction per task and the workload distribution (speedup). With use of MPI the MUMPS library is parallelized basing on asynchronous static and dynamic scheduling algorithms. Moderate speedups of 14 on 32 processors [8] have been reported. Nearly linear scaling for up to 4 tasks and speedup of 6 on 8 tasks have been reported for the most recent version of MUMPS [11]. Noticeably, the parallel performance reported strongly varies with the size and type of the left-hand-side matrix [12, 13].

For this paper we have compiled the CCNM program using the Intel Fortran compiler version 11. For the parallel version of the code the Intel MPI library was used on the Opus cluster and HP-MPI library on the XC 3000 (HC3). For LAPACK, BLAS, BLACS and ScaLAPACK that are needed by MUMPS and ARPACK the Intel Math Kernel Library version 10 was linked. For profiling and debugging purposes gprof and DDT, respectively, were used.

2.4 Simulation protocol and parameters

We started our runs on the systems Opus (IBM x3550 with Intel Xeon E5430 processors and DDR InfiniBand interconnect) and the HC3 (HP XC3000 with Intel Xeon E5540 processors and QDR InfiniBand interconnect) at the Steinbuch Centre for Computing (SCC). For the benchmarking we considered the same parameterization of the two models PCC and defined above. The system size, L, is defined in terms of number of links in one direction of the square lattice which was varied from 128 up to 512. For the SOC model we choose the following combination of spatial distances to calculate the correlation function $\mathscr{K}_2$, $\mathbf{r}_1 - \mathbf{r}_2 = \mathbf{r}_3 - \mathbf{r}_4 = 1$ and $\mathbf{r}_1 - \mathbf{r}_3 = 3$. For the benchmarking purpose in the PCC model we measure the transmission amplitude, T, where the injected current link and the draining current link is differed by one lattice site. In each of the two models we only calculate 8 eigenvalues (with wavefunctions) per sample.

3 Computational performance

Parallelization of the disorder averaging is coarse-grained and widely latency insensitive. In addition, it requires exchange of very small messages and the communication times do not depend on the interconnect's bandwidth. Thus, the parallelization of the disorder averaging

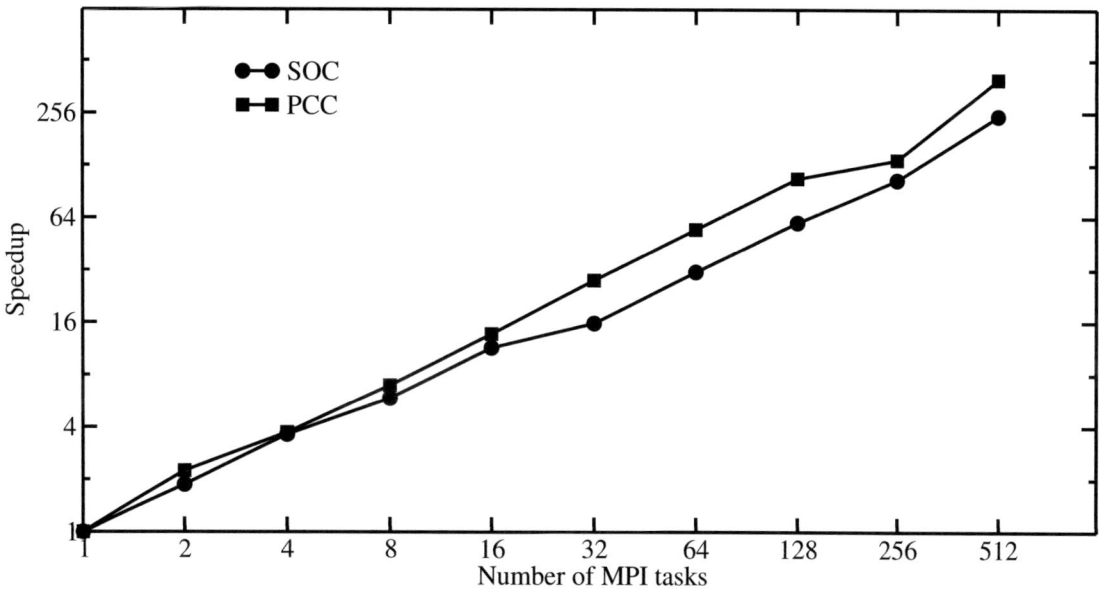

Figure 2: Speedup of parallel disorder averaging for the SOC and PCC models (both with $L = 512$ links) denoted by circles and squares, respectively.

scales very well for very large number of MPI tasks as shown on Fig. 2. Due to the widely dominating parallel section for the sampling tasks ($> 99.99\%$ for models with $L = 512$ links) the speedup is nearly linear for up to 512 MPI tasks. However, the observed slope is notably smaller than that of the ideal speedup. As introduced in the methods section, we have implemented a synchronous algorithm to parallelize disorder averaging. Because each disorder realization takes slightly different time due to the iterative solver this leads to load imbalance which gives rise to overall smaller slope of the speedup. We have analyzed the measured time profiles of all parallel sections and arrived to approx. 13% average load imbalance as determined as the ratio of the standard deviation and the mean of parallel section times for both SOC, and PCC models. Moreover, we identified load imbalance peaks (from the ratio of the mean and the maximum of parallel section times) amounting to approx. 47% and 40% for the SOC and the PCC model, respectively. In agreement, the PCC model exhibits a better performance, i.e. a speedup slope in Fig. 2 that is closer to the ideal one than for the SOC model. Because load imbalance does not depend on number of tasks, the speedup is evenly affected for small and large number of tasks and thus it is linear (cf. Fig. 2). In future development, the load imbalance issue can be efficiently remedied using an asynchronous parallelization of the disorder averaging, e.g. such one based on a master–slave concept.

Besides parallelization of disorder averaging we also exploited parallelism available in the linear solver library MUMPS. As noted previously, parallelization of this kind is already known to scale only moderately [12, 13], however, the possibility to distribute the data, which for the

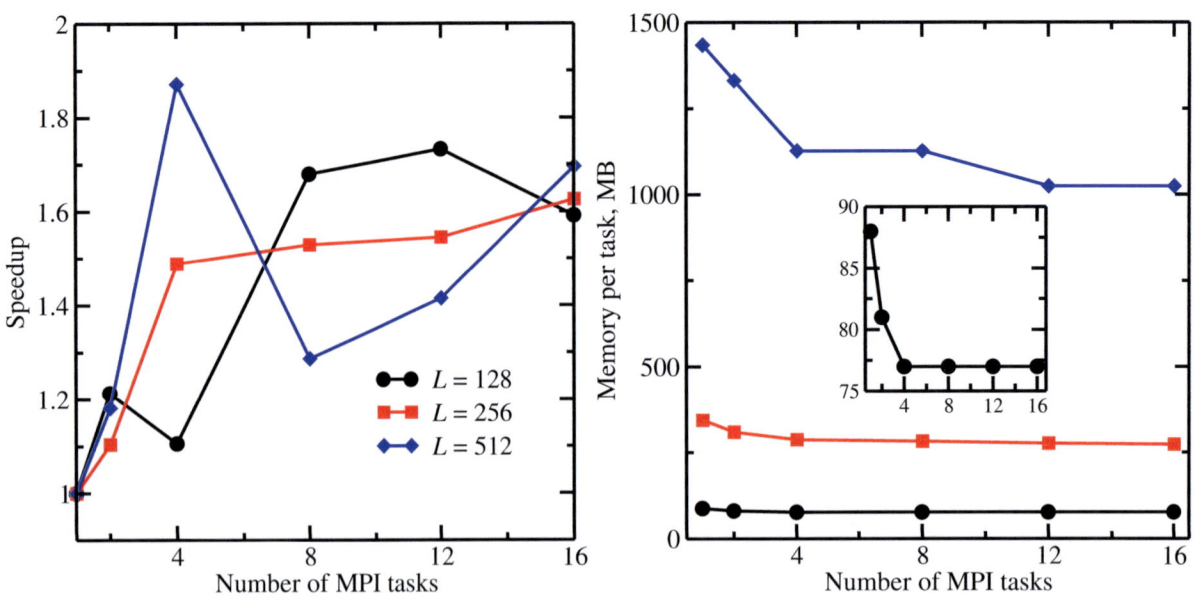

Figure 3: Speedup (left plot) and memory usage per task (right plot) for the SOC model with parallelized linear solver. Measured data for $L = 128$, 256 and 512 links are denoted by black circles, red squares and blue diamonds, respectively.

CCNM scales like L^4, enables carrying out computations for $L > 2000$ links, i.e. when the available memory on the compute node for one MPI task becomes a limitation. As a benchmark we show the measured speedup and memory decrease per task for the two models on Figs. 3 and 4.

For two and four tasks an initial increase of the speedup is observed. Then the speedups for $L = 128$ and $L = 256$ links additionally increase while the speedup for the models with $L = 512$ links drops somewhat with 8 MPI tasks. The best speedup found for the SOC model is 1.9 and for for the PCC model 2.1 for the case with the largest number of links. The speedup for both 128-link models decreases going past 16 MPI tasks while the gain for the 512-link models is insignificant. Note that the speedup only due to calls to MUMPS has been discussed. The code parts that do not belong to the linear solver, amounting to 35% and 15% for SOC and PCC, respectively, are not considered. On the right panels of Figs. 3 and 4 we plotted the reduction of memory usage per task with the degree of parallelization. Largest decrease of factor of two is found for the PCC model for all network sizes. Relatively moderate memory benefits can be made with the SOC model variable from 10 up to 30%, from the smallest to the largest network sizes, respectively. For all sizes and both models the memory usage decreases monotonously with task number. However, no further gain was measured for number of tasks larger than 16. To summarize, the linear solver as available in the MUMPS library can perform only moderately in parallel utilizing efficiently up to 2-4 MPI tasks. Additional speedup improvement may be achieved using threaded BLAS calls as has been reported in Ref. 11 with up to 4 threads per

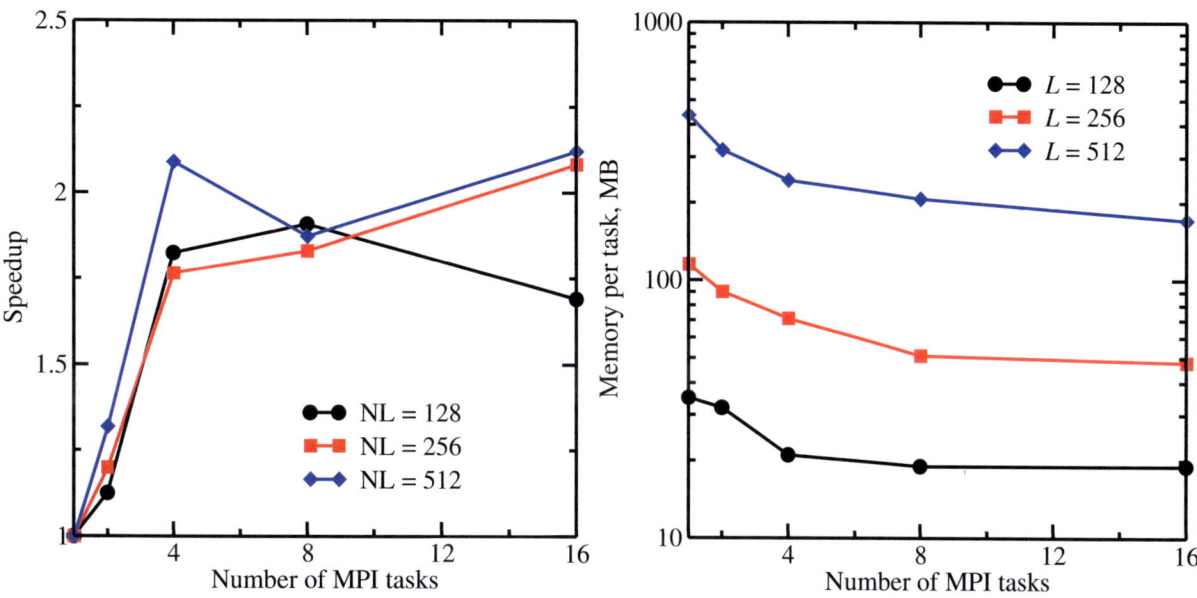

Figure 4: Speedup (left plot) and memory usage per task (right plot) for the PCC model with parallelized linear solver. Measured data for $L = 128$, 256 and 512 links are denoted by black circles, red squares and blue diamonds, respectively.

task. Furthermore, the data distribution can be optimized using another partitioning algorithm [14]. Also in this case, a trade-off between performance gain and resource utilization has to be made with up to 16 tasks.

4 Conclusion

In this paper, we have reported on a efficient parallel implementation of the Chalker–Coddington network model. Currently, the code can be efficiently used on massively parallel computers, like the HC3 at SCC, to solve the model and average the solutions over disorder within a single day. For matrices for network size of $L \approx 1000 - 2000$ an improved parallelization of the linear solver can yield additional speedup and, at certain extent, alleviate the existing memory bottleneck per task.

In current and future work we consider using ParMETIS [14, 15] or PT-SCOTCH [16] for factorization/reordering to improve the scaling in terms of speedup and memory usage per core. In addition, using multi-threaded BLAS on 2-4 threads can improve the speedup. In order to minimize and eliminate load imbalance due to parallelization of disorder sampling, an asynchronous scheduling algorithm is currently being implemented. Another optimization aspect is the reduction of code parts not belonging to the linear solver via serial optimization.

Acknowledgment

Financial support from the CFN (project number C4.11) at KIT and the Program "Supercomputing" of the Helmholtz Association is gratefully acknowledged.

References

[1] J. T. Chalker and P. D. Coddington. Percolation, quantum tunnelling and the integer Hall-effect. *J. Phys. C: Solid State Phys.*, 21:2665, 1988.

[2] B. Kramer, T. Ohtsuki, and S. Kettemann. Random network models and quantum phase transitions in two dimensions. *Phys. Rep.*, 417:211, 2005.

[3] R. Klesse and M. Metzler. Universal multifractality in quantum hall systems with long-range disorder potential. *Europhys. Lett.*, 32:229, 1995.

[4] I. Burmistrov, S. Bera, F. Evers, I. Gornyi, and A. Mirlin. Wave function multifractality and dephasing at metal-insulator and quantum Hall transitions. *arXiv:1011.3616*, 2010.

[5] M. Janssen, M. Metzler, and M. R. Zirnbauer. Point-contact conductances at the quantum hall transition. *Phys. Rev. B*, 59:15836, 1999.

[6] R. B. Lehoucq, D. C. Sorensen, and C. Yang. *ARPACK Users Guide: Solution of Large Scale Eigenvalue Problems by Implicitly Restarted Arnoldi Methods*. Society for Industrial and Applied Mathematics, Philadelphia, PA, 1998.

[7] P. R. Amestoy, I. S. Duff, J. Koster, and J.-Y. L'Excellent. A fully asynchronous multifrontal solver using distributed dynamic scheduling. *SIAM J. Matrix Anal. Appl.*, 23:15, 2001.

[8] P. Amestoy, I. S. Duff, J.-Y. L'Excellent, and J. Koster. MUMPS: A general purpose distributed memory sparse solver. In *Proceedings of the 5th International Workshop on Applied Parallel Computing, New Paradigms for HPC in Industry and Academia*, PARA'00, pages 121–130, Springer, 2001.

[9] P. R. Amestoy, A. Guermouche, J.-Y. L'Excellent, and S. Pralet. Hybrid scheduling for the parallel solution of linear systems. *Parallel Computing*, 32(2):136, 2006.

[10] J. Schulze. Towards a tighter coupling of bottom-up and top-down sparse matrix ordering methods. *BIT*, 41:800, 2001.

[11] J. Y. L'Excellent. MUMPS: A multifrontal massively parallel solver. URL: http://www.ci-ra.org/Documents/Seminaires/11-2010/JY-Lexcellent.pdf.

[12] L. Grasedyck, W. Hackbusch, and R. Kriemann. Performance of H-LU preconditioning for sparse matrices. *Comp. Methods Appl. Math.*, 8:336, 2008.

[13] M. Fournié, N. Renon, Y. Renard, and D. Ruiz. CFD parallel simulation using GetFEM++ and MUMPS. In Pasqua D'Ambra, Mario Guarracino, and Domenico Talia, editors, *Euro-Par 2010 - Parallel Processing*, volume 6272 of *Lecture Notes in Computer Science*, pages 77–88. Springer, 2010.

[14] G. Karypis and V. Kumar. A parallel algorithm for multilevel graph partitioning and sparse matrix ordering. *J. Par. Distr. Comp.*, 48:71, 1998.

[15] G. Karypis, K. Schloegel, and V. Kumar. ParMETIS: Parallel graph partitioning and sparse matrixordering library. Technical report, University of Minnesota, Department of Computer Science and Engineering, 1997.

[16] F. Pellegrini and J. Roman. SCOTCH: A software package for static mapping by dual recursive bipartitioning of process and architecture graphs. In *Proceedings of HPCN'96, Brussels, Belgium*, volume 1067, pages 493–498. Springer, 1996.

All-Atom Replica Exchange Simulations of Denaturant Induced Partial Unfolding of RNaseH

Simon Widmaier[1], Ivan Kondov[2], and Wolfgang Wenzel[1]

[1] Institute of Nanotechnology, [2] Steinbuch Centre for Computing, Karlsruhe Institute of Technology, Hermann-von-Helmholtz-Platz 1, 76344 Eggenstein-Leopoldshafen Germany

Abstract

The unfolding of Ribonuclease H (RNaseH) in water/guanidinium chloride solvent at 300K can be analyzed by means of single-molecule fluorescence resonance energy transfer (FRET) experiments, from which a deduction on a stable, partially unfolded configuration is possible. Highly effective biomolecular simulation methods, like replica exchange, allow a fast sampling of the energy landscape of complex biomolecules and are applicable for the quest for partially unfolded configurations of RNaseH.

We here present the results of two comparative all-atom replica exchange simulations performed on *E. Coli* RNaseH (2RN2) using water as well as denaturant guanidinium chloride solvent. The combinatory influence of temperature and denaturant solvent reveal distinct unfolding mechanisms depending on the choice of the solvent type. GdmCl solvent based replica exchange simulations can amplify the induction of destabilizing effects in replica exchange simulations, particularly at moderate temperatures and therefore accelerate the search for representative structure ensembles.

1 Introduction

RnaseH is an enzyme that cleaves RNA via a hydrolytic mechanism and is commonly used as model to study folding and unfolding of soluble proteins. Partial unfolding of proteins is traditionally achieved in biomolecular simulation by increasing the kinetic energy of the simulated system. Recent studies apply denaturant solvents in molecular dynamics simulations and compare the solvent effect on the unfolding efficiency [1].

As shown in Fig. 1, experiments on surface-immobilized RNaseH performed by Kuzmenkina et al. [2], indicate a thermodynamically stable, partially unfolded configuration of the RnaseH molecule. Due to the large and highly complex energy landscape of proteins and the duration of unfolding events in the microsecond timescale, traditional molecular dynamics simulations are a computationally very costly approach to produce representative ensembles of unfolded states.

Hence, we performed comparative replica exchange simulations on RNaseH one system using water solvent and a second with mixed guanidinium chloride (GdmCl) / water denaturant

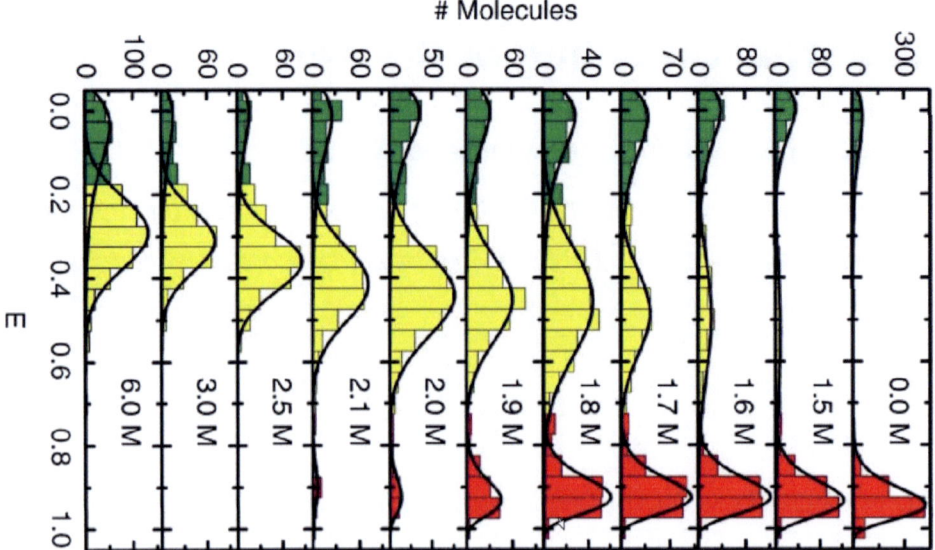

Figure 1: Experimental histograms derived from [2] (rescaled). FRET efficiency values E at concentrations from 0.0 M to 6.0 M of GdmCl. Three populations can be distinguished: red, folded molecules; yellow, unfolded molecules; green, molecules labeled with a donor only. The distributions are fitted with two log-normal and one Gaussian (unfolded population) distributions to determine the average FRET efficiency and width for each subpopulation.

solvent. In the course of the simulation, the protein is exposed to multiple denaturant effects, most importantly the system temperature and the denaturant solvent. The replica exchange approach allows a fast sampling of the energy landscape and paves the way for ensemble generation for further analysis. For comparison, one system with TIP3 water and a second with mixed guanidinium chloride / TIP3 solvent was constructed.

2 Methods

2.1 Simulation protocol

The systems were built and parameterized using the crystal structure of *E. Coli* RNaseH, PDB code 2RN2, using CHARMm [3] version c35b5. The water solvent was included in the simulation within the TIP3P water model as implemented in CHARMM. The TIP3P water model specifies a three-site rigid water molecule with charges and Lennard-Jones parameters assigned to each of the three water atoms [4]. The water/GdmCl ratio of RNaseH-DEN was chosen 35.27 which approximately corresponds to a molarity of 1.42 M. This guanidinium concentration is in the lower molarity range for experimentally observed unfolding at ambient conditions (cf. Fig. 1). Parameters for the guanidinium solvent molecules were generated derived from the

Table 1: Comparison of parameters of the two simulated systems.

	(RNaseH-WAT)	(RNaseH-DEN)
Environment	water	GdmCl + water
Water molecules	24828	22361
Guanidinium molecules	-	634
Chloride ions	2	636
Atoms	76941	76515

CHARMm 27 forcefield for arginine as described in Ref. [5]. Replica exchange simulations were performed using the code NAMD [6, 7] version 2.7b2. Eight systems were treated in parallel applying eight equidistant temperature steps between 300 K to 600 K. In Table 1 we have summarized the most important parameters of the two simulations. The RNaseH-DEN system has been simulated 8 ns and the RNaseH-WAT 9 ns. Snapshots of the structures we taken in 1 ns intervals and used for analysis. In both simulations, 1 ns was carried out at the cost of 10 wall hours on the HP XC3000 machine HC3 (see below).

2.2 Replica exchange

To compile the NAMD code we have used the Intel Compiler 11. For parallelization basing on both multi-threading and message passing (MPI) we have employed the Charm++ library [8, 9]. The parallel NAMD code was optimized and adapted for use on the distributed memory parallel computer HP XC3000 (HC3) at the Steinbuch Centre for Computing. Each node of HC3 has eight Intel Xeon processor cores and thus suitable for multi-threading of parts of the simulation running on the same node. In particular, we implemented a modulefile which automatically configures the runtime environment for either multi-threaded or MPI versions of NAMD depending on the resources allocated in the user job.

In the modulefile for replica exchange molecular dynamics (REMD) we have deployed the multi-threaded version of the code. The module analyses the resources available for the job and assigns replicas on different nodes. On each node the replica can run then on up to eight threads utilizing one processor core per thread. Thus a REMD job with this module can use multiple nodes but not more nodes than replicas. The number of tasks may not be less than the number of replicas. In addition, the number of tasks assigned by the batch system must be the same for each node.

3 Results

Denaturation occurs at much lower temperatures in the mixed GdmCl/water solvent (RNaseH-DEN) as compared to RNaseH in pure water solvent (RNaseH-WAT). As shown in Figs. 2 and 3, the root mean square deviation (RMSD) of the spatial coordinates of the centered protein compared to the initial reference structure has a temperature dependence in RNaseH-WAT, whereas RNaseH-DEN exhibits fluctuations that are not consistent with the native structure at ambient conditions.

The RNaseH-DEN system shows a significant RMSD offset (Fig. 3) at ambient temperature conditions and confirms the denaturant effect of GdmCl/water at 300 K. At higher temperatures of 550-600 K, the difference between the RMSDs of water and GdmCl/water systems are negligible indicating that temperature denaturation outweighs solvent-induced effects.

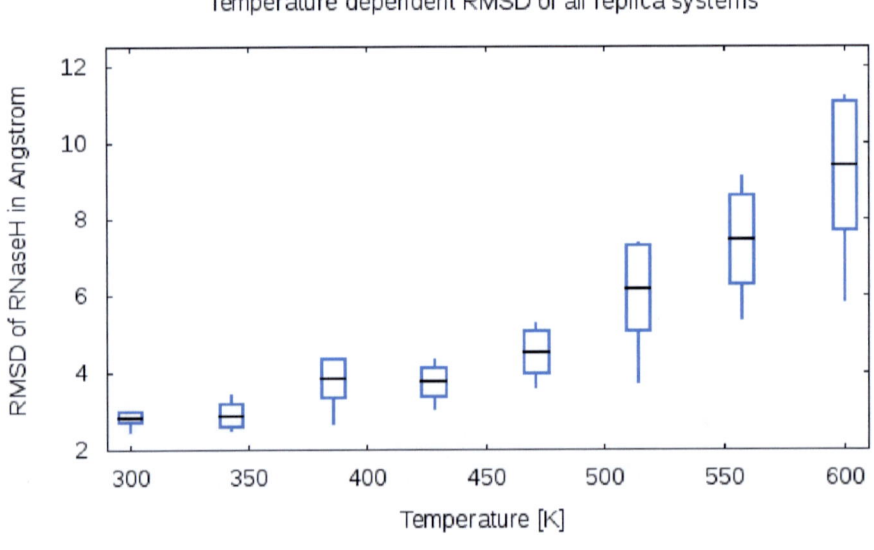

Figure 2: Root Mean Square Deviation (RMSD) of RNaseH-WAT with pure TIP3 water solvent. All eight replica simulations were conducted at equidistant temperatures between 300 K and 600 K. The black dashes depict the mean RMSD values, the rectangular bars denote the standard deviation, and the vertical lines connect the minimum and maximum RMSD values for each temperature. The RMSD reveals a significant temperature dependence of unfolding.

This result shows that the RNaseH-DEN system is exposed to two distinct destabilizing effects. Due to the repetitive exchange events during the simulation, the average RMSD values fluctuate and show higher values in systems with lower temperatures, as the unfolded states are stabilized by the denaturant solvent even at lower temperatures.

Another analysis method to quantify denaturation is provided by the radius of gyration of the protein. The radius of gyration can be estimated experimentally by light scattering and therefore is commonly used to quantify the folding state of polymer chains. As illustrated in Figs. 4 and 5, the GdmCl system shows a large offset of approximately 17 Å and no temperature dependence. Surprisingly, between 300 K and 450 K the denaturant effect decreases with increasing temperature. At 600 K, RNaseH-WAT shows slightly larger fluctuations of the radius of gyration than RNaseH-DEN at the same temperature.

These results indicate that RNaseH populates non-native conformations in GdmCl/water solvent at room temperature. The denaturant effect of GdmCl shows no temperature dependence at ambient conditions and confirms the difference between heat and solvent induced unfolding mechanisms.

In contrast to solvation in pure water, the two-phase mixture of GdmCl/water has a stabilizing effect on globular RNaseH structure with increasing temperature. This effect is presumably due to the higher evaporation temperature of the GdmCl/water environment. Alternatively, for high

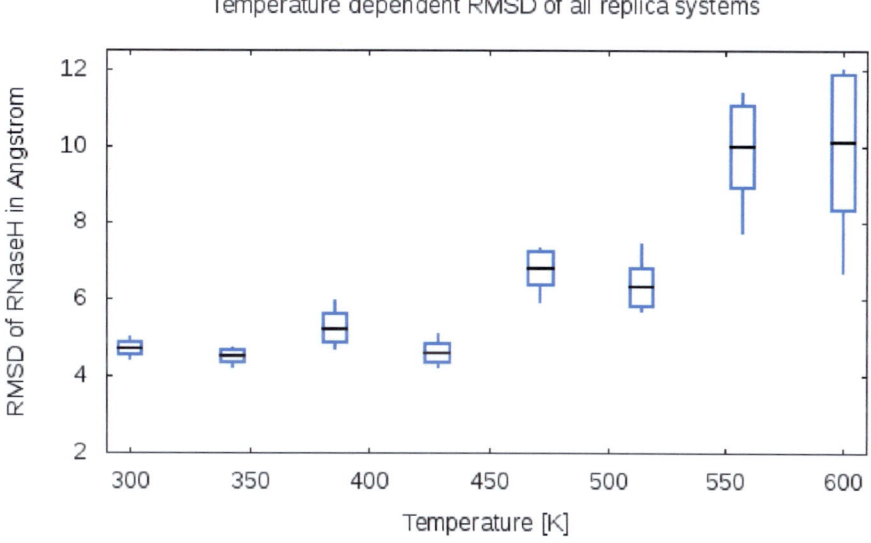

Figure 3: Root Mean Square Deviation (RMSD) of RNaseH-DEN with denaturant mixed guanidinium chloride (GdmCl)/water solvent. The black dashes depict the mean RMSD values, the rectangular bars denote the standard deviation, and the vertical lines connect the minimum and maximum RMSD values for each temperature. For low temperatures, the RMSD does not show a correlation between temperature and unfolding, but a significant offset at 300 K. This indicates distinct denaturation effects induced by heat on the one hand and solvent interactions on the other.

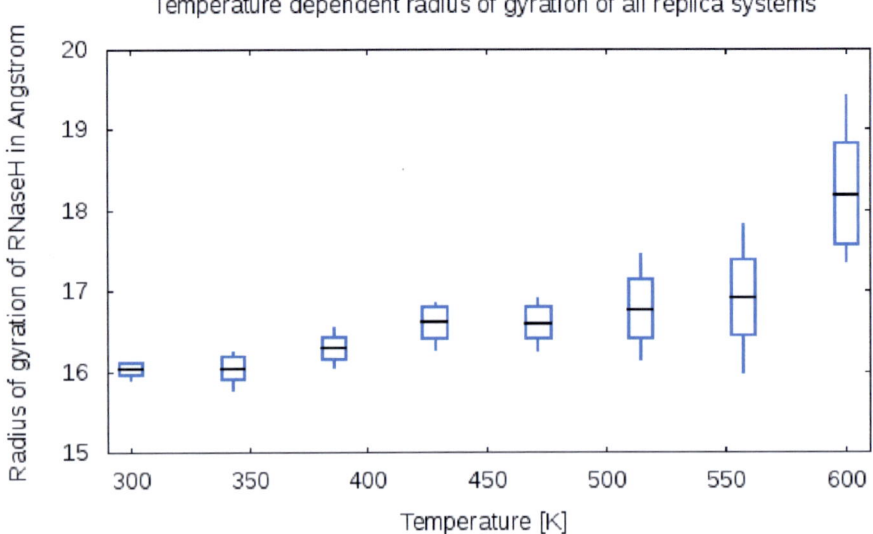

Figure 4: Radius of gyration of RNaseH-WAT with pure TIP3 water solvent. All eight replica simulations were conducted at equidistant temperatures between 300K and 600K. The black dashes depict the mean radii of gyration, the rectangular bars denote the standard deviation, and the vertical lines connect the minimum and maximum radii for each temperature. The radius of gyration shows a stepwise temperature dependence with increasing average values, standard deviations and extreme values.

temperatures the water seems to dissociate more effectively as GdmCl the H-bonds and the ionic contacts in the protein. Thus the stabilization of native state is due to an interplay between the ionic bridges with denaturant ions located at the globular surface.

4 Conclusion

The identification of a stable, partially unfolded structure, which is representative for the results of single-molecule FRET experiments, by replica exchange allowed subsequent molecular dynamics simulations and a detailed analysis of the unfolding mechanisms of mixed water/guanidinium chloride solvent.

Future work may yield the representative partially unfolded structures derived from our all-atom replica exchange simulations in denaturant solvent for detailed analysis in subsequent molecular dynamics simulations. In other studies we will address the expansion of traditional temperature cascading replica exchange methods by integration of denaturant baths with unaltered temperature as second denaturation dimension and the establishment of a highly efficient unfolding method comprising multiple denaturant effects.

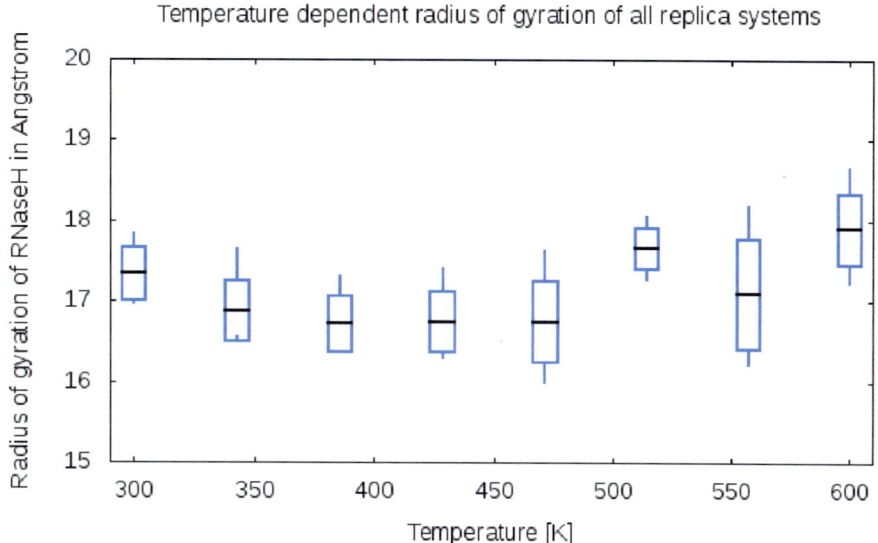

Figure 5: Radius of gyration of RNaseH-DEN with denaturant mixed guanidinium chloride (GdmCl)/water solvent. The black dashes depict the mean radii of gyration, the rectangular bars denote the standard deviation, and the vertical lines connect the minimum and maximum radii for each temperature. In comparison to RNaseH-WAT, the radius of gyration shows an inverse development for replicas, significantly higher standard deviations and maximal values.

Acknowledgment

Financial support from the Deutsche Forschungsgemeinschaft and the Helmholtz Association (Program Supercomputing) is gratefully acknowledged.

References

[1] C. Camilloni, A. G. Rocco, I. Eberini, E. Gianazza, R. A. Broglia, and G. Tiana. Urea and guanidinium chloride denature protein l in different ways in molecular dynamics simulations. *Biophys. J.*, 94:4654, 2008.

[2] E. V. Kuzmenkina, C. D. Heyes, and G. U. Nienhaus. Single-molecule fret study of denaturant induced unfolding of rnase h. *J. Mol. Biol.*, 357:313, 2006.

[3] B. R. Brooks, R. E. Bruccoleri, B. D. Olafson, D. J. States, S. Swaminathan, and M. Karplus. Charmm: A program for macromolecular energy, minimization, and dynamics calculations. *J. Comp. Chem.*, 4:187, 1983.

[4] W. L. Jorgensen, J. Chandrasekhar, J. D. Madura, R. W. Impey, and M. L. Klein. Comparison of simple potential functions for simulating liquid water. *J. Chem. Phys.*, 79:926, 1983.

[5] P. E. Mason, G. W. Neilson, J. E. Enderby, M.-L. Saboungi, C. E. Dempsey, A. D. MacKerell, and J. W. Brady. The structure of aqueous guanidinium chloride solutions. *J Am Chem Soc*, 126:11462, 2004.

[6] NAMD was developed by the Theoretical Biophysics Group in the Beckman Institute for Advanced Science and Technology at the University of Illinois at Urbana-Champaign.

[7] J. C. Phillips, R. Braun, W. Wang, J. Gumbart, E. Tajkhorshid, E. Villa, C. Chipot, R. D. Skeel, L. Kale, and K. Schulten. Scalable molecular dynamics with NAMD. *J. Comp. Chem.*, 26:1781, 2005.

[8] Charm++ was developed by the Parallel Programming Laboratory in the Department of Computer Science at the University of Illinois at Urbana-Champaign.

[9] L. V. Kale and S. Krishnan. Charm++: Parallel programming with message-driven objects. In *Parallel Programming using C++*, G. V. Wilson and P. Lu (Eds.), pages 175–213, MIT Press, 1996.

Conductance and Noise Correlations of Correlated Nanostructures

A DMRG Perspective

Peter Schmitteckert

Institute of Nanotechnology, Karlsruhe Institute of Technology

Hermann-von-Helmholtz-Platz 1, 76344 Eggenstein-Leopoldshafen, Germany

E-mail: peter.schmitteckert@kit.edu

Abstract

The study of transport in and out of equilibrium, strongly interacting systems, is of crucial importance for technological applications. It also addresses some of the most challenging fundamental questions, from the possibility of fluctuations theorems out of equilibrium, to the time evolution of quantum many body entanglement. While experimental progress in this area has been swift and steady, the theory has been held back by considerable technical difficulties. The physics of interest occurs usually in non perturbative regimes, where analytical methods are few and limited. Numerical approaches require real-time simulations, which up to recently had been notoriously hard. In our project we apply the Density Matrix Renormalization Group (DMRG) to perform time dependent simulations for strongly interacting quantum systems. As an introduction to the approach and to a remarkable consequence of electron-electron interaction, we present our results concerning the spin-charge separation in one-dimensional wires. We then continue with the main results of our project, namely the extraction of conductance and current correlations from time dependent simulations. We present results for the interacting resonant level model (IRLM) at the self dual point, where we were also able to obtain analytical results based on the thermodynamic Bethe ansatz. Both approaches lead to an excellent agreement and are by now already an established benchmark for other approximative approaches. Most strikingly, we find a negative differential conductance regime for high voltages and the measurement of the shot noise allows us to determine the effective charge of the charge carriers. Finally we provide first results for the Kondo system and discuss our current approach to obtain higher order cumulants. Our code is currently SMP parallelized within a master-worker approach using Posix threads, where the workload can be distributed on worker threads either running on CPUs or GPUs. The simulations for the IRLM are performed on the XC2 at the Steinbuch Centre for Computing (Karlsruhe) and the Kondo calculation on the JUROPA cluster at the Jülich supercomputing centre.

1 Introduction

Transport properties of strongly interacting quantum systems are a major challenge in todays condensed matter theory. While much is known for transport properties of non-interacting electrons, based on the Landauer–Büttiker formalism [1, 2, 3], the non equilibrium properties of interacting fermions are an open problem. Due to the vast improvements in experimental techniques there is an increasing theoretical interest in one-dimensional quantum systems. Since in low dimension the screening of electrons is reduced the effective interaction gets increased and can drive the electron systems into new phases beyond the standard description of a Fermi liquid, e.g. into a Luttinger liquid. Formally the conductance of a quantum device attached to leads is given by the Meir Wingreen formula [4]. Besides the special case of proportional coupling, the Meir Wingreen can only be treated within perturbative approaches.

The Density Matrix Renormalization Group (DMRG) method [5, 6, 7] is a well established method to study low dimensional strongly correlated quantum systems. The method is controlled in the sense that it has a single control parameter, namely the number of states N_{Cut} kept per block, and that the results become exact once the control parameter is large enough. However, the calculations are getting very expensive in memory and CPU time for large N_{Cut} leading to the necessity of using high performance computing infrastructure. The major difficulty in developing a high performing DMRG implementation lies in the large amount of book keeping needed to keep track of the quantum numbers/symmetries. Therefore we have chosen C++ as the core language relying heavily on the standard template library (STL) and to some extend on boost.org. The execution of the code is however dominated by the use of BLAS 3 calls, most dominantly dgemm leading to a high performing code. As explained in Section 4 our parallelization is implemented via Posix threads, which allows for a high concurrency within our master-worker approach. We could extend our parallelization to distributed computing by implementing MPI workers, like we have done for GPU workers. However, to obtain data like current–voltage (I/V) characteristics we have to run the code many times for different voltage leading to an intrinsic embarrassingly parallel problem.

2 Spin charge separation in a transport setup

One of the striking properties of interacting one-dimensional Fermi systems is the possibility of a separation of spin and charge degrees of freedom, for an overview see Ref. 8. As already described in Ref. 9 wave packets in a repulsive Hubbard model undergo a spin charge separation. The question we ask in this section is whether one should be able to observe the spin charge separation in a transport setup. We have therefore attached an interacting region to noninteract-

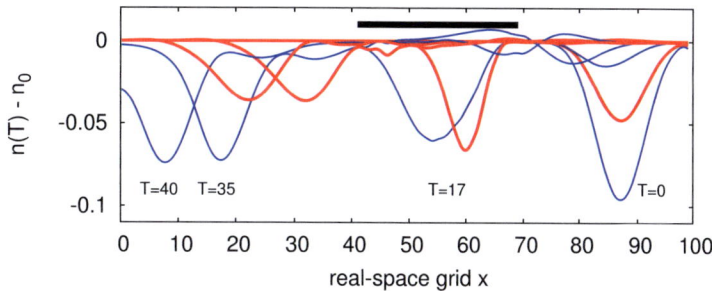

Figure 1: Spin charge separation in a transport experiment: Spin (thick, red) and charge (thin, blue) densities were substracted from the background of the ground state system without an additional excitation. A created hole in the right lead (T=0) passes the interacting nanostructure undergoing SCS (T=17). In the left lead spin and charge densities travel independently with equal velocity (T=35,40).

ing leads. We then created a single, left moving hole excitation in the right lead and let it evolve. At the end of this scattering process of a single electronic excitation, one may ask what we end up with. The main question that arises is, whether the outcome will be well defined spin-charge separated wave packets, or should a hole be reconstructed, since we took out one electron of the system in the beginning.

The transport setup consists of 100 sites, divided into 41 left lead sites, 29 interacting sites and 30 right lead sites. Upon the ground state we created a single hole excitation in the right lead using a Gaussian distribution of annihilation operators with momenta k, around k_0 and of width σ.

$$\frac{1}{N} \sum_k e^{-\frac{(k-k_0)^2}{2\sigma^2}} c_k |\Psi_0\rangle \tag{1}$$

With 48 down and 48 up electrons the non-interacting system was at half-filling and the interacting system with an onsite Hubbard interaction was kept at a filling of ~ 0.43 and the injected hole had an average momentum of $k_0 = 0.43\pi - 2\sigma$, where $\sigma = 0.03$. This ensured the ability of the hole to tunnel into and out of the interacting region and keeping the transmission amplitude maximal.

In Fig. 1 we display the time evolution of the hole excitation for several time steps, where we have subtracted the background density of the system (n_0) without an excitation. Additionally, we averaged over Friedel osczillations of $2k_F$. The system was calculated with a maximum with 800 number of states per block, using adaptive RT-DMRG only. The data nicely shows that the wave packet undergoes a spin-charge separation and finally one ends up with a charge and a spin excitation travelling separately but with equal speed in the left lead. To this end, there is no reason for a recombination of spin and charge degrees of freedom to a single hole excitation. Nevertheless the outgoing wave packets are well defined and, in principle, the charge density and the spin density are measurable in a time-resolved measurement of a spin-polarized charge density. In Ref. 8 we have shown that by studying spin charge separation in a polarized system one can actually determine the charge and spin nature of excitation peaks in ARPES measurements.

3 Transport Properties of Strongly Correlated Nanostrucutres

The major problem in non-equilibrium dynamics consists in the fact that the stationary Schrödinger equation is now replaced by the time-dependent Schrödinger equation. Therefore, an *eigenvalue problem* is replaced by a *boundary problem* and one has to take care of the initial state. Therefore, one has to be very careful in sending all difficulties to time equal minus infinity since at some time t_0 one hits the initial state. In our approach we simulate the transport through nanostructures attached to non-interacting leads by the time evolution of an applied voltage quench. While on finite system one can never reach steady state dynamics we are looking for an intermediate time scale in which the response corresponds to the steady state system. To this end, we perform the full time integration of the time dependent Schrödinger equation via a time evolution operator given by the matrix exponential. The details of this approach have been explained in Refs. 10, 11, 12 where first results have already been reported in Ref. 12 and is reviewed in Ref. 13.

The main achievement consists in the fact that we have been able to make quantitative comparison with analytical calculations on a continuum version of the interacting resonant level model (IRLM) in the framework of Bethe ansatz and a dressed Landauer–Büttiker approach and the time dependent simulation on a lattice version of the IRLM.

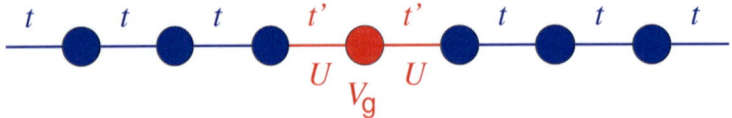

Figure 2: Sketch of the IRLM model. t' denotes the coupling of the impurity to the left and right lead, $t = 1$ is the hopping element in the leads, U is the interaction on the contact link, and V_g is a gate voltage which is set to zero in this work.

Using a field theoretical treatment of the IRLM based on the thermodynamic Bethe ansatz [14] one can map the problem of interacting fermions on noninteracting Bethe particles which scatter only by a phase shift. Therefore one can employ a Landauer–Büttiker-like treatment of the transport problem. However, in the mapping of the original fermions to the Bethe particles one mixes in general particles from the left and right lead and it is in no way clear how the charge operator $e(N_L - N_R)$ translates into the new basis. Interestingly, the continuum version of the IRLM displays a so-called self dual point where a mapping between small and large U maps on the same model. Exactly at this point of interaction the most complicated terms in the mapping of the charge operator cancel and the procedure can actually be carried out analytically [14]. Since in the field theory the leads are taken to be continuous with linear dispersion the model is scale free and can not be compared directly to the lattice version. For this one has to regularize the field theoretical result by introducing scales for the observables, which is for example well known in the context of Kondo physics, where one has to introduce a scale T_K. Also here, since at small voltages we have a linear conductance of one, a single scale for the current and voltage axis is sufficient, which we denote by T_B.

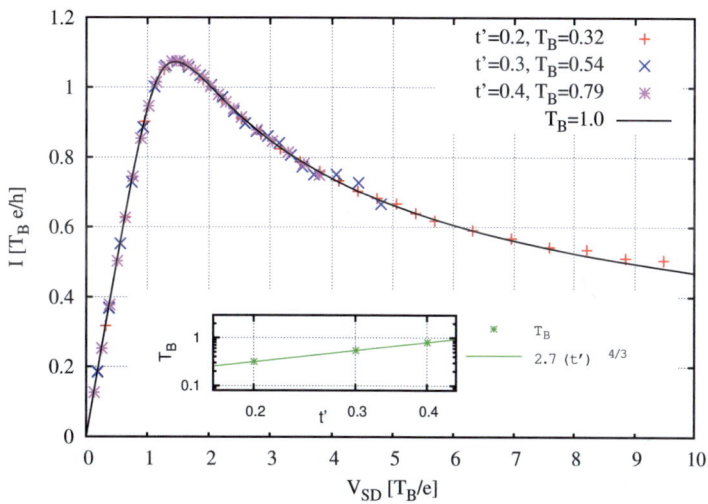

Figure 3: Comparison between analytical and DMRG results at the self dual point. For each t' the numerical data have been fitted using a single parameter T_B to the analytical result. Finally T_B was fitted against t' leading to the proposed $T_B = c(t')^{4/3}$, $c \approx 2.7$.

In Fig. 3 we have rescaled our numerical results for $U = 2.0t$ by fitting the scale T_B for $t' = 0.2, 0.3, 0.4$. Remarkably all the results collapse on the predicted analytical result. It is interesting to note that this scaling works still in the voltage regime where the dispersion of the cosine band of the nearest-neighbour hopping chain in the leads can not be neglected. Even the predicted dependence of T_B on t', $T_B \sim (t')^{\frac{4}{3}}$ fits very well as shown in the inset with a prefactor of 2.7. Therefore, this prefactor accounts for the complete regularization of the field theory.

Motivated by the success of the I/V characteristics we extended our approach to obtain current-current correlations, e.g. shot noise, for interacting quantum systems

$$S(t,t') = \langle \Delta\hat{I}(t)\Delta\hat{I}(t')\rangle_\Psi, \quad \Delta\hat{I}(t) = \hat{I}(t) - \langle\hat{I}(t)\rangle_\Psi, \tag{2}$$

$$\hat{I}(t) = e^{i\hat{H}t}\,\hat{I}\,e^{-i\hat{H}t}, \quad \langle\cdot\rangle_\Psi = \langle\Psi|\cdot|\Psi\rangle. \tag{3}$$

For this we first have to reach the quasi stationary regime at time t_0 in response to our voltage quench. Then we can start to calculate the current–current correlation in time domain, which then gives the $S(\omega)$ after a Fourier transformation. Of course, all of these steps are sensitive to finite size effects and a careful analysis has to be performed. The details are explained in Ref. 15 and results for the IRLM are given in Ref. 16.

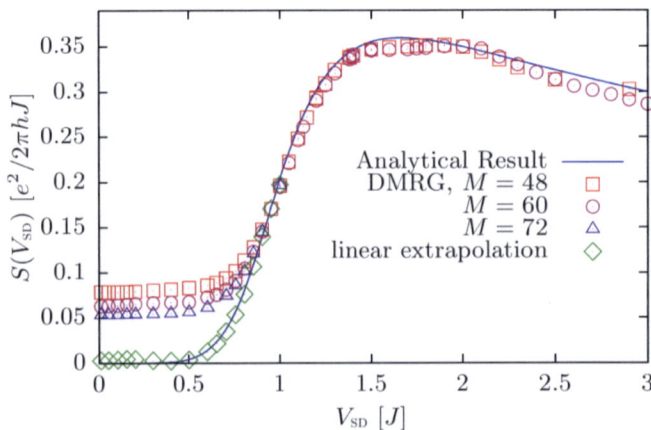

Figure 4: Linear extrapolation of the numerical shot noise data. The linear scaling of the low voltage finite size error is exploited to perform a linear extrapolation $1/M \to 0$. We find nice agreement of numerical and analytical results.

As shown in Fig. 4 the simulations lead to finite shot noise even in the absence of current at zero voltage. The reason for this intriguing result is given by the finite size of the samples used in the the numerics. As a consequence one performs the simulation not at zero frequency but at $\omega \sim 1/M$, where M is the number of sites used in the simulation. We could show [15, 16] that in our case the finite frequency correction is proportional to G^2/M.

4 Parallelization

In our implementation we use a master-worker approach within the framework of Posix threads as displayed in Fig. 5. The code performing all the book keeping is running as a serial master scheduling all major work load to the master queue, from which the worker pick their work load. The advantage of Posix threads is the high flexibility in scheduling the work load. The reason

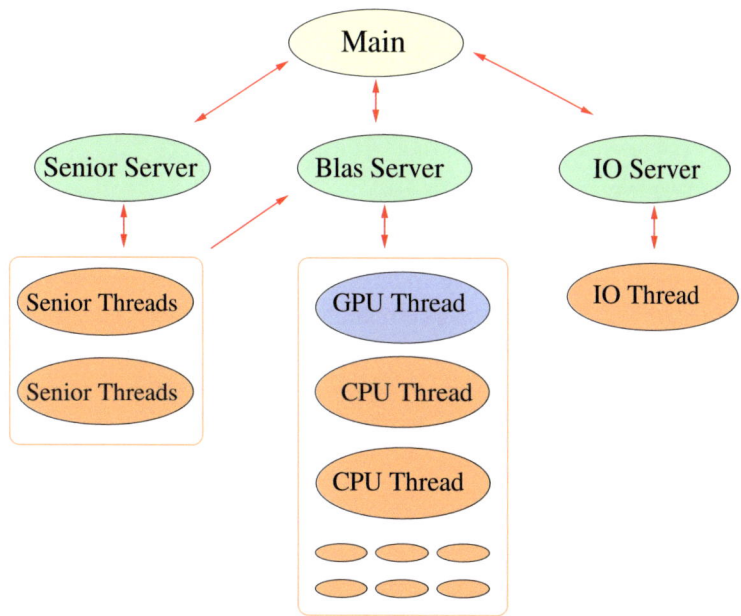

Figure 5: The three-master approach to DMRG. All three servers are instances of the same master class. However, they are used for different tasks. The workers can run on CPUs as usual Posix threads or as threads which offload their actual work to acceleration cards.

why this approach scales is that the book keeping itself takes basically no time in comparison to the scheduled matrix operation. In addition, most of the book keeping and scheduling can be done concurrently, see Ref. 9 for a detailed discussion. Another advantage of the Posix thread approach is that we can schedule arbitrary subroutines. We exploit this feature by reusing the master class for scheduling larger work units. For this purpose we create a second instance, which we call senior server, which takes extended subroutines, like a sparse matrix exponential, a sparse matrix diagonalization, or the evaluation of observables as argument. We can therefore not only exploit the parallelism of the algorithms, but include the concurrent evaluation of large work units to reduce idling due to inherently serial parts of a subroutine. In addition we are in the process of moving the IO load into a third instance of the server, in order to perform our IO operations asynchronously.

Finally, within this parallelization scheme we are not restricted to a single type of worker, but we can schedule different types of workers. Currently we have implemented worker which can schedule dgemm on AMD and and the full range of BLAS 3 and LAPACK calls on NVidia graphics cards. We provide some benchmarks in Ref. 17. It is clear from our approach displayed in in Fig. 5 that it is a simple task to an MPI work, if we would have access to sufficient CPU time. For such an approach it would be interesting if we could run the main code on a fat node e.g. a node with large amount of memory, while the workers could run on thin nodes.

References

[1] R. Landauer. Spatial variation of currents and fields due to localized scatterers in metallic conduction. *J. Res. Dev.*, 1:233, 1957.

[2] R. Landauer. Electrical resistance of disordered one-dimensional lattices. *Phil. Mag.*, 57:863, 1970.

[3] M. Büttiker. Four-terminal phase-coherent conductance. *Phys. Rev. Lett.*, 57(14):1761–1764, 1986.

[4] Y. Meir and N. S. Wingreen. Landauer formula for the current through an interacting electron region. *Phys. Rev. Lett.*, 68(16):2512, 1992.

[5] S. R. White. Density matrix formulation for quantum renormalization groups. *Phys. Rev. Lett.*, 69:2863, 1992.

[6] S. R. White. Density matrix renormalization group. *Phys. Rev. B*, 48:10345, 1993.

[7] I. Peschel, X. Wang, M.Kaulke, and K. Hallberg (Eds.), *Density Matrix Renormalization*, 1999.

[8] T. Ulbricht and P. Schmitteckert. Tracking spin and charge with spectroscopy in polarised systems. *EPL*, 89:47001, 2010.

[9] P. Schmitteckert and G. Schneider. Signal transport and finite bias conductance in and through correlated nanostructures. In *High Performance Computing in Science and Engineering '06*, W. E. Nagel, W. Jäger, and M. Resch (Eds.), pages 113–126. Springer, Berlin, 2006.

[10] G. Schneider and P. Schmitteckert. Conductance in strongly correlated 1d systems: Real-time dynamics in DMRG. *(unpublished)*, 2006.

[11] P. Schmitteckert. Signal transport in and conductance of correlated nanostructures. In *High Performance Computing in Science and Engineering '07*, W. E. Nagel, D. B. Kröner, and M. Resch (Eds.), pages 99–106. Springer, Berlin, 2007.

[12] T. Ulbricht and P. Schmitteckert. Signal transport in and conductance of correlated nanostructures. In *High Performance Computing in Science and Engineering '08*, W. E. Nagel, D. B. Kröner, and M. Resch (Eds.), pages 71–82. Springer, Berlin, 2008.

[13] A. Branschädel, G. Schneider, and P. Schmitteckert. Conductance of inhomogeneous systems: Real-time dynamics. *Annalen der Physik*, 522:657, 2010.

[14] E. Boulat, H. Saleur, and P. Schmitteckert. Twofold advance in the theoretical understanding of far-from-equilibrium properties of interacting nanostructures. *Phys. Rev. Lett.*, 101(14):140601, 2008.

[15] A. Branschädel, E. Boulat, H. Saleur, and P. Schmitteckert. Numerical evaluation of shot noise using real-time simulations. *Phys. Rev. B*, 82(20):205414, 2010.

[16] A. Branschädel, E. Boulat, H. Saleur, and P. Schmitteckert. Shot noise in the self-dual interacting resonant level model. *Phys. Rev. Lett.*, 105(14):146805, 2010.

[17] A. Branschädel, T. Ulbricht, and P. Schmitteckert. Conductance of correlated nanostructures. In *High Performance Computing in Science and Engineering '09*, W. E. Nagel, D. B. Kröner, and M. Resch (Eds.), page 123. Springer, Berlin, 2009.

Simulation Laboratory Astro- and Elementary Particle Physics

Gevorg Poghosyan, David Seldner, and Frank Schmitz

Steinbuch Centre for Computing, Karlsruhe Institute of Technology

Abstract

For integrating of scientific application software into modern e-Infrastructures, simulation laboratories (SimLab) are established at the Steinbuch Centre for Computing (SCC) of the Karlsruhe Institute of Technology (KIT). SimLab for "Astro- and Elementary Particle Physics" (SimLab A&E Particle) is supporting researchers in homonymous scientific fields in developing scientific simulation codes and porting them into up-to-date super-computing infrastructures. Currently we are working on parallelization of the CORSIKA code for simulation of cosmic rays/air showers, standardization of the KB3D code for simulation of heavy ion collisions or laser excited semiconductor systems and adaptation of codes from numerical relativity for simulation of nuclear matter at high densities in compact astrophysical objects.

1   Introduction

While the more hardware-oriented revitalisation, restructuring and strengthening of high-performance computing (HPC) infrastructures in Europe is making good progress, the challenges of high-quality user support and modern software development in the era of multi-core processors have not yet been sufficiently mastered. The complementary question of software development and productive usage of current and future high-end systems has not yet been addressed. It should be a joint endeavour of supercomputing centres and the scientific and engineering research communities. These will have to go well beyond the traditional support desk favoured by many contemporary computer centres (Attig, et al., 2008).

In an effort to improve this situation, an innovative research and support structure, so-called Simulation Laboratories, are currently being established at different sites in Germany. In particular "SimLab A&E Particle" is getting its shape at SCC of KIT. These will provide support for researchers in KCETA competence field of KIT, as well as for other groups in Germany and Europe focused on research in homonymous scientific fields.

2   Concept of S.P.O.R.A.D.I.c service and objectives of Simulation Lab

Computational Software during the past decades became a fundamental tool for scientific research in particle physics. Rarely, solution of modern scientific problems in astro- and elementary particle physics is being achieved without development of computer simulation software. But adaptation of even off-the-shelf scientific simulation codes into up-to-date HPC and distributed computing infrastructures like Grid or Cloud Computing oft requires not only substantial knowledge of how to use those modern computing systems, as well as it leads to necessary essential changes in the scientific simulation code.

Necessity of optimal and effective use of limited computational time is one of the main challenges for any HPC user, often resulting in implementing newer effective algorithms into the scientific software used. Seldom, the latter can be reached without re-engineering the own codes, resulting in changes of the scientific concepts and architecture, practically leading to fundamentally new software.

Simulation Laboratories are aiming to support or even to fully take over the part of research activities of scientific groups related to computational, often initially unplanned subjects. We support scientific groups in mastering S.P.O.R.A.D.I.C. changes in their simulation codes and conduct necessary tests and productive runs for proofs of correctness of scientific results by improving scientific codes (Thiara, et al., 2009).

Under S.P.O.R.A.D.I.C. service for scientific simulation software, "SimLab A&E Particle" provides:

*S*tandardization – making codes object oriented, adapting Input-Output to modern standards,

*P*arallelization – scientific exploitation of the code to find parallelization strategies,

*O*ptimization – infrastructure dependant performance-analysis: infrastructure dependant profiling

*R*elease – providing deduced parts of code and simulated results as publicly available libraries

*A*daptation – porting code to up-to-date HPC, Grids and Clouds infrastructures

*D*ata – managing huge amount of data produced by large-exascale simulations

*I*ntensive – data mining, visualisation, statistic

*C*omputing – monitoring of computing time used, bookkeeping for large scale parameter studies

2.1 "Standardization"

During the last decades of formation of computing technologies, many codes that are used to solve scientific problems on available HPC infrastructures, have been developed without significant necessity to use them on other systems. Very often the author is an important "portion" of the code, when somebody else is going to use parts of it or an adaptation of the old scientific software to new computational infrastructures must be done. Often codes stay on the same level as long as the problems they solve stay "small" and computation technologies for which they were initially developed are still available.

SimLabs has an objective work on standardization of old codes developed in last decades by scientific communities, e.g. by separating different objects, functions, subroutines of code, in form that they could be used as library from newer simulation software. By deploying object oriented architecture, promoting appropriate software standards one can improve also scalability, interoperation and better implement scientific simulation codes to multi-threaded, highly parallel, hierarchical computing architectures newly available in Europe and worldwide.

When more HPC resources are available, more detailed and complex problems can be solved with the same code than before. Especially in distributed memory computing infrastructures like grid/cloud, standardization of I/O data is significant. Exploitation of data read and produced by a code, helps us to standardize its formats for easily mastering problems arising during distribution of increased data productions.

2.2 "Parallelization"

Current trends in computer hardware are dictating a gradual shift towards the use of clusters, multi-core workstations or massively parallel processing machines (Vatsa, 1999). Many scientific groups are facing this challenge to master more complex simulations for their research on new HPC systems. But such a simulation with non parallelized versions of codes previously running optimal on single computers would result in only a very small gain of performance, when run without change on massively parallel, multi-core systems. To exploit the available processor cores, software developers must design and implement applications with a high degree of concurrency. But the development of parallelized applications is error prone and time consuming (Lee, 2006). Software architects and developers are thus confronted with the question of when the additional effort for introducing concurrency into their application pays off (Happe, 2009).

Here SimLab supports scientific groups in helping to master above mentioned time consuming developments. This means for example, implementing mathematical libraries, algorithms parallelized, optimized and provided from HPC hardware developer companies. Thus, minimal deviation from the original code is assured and relatively quick solutions can be achieved.

2.3 "Optimization"

The possible benefit in software performance may be limited due to bottlenecks or inherently sequential parts of the application (Amdahl's Law (Rodgers, 1985)). One major hurdle in porting scientific codes to distributed computing platforms is the difficulty encountered in partitioning the problem so that the computation-to-communication ratio for each compute node (process) is maximized and the idle time during which one node waits for other nodes to transfer data is minimized (Vatsa, 1999). SimLab A&E Particle have building competences and provides support in optimizing the performance of parallelized codes by identifying bottlenecks, for instance by varying certain parameters of simulations, e.g. various astrophysical objects, stellar matter or testing different types of elementary particle.

2.4 "Release"

Simulation software with broad impact in a research field and users from many countries all over the world often needs to be made freely available. For instance, in distributed computational infrastructures like grid/cloud, computing elements need to automatically obtain the latest version of simulation software, from the centralised repository, so that codes involved in many big international projects are up to date. Building such a centralised system, involved user communities could be informed of new improvements in functionalities, new data and documentations. As well, appropriate licensing schemes for open source software must be provided. Here SimLab will serve communities defining the license standards, as well as making easy-to-use and user friendly portals/repositories for download, support and bug fixing systems.

2.5 "Adaptation"

Many scientific simulation codes from the past decades are at most optimized for given machines available for particular community and are not easily portable to latest distributed computing environments without changes. The adaptation of codes is well suited in SimLab services. For this, we use specialized computation programs and standardised libraries optimized for solution of different problems on different parallel and distributed computational environments. Even if fundamentals of mathematics and physics or chemistry are not changing, use of new already well temporized numerical libraries (like matrix operations, sorting and searching or solution of linear differential equations) is of crucial importance for reaching higher performance, accuracy on a given computational infrastructure.

2.6 "Data Intensive Computing"

In SimLab A&E Particle we improve scientific simulations to process big amount of input data or collect large output data when using local HPC storage systems, as well as resources distributed in e-science infrastructures, like Grid and Cloud Computing. Here, workflow orchestration tools play an important role not only when partitioning of different simulation jobs along grid or HPC blocks is the challenge, but also when balancing computation needs and data transfer bandwidth has to be organised. Especially when using Grid and Cloud, improvements or re-engineering of simulation code is often required to organize correct access of data. Seldom, data blocks could be stored on the same node where the simulation is running, but have to be distributed to the next available or even on different ones. Here, the use of some standard protocols for data exchange and interfaces for access and monitor the computation has to be implemented into codes to master up-to-date EU computational infrastructures and to ones distributed all over the world.

Often construction of graphical visualizations from simulated or experimental results is itself a complicated investigation, especially when analyses are carried out by hand. Here partially automated procedures using general-purpose scripting languages could be implemented. As well large amount of data could be distributed on different storage elements has to be examined, data generated from different scientific simulation steps must be organized, before mining of data helps to find something "useful" and "new". Such a bookkeeping provenance of information is a major challenge for scientists. Here SimLab aims to cover the lack by using own developed and standard tools for capturing information already during simulations. This could help to decrease difficulty of interpretation of data produced by simulations using intensive computations, keep data accurately and reliably reproducible.

3 Current Activities and Co-operations in SimLab A&E Particles

Many groups in KIT and beyond researching in fields of Cosmic Rays, Heavy Ion collisions, Compact Astrophysical Objects by use of scientific simulation software are in cooperation with SimLab A&E Particle. We support them in parallelization and porting of their codes into modern European HPC, Grid and Cloud infrastructures to which SimLabs provides access.

3.1 "CORSIKA" simulation of cosmic rays

During the past 20 years a code CORSIKA has been developed at KIT and became a worldwide standard instrument for scientists, studying the complex simulation of air-showers induced by cosmic rays in the atmosphere (Heck, et al., 1998). But simulation for ultra high energy cosmic rays (UHECR) with energies as high as 10^{20} eV with the present version of CORSIKA applicable for sequential runs only, could take decades on single computers. Hence, implementation of a new methodology for parallelization is vital to manage simulation for such UHECR at mentioned energies in acceptable time. Moreover, large amount of data generated during such a simulation must be analyzed and compared with experimental results in real-time. The latter makes it indispensable to develop and implement modern data recording and analyzing algorithms into the CORSIKA code.

Parallel execution of CORSIKA simulated air showers is created in SimLab A&E Particle in cooperation with the Institute of Nuclear Physics of KIT. It is realised in form of scientific workflow management systems. In particular, splitting input data for corresponding individual jobs in a workflow is performed and for each calculation of separate new sub-showers parallel own node/computer/core could be used, even if no parallelization in the CORSIKA source-code itself was attempted.

Next the strategies for balancing computation needs of different sub-shower types and data transfer bandwidth have to be developed. Also an automated tracking and storage of bookkeeping information promises to be a major advantage for improving the efficiency of workflow system for cosmic rays simulations. In cooperation with the University of Westminster SimLab A&E Particle develops a system for scheduling CORSIKA jobs in BOINC (Anderson, 2004) driven environments.

3.2 "KB3D" Code for solution of Kadanoff–Baym equations

In SimLab A&E Particle within cooperation with Goethe University of Frankfurt a standardization of code for solving Kadanoff-Baym 3D equations is made. Code KB3D is Fortran77 code for simulation of evolution in excited systems (Köhler, et al., 1999). For instance, simulation of a flash of laser on the semiconductor or heavy ion collisions(HIC), when spin polarized protons accelerated up to 100 GeV are colliding with another proton or Gold or Copper atoms. In KB3D the process of equilibration – thermalization is modelled using non-equilibrium Green Functions. Green Functions convolutions in this code is computed using Fast Fourier Transformation Mathkeisan commercial libraries, specially available only on Cray, SGI, NEC supercomputers. The use of other standard FFT libraries will be implemented and also a potential speedup when use of GPU for FFT calculations is planned.

3.3 Modelling matter at high densities and temperatures in Compact Stars

We are also involved in compact star community, studying the evolution of compact astrophysical objects, like binary star systems (neutron star and white dwarf) (Blaschke, et al., 2008). Here the interesting evolution is the behaviour of neutron star, known also as pulsar. Observable signals from neutron star are sensitive to interior processes and following the evolution of this system one can conclude which kind of processes are happening in dense stellar matter. One can simulate this evolution when different types of equations of states (EoS) for description of interior of star are chosen – with quarks, without quarks and hybrid. Depending on the type of matter the rotational frequency of star gets stuck in some special regions where star is „waiting" for some millions of years. So one can say that there is a possible region of frequencies, where such a system (Low Mass X-Ray Binaries) could be found with the highest probability (Poghosyan, et al., 2001).

So it is vital to test all possible parameters of systems and degrees of freedom in order to perform some statistics. This will be only possible when one standardizes the usage of many EoS and their parameters as well as parallelization of different simulations needed to manage thousands of possible scenarios. In framework of SimLab A&E Particle in cooperation with University Wroclaw and Yerevan State University, we are developing a scientific workflow system for simulation of rotating compact stars systems. Here the large parameter studies can effectively be performed using parallelized systems.

References

[1] Anderson D.P. BOINC: A system for public-resource computing and storage [Conference] // FIFTH IEEE/ACM INTERNATIONAL WORKSHOP ON GRID COMPUTING, PROCEEDINGS. - Pittsburgh, PA, NOV 08, 2004 : IEEE, Task Force Cluster Comp; ACM; Microsoft Corp, 2004. - Vols. pages 4-10.

[2] Attig N., Esser R. and Gibbon P. Simulation Laboratories: An Innovative Community-Oriented Research and Support Structure [Conference] // Proceedings of the Cracow Grid Workshop (CGW'07). - 16. - 18. Oktober 2007, Krakow, Polen : eds.: M. Bubak, M. Turala, K. Wiatr. - ACC CYFRON ET AGH, 2008. - 978-83-915141-9-1.

[3] Blaschke D, Poghosyan G and Grigorian H Mapping the QCD Phase Transition with Accreting Compact Stars [Conference] // International Workshop on Decade of Accreting Millisecond X-Ray Pulsars, APR 14-18. - Amsterdam, NETHERLANDS : AIP CONFERENCE PROCEEDINGS, 2008. - Vols. DECADE OF ACCRETING MILLISECOND X-RAY PULSARS, 1068: 191-198 2008.

[4] D.P. Anderson BOINC: A system for public-resource computing and storage [Conference] // FIFTH IEEE/ACM INTERNATIONAL WORKSHOP ON GRID COMPUTING, PROCEEDINGS. - Pittsburgh, PA, NOV 08, 2004 : IEEE, Task Force Cluster Comp; ACM; Microsoft Corp , 2004. - Vols. pages 4-10.

[5] Happe Jens Predicting software performance in symmetric multi-core and multiprocessor Environments [Book]. - Universitätsverlag Karlsruhe, Karlsruhe : The Karlsruhe Series on Software Design and Quality / Ed. by Prof. Dr. Ralf Reussner, 2009. - Vols. ISBN 978-3-86644-381-5 .

[6] Heck D. [et al.] CORSIKA: A Monte Carlo Code to Simulate Extensive Air Showers [Report]. - 90 pages, 10 figures : Forschungszentrum Karlsruhe Report FZKA 6019 , 1998.

[7] Köhler H. S., Kwong N. H. and Yousif Hashim A. A Fortran code for solving the Kadanoff-Baym equations for a homogeneous fermion system [Article] // Computer Physics Communications. - 1999. - vol. 123,. - pp.123-142 : Vols. Issue 1-3,.

[8] Lee E.A. The Problem with Threads [Article] // IEEEComputer. - 2006. - Vols. 39(5):33–42 .

[9] Poghosyan G., Grigorian H. and Blaschke D. Population clustering as a signal for deconfinement in accreting compact stars [Article] // ASTROPHYSICAL JOURNAL LETTERS. - [s.l.] : UNIV CHICAGO PRESS, 1427 E 60TH ST, CHICAGO, IL 60637-2954 USA, 2001. - 551. - Part 2 : Vol. 1.

[10] Rodgers David P. Improvements in multiprocessor system design [Article] // ACM SIGARCH Computer Architecture News. - 1985. - 13(3):225–231.

[11] Thiara G., Poghosyan G and Schmitz F. SCC works on development of different scientifc simulation codes [Journal]. - Karlsruhe : Steinbuch Centre for Computing, 2009. - 2 : Vols. SCC-NEWS.

[12] Vatsa V. N. Parallelization of a multiblock flow code: an engineering implementation [Article] // Computers and Fluids. - 1999. - 38. - 603-614 : Vols. 4-5.

Computing needs of gravitational wave experiments

Gergely Debreczeni on behalf of the Virgo Collaboration

Research Institut for Particle and Nuclear Physics of
the Hungarian Academy of Sciences, Budapest

Extended Abstract

Einstein's theory of general relativity predicts in 1916 the existence of gravitational waves propagating through the space-time at the speed of light, likes ripples on the surface of water. These waves can be generated when masses move or interact and could be observed if the masses are large enough. Despite of the solid theoretical foundation and very strong indirect evidences their existence has never been confirmed directly by any experiment. The primary goal of the Virgo experiment is the first direct observation of such a gravitational wave.

The Virgo detector for gravitational waves (http://www.virgo.infn.it) consists mainly in a Michelson laser interferometer made of two orthogonal arms being each 3 kilometres long. The effect of an incident gravitational wave on the detector is a measurable strain of its arms. Comparing the fluctuations of the arm lengths to the theoretical predictions one can search for gravitational wave signal in the noisy detector output.

Such searches are computationally very expensive. The arithmetic density of the algorithms used in the data analysis varies between several orders of magnitudes up to the practically almost impossible ranges. Depending on the type of search, one has to match the data with several tens of thousands of theoretical waveform template, look for temporal power excesses in the detector output, or analyze the data of several detectors and find correlations. Furthermore when searching for signals emitted by rotating neutron stars one has to perform very high resolution many-dimensional parameter scan in long baseline data stretches, where available computing power directly translates to detector sensitivity, as such is of utmost importance from the first discovery point of view !

These are the reasons why Virgo experiment is continuously trying to exceed the limits of actual computing limitations. Because of the wide variety of data analysis algorithms used the Virgo experiment can make efficient use of Grid technologies, many-core computing techniques and HPC solutions.

Challenges of simulating air showers at ultra-high energy

Dieter Heck[1], Ralph Engel[1], Tanguy Pierog[1], Gurpratap Thiara[2], Shenan Karla[2], Himani Singla[2], Gevorg Poghosyan[3], David Seldner[3], Frank Schmitz[3]

[1]*Institute for Nuclear Physics, Karlsruhe Institute of Technology* [2]*PEC University of Technology, Chandigarh, India;* [3]*Steinbuch Centre for Computing, Karlsruhe Institute of Technology*

Abstract

In this contribution we describe the work on the parallelization of the Monte Carlo code CORSIKA to master the challenges of simulations for development of an Extensive Air Shower initiated by cosmic ray particles at the highest energies of 10^{20} eV. We have implemented workflow system for parallel execution of CORSIKA on distributed computing infrastructures and make preliminary tests simulations for energies up to 10^{18} eV. It allows us to estimate computational needs and challenges for productive simulations at higher energies to escape possible overflows when using parallel job scheduling systems.

1 Introduction

One of the problems in simulating Extensive Air Showers (EAS) initiated by cosmic rays at the highest observed energies comes from the huge number of 10^{11} particles which are created within the avalanche by the consecutive interactions with air. Their fate is determined by the flight path between their creation and their interaction or decay, and their nature and energy determines the number, types, energies and directions of the secondary particles generated in the interactions. These stochastic processes are well modelled by Monte Carlo (MC) methods to get correctly not only the mean values (which might be given eventually by analytical approximations) but also the fluctuations and correlations of the measurable shower observables as e.g. lateral distribution of the particles at ground or energy spectra of those particles at different distances to the shower axis. A solution of following this huge number of particles might be the parallelization of the MC code CORSIKA (COsmic Ray SImulations for KAscade) (Heck et al. 1998) to treat independent sub-showers by different cores in parallel. Already in an early stage of the development of the CORSIKA code several possibilities to circumvent the long CPU times which increase nearly linearly with increasing energy of the initiating cosmic particle, were considered (Gils et al. 1993) including various structures of a multi-Transputer computer farm (Gils et al. 1989).

Today the availability of multi-core processor systems has revived the parallelization ideas. To master challenges of productive usage of current and future high-end multi-core processors systems an innovative research and support structure, so-called Simulation Laboratories (SimLab), are currently being established at different supercomputing centres in Germany. In particular "SimLab Astro- & Elementary Particle Physics" (SimLab A&E Particle) at SCC of KIT is providing support on parallelization of scientific application CORSIKA and porting it into up-to-date distributed and super-computing infrastructures in Europe (Thiara, Poghosyan und Schmitz 2009).

2 Outline of Problem

2.1 Ultra-high energy Cosmic Rays

The highest energies of cosmic rays observed so far exceed 10^{20} eV. To accelerate protons to those energies with the present technologies of the LHC-collider, one needs an accelerator ring with the diameter of Mercury's orbit around the Sun and an acceleration time of more than 800 years. Nevertheless such Ultra High Energy (UHE) particles bombard the Earth's atmosphere from space and the resulting shower cascades are observed in experiments. To interpret these observations correctly simulation software is necessary which can model such events.

2.2 "CORSIKA" simulation software

During the past 20 years the code package CORSIKA (Heck et al. 1998) for the simulation of EAS has been developed at KIT and became a worldwide standard instrument for scientists, studying the complex simulation of air-showers induced by cosmic rays in the atmosphere. CORSIKA is based on the MC technique and allows the realistic simulation of interaction, propagation, and decay of particles in extensive particle cascades initiated by high-energy cosmic rays from our Galaxy or extragalactic objects. CORSIKA has become the worldwide standard tool for EAS simulations. More than 750 users apply this code in about 40 experiments worldwide.

One method to reduce the CPU-time is the so called "thinning" (Kobal 2001). In this method after a certain stage of the shower development only statistically selected particles are followed while the bulk of particles are dropped. The particles followed get a weight to keep the energy balance within the EAS. The drawback is additional artificial fluctuations of observable shower quantities, and it is highly desirable to verify that the results are not biased by the thinning procedure in any respect. This needs the verification by fully simulated EAS without thinning even at UHEs.

But simulation for UHECR with energies as high as 10^{20} eV with the present version of CORSIKA applicable for sequential runs only, could take decades on single computers (Knapp et al. 2003, Schmidt and Knapp 2005). Hence, implementation of a new methodology for parallelization is vital to manage simulation for such UHECR at mentioned energies in acceptable time.

2.3 Scientific Workflow for Parallel executions of "CORSIKA"

First runs of parallel CORSIKA executions were performed on the Karlsruhe multi-Transputer system (Gils et al. 1989) simulating 10000 showers with up to 10^{15}eV for energies. The limitation for output was set by the size of the storage discs, at that time (1989) 500 MByte.

Currently we developed scientific workflow management systems for parallel; generation-type execution of CORSIKA simulated air showers. It allows splitting and distributing input data for corresponding sub-showers to start individual parallel jobs per secondary particle on own node/computer/core. Considering simulation of separate sub-showers as new initial simulations, the parallel runs are fully independent and simulation easily scalable on any distributed computational system. Different amount of sub-showers could be generated by varying the input parameters for energy gap. Secondary particles energy of which is lying in the given gap are grouped or separately simulated.

Implementing initial book keeping system, we limit cascade-like structures into generations to balance computation needs of simulations on computational infrastructure, where the simulation must run. It could be adapted and optimised, for instance to escape long jobs waiting in queues or overflowing the scheduling system.

Hitherto, we performed test runs using LoadLeveler driven computing infrastructure of SCC called Opus Cluster. We have simulated proton induced showers with initial energies 10, 100 and 1000 Peta electron Volt (PeV=10^{15}eV), when higher limit of energy gap to start separation of secondary shower simulations are varied from 0.01 PeV till initial energy. For particle at energies lower than "ground" limit of gap equal to 0.001 PeV, no any separate simulations started.

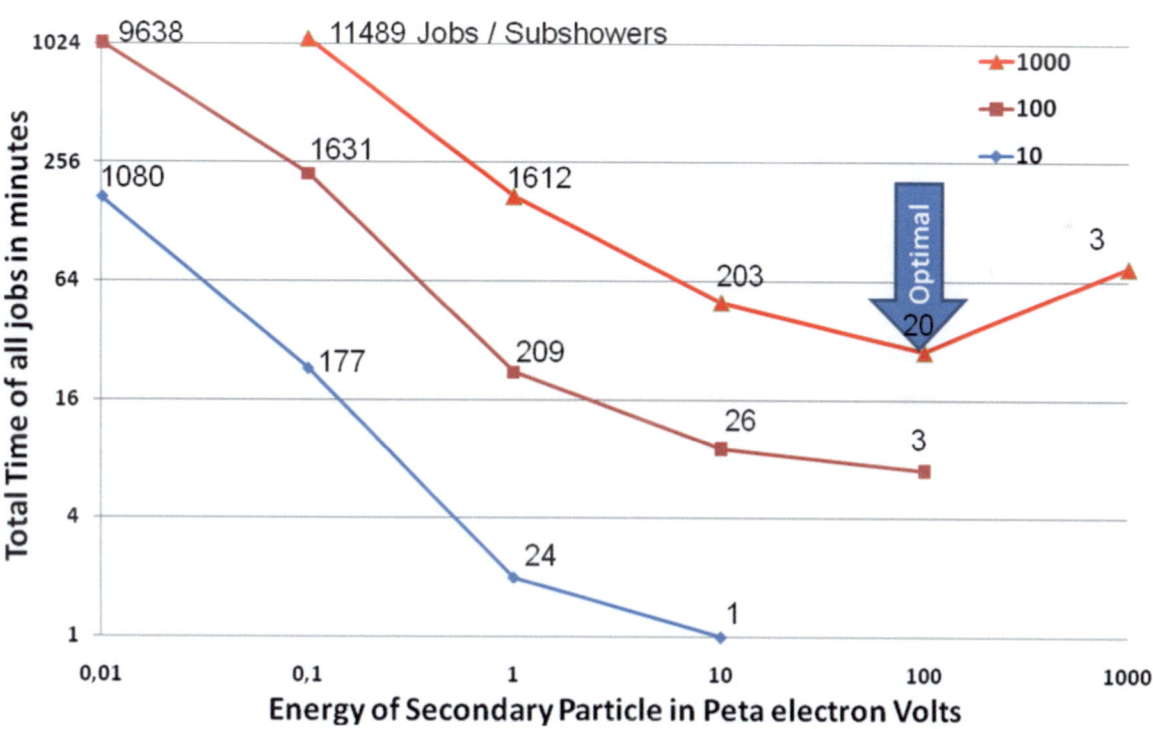

Fig. 1 Total time spent for simulation of proton induced showers with different initial energies and energy gaps. Numbers on graph, show amount of jobs/subshowers. It could be seen that parallel simulations could be optimally used only starting at high energies and enough subshowers.

In present system, each parallel calculation stores results into local or shared disk space accessible from particular node, where it is running. Here the variation of parameters allows escaping limitations on storage space available on particular node/system, when more sub-showers with smaller outputs would be used. Hereafter, automated tracking and book keeping system must be improved as of large amount of data up to 10^6 files with total size of up to 200GB per EAS is expected to be generated during full simulation. The last must be analyzed and compared with experimental results in "real-time".

3   Challenges – Work in Progress

It is indispensable to implement modern data recording and analyzing algorithms into the developed Workflow system or CORSIKA code itself. Parallel runs and possible generation of hundred of thousand small files will consequence of troubles in file system, when even simply trying to read, analyse such amount of files. In addition, the problem of uncompleted or improperly simulated sub-showers could raise the complexity of management for generated big data amount, as of revealed fault sub-showers and corresponding resulting files must be simulated again. Here an algorithms of identification of sharing and re-running identified sub-showers will be improved.

Subsequently optimization and internal parallelization in the CORSIKA source-code itself will be next attempted with goal to reach maximal scalability of code on distributed and supercomputing systems.

References

[1]   Gils H.J., Heck D., Oehlschläger J., Schatz G. and Thouw T., Computer Physics Communications 56 (1989) 105

[2]   Gils J. , Heck D., Oehlschläger J., Schatz G. and Thouw T., *A Multi-Transputer System for Parallel Monte Carlo Simulations of Extensive Air Showers*, in: Report KfK 5185 (1993), ed. W. Hohenhinnebusch

[3]   Heck D., Knapp J., Capdevielle J.N., Schatz G., and Thouw T.. *CORSIKA: A Monte Carlo Code to Simulate Extensive Air Showers*. 90 pages, 10 figures: Forschungszentrum Karlsruhe Report FZKA 6019 (1998)

[4]   Knapp J. et al., Astropart. Phys. 19 (2003) 77

[5]   Kobal M., Astropart. Phys. 15 (2001) 259

[6]   Schmidt F. and Knapp J.: *Results from the simulation of an unthinned proton shower at 5x10^18 eV*, GAP note 2005-095 (www.auger.org/admin/GAP_Notes/)

[7]   Thiara G., Poghosyan G. and Schmitz F. "*SCC works on development of different scientific simulation codes.*" SCC-NEWS, no. 2 (2009)

Massive and massless four-loop integrals

P. Marquard[*]

Institute of Theoretical Particle Physics

Karlsruhe Institute Of Technology,D-76128 Karlsruhe,Germany.

1 Introduction

The problems treated within our projects aim for the evaluation of so-called Feynman diagrams which in turn lead to quantum corrections within a given quantum field theory like Quantum Electrodynamics or Quantum Chromodynamics but also supersymmetric theories. Among the various physical applications are predictions for high-energy reactions to be measured in experiments like the Large Hadron Collider (LHC) at CERN in Geneva but also precise determinations of fundamental parameters like quark masses and coupling constants.

Quantum corrections can be classified by closed loops appearing in the Feynman diagrams. In general the mathematical input for a Feynman diagram is rather compact. However, in the process of evaluating the corresponding integrals at the higher loop level one often obtains intermediate expressions which can easily reach up to several tera bytes. Several manipulations have to be applied before finally the final expression, which is again relatively compact, emerges. The typical CPU time reaches from several hours to several months depending on the concrete problem under consideration.

In order to be able to manipulate huge expressions a special tool is necessary. Our workhorse for such calculations is the computer algebra program FORM [1] and its parallel versions ParFORM [2] and TFORM [3].

E-Mail:*peter.marquard@kit.edu*

FORM's method of operation is shown in Fig. 1. As can be seen it works on a term by term basis which leads to a quite simple way of parallelization: The original expression is divided

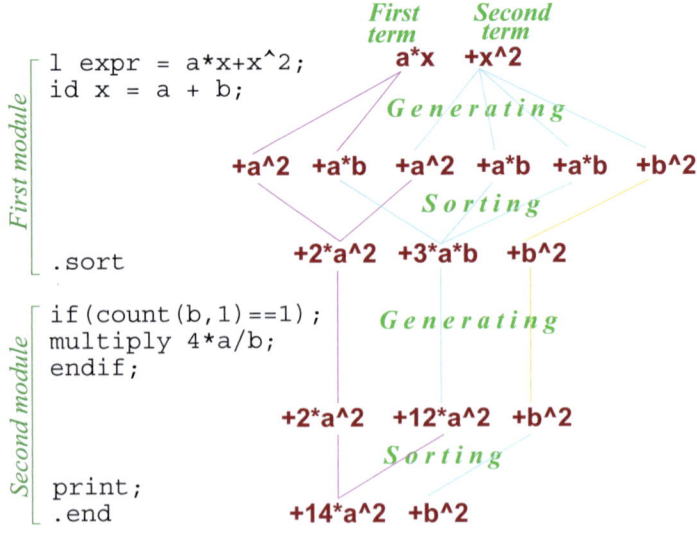

Fig. 1: Method of operation of FORM

into several pieces which are then distributed to the individual processors or cores (workers). Once the workers have finished their job the resulting expressions have to be collected by one processor which combines the results. This step is important in order to take into account the cancellations of the analytical expressions. However, this step also constitutes the main bottleneck both for ParFORM and TFORM since it may happen that the expressions are still quite big. Thus one expects that starting from a certain number of parallel workers the speedup of the parallelization slows down and a saturation is observed.

Note that the very concept of parallelization for our algebraic calculations is different from the "conventional" parallelization like a Monte Carlo task or computations in connection to finite element applications where only quite small expressions have to be transfered between the individual processors. In our case the final sorting, which in general still contains huge expressions, has to be performed by one worker. In particular, a computer architecture running ParFORM or TFORM requires a fast connection to the (in general) local hard disks which should be of the order of one tera byte per core.

2 New features of ParFORM

In this Section we describe recent progress in the development of ParFORM. In particular, we describe the parallelization of "Dollar variables", "Right-hand side expressions" and "InParallel".

A. Dollar variables

There are special variables in FORM which are, as far as their behaviour is concerned, a mixture between local and global variables, so-called dollar variables. These are very useful in connection with the flow control of a program. Since these variables can be modified by each compute node independently it might occur that a dollar variable is set to some value by one node which (unintentionally) influences the result of another node. For this reason the user has to specify at the end of each module involving dollar variables the treatment of the latter with the help of a so-called module option.

It should be mentioned that the practical implementation is straightforward in the case of TFORM since the master process can directly access the memory of all workers whereas in ParFORM the dollar variables have to be sent to the individual workers. They have to be re-collected by the master at the end of the module.

B. Right-hand side expressions

Right-hand side (RHS) expressions can appear in two variants: An already defined expression appears either on the right-hand side of the definition of a new expression or within an id statement. This is illustrated by the following two short examples:

Type I:	Type II:
L F = a + b;	L F = a + b;
L G = x + F;	L G = c + d;
	id a = G;

Within TFORM RHS expressions are no problem since all threads work with the same file system. In ParFORM, however, the expression which appears on the right-hand side may be situated in the respective scratch file of different nodes and thus may belong to a different file system.

In order for ParFORM to be able to operate in the parallel mode in case RHS expressions of type I are present the master sends the required expression to the worker and the execution proceeds as usual. This simple solution is not possible for RHS expressions of type II since then all workers must have access to the expression appearing on the right-hand side. Since up to now the scratch files of the workers have been used as MPI input/output buffers the structure of ParFORM has been changed in order to allow for local scratch files. Afterwards the master can distribute the expressions to the workers and the replacement as required by the id statement can be performed.

C. InParallel *statement*

In situations when there are several active expressions within a module they are executed one-by-one where the master distributes the individual terms of an expression to the workers. In case the expressions are small this is quite inefficient because there is a certain amount of overhead in the individual operations. For this reason a different form of parallelization, initiated by the keyword InParallel, has been implemented in ParFORM and TFORM which allows to distribute complete expressions to the workers such that worker 1 deals with expression 1, worker 2 with expression 2, etc.

Since for TFORM all workers run on the same node the implementation is quite simple: the master has to tell each worker which expression to treat next; afterwards the worker is responsible for obtaining its input and writing its output.

In the case of ParFORM the workers might run on different nodes and thus the implementation of this statement is not straightforward. It has turned out to be most practical to let the master send the complete expression (in a compressed form) directly from its scratch file to the one of the worker. Afterwards the worker processes the expression in usual way.

The novations described in A, B and C are exemplified in Fig. 2 where the program MZV [4] is used with parallel mode for dollar variables, RHS and InParallel switched on and off. In all three cases a significant improvement is visible leading to a speedup of 5 for 7 workers.

In Fig. 3 the performance of ParFORM is shown for a typical job where up to 60 processor cores have been used. The most important characteristic of scalability is a speedup on p parallel workers, $S(p) = T_1/T_p$, the ratio of the time spent by one worker for solving the problem to the time spent by p workers.

We compare the present result for the XC4000 cluster (XC4000.08) with the previous one (XC4000.07) and with the results obtained on the old cluster XC6000 which has Itanium2 processors and consists of 108 2-way nodes and twelve 8-way nodes with Quadrics QsNet2 interconnection.

For XC6000 a good scaling behaviour is observed up to about 16 processors. Above approximately 24 processors the saturation region starts and only a marginal gain is observed once 60 processors are employed. The cluster XC6000 has only about 300 processor cores, and the communication media, QsNet2, has dynamical balancing while the XC4000 cluster is much larger and the communication media, InfiniBand, does not have dynamical balancing. This is probably the reason that for the XC4000 the situation is much worse.

In 2007 we observed beyond about 32 cores that the system was very unstable. Sometimes this instability even occurred earlier, after using about 10 cores. The situation concerning the stability has improved considerably since then and nowadays the system is much more stable. However, the saturation region still starts around 16 cores which is probably due to the less efficient connection to the hard disks and interconnections of the individual nodes.

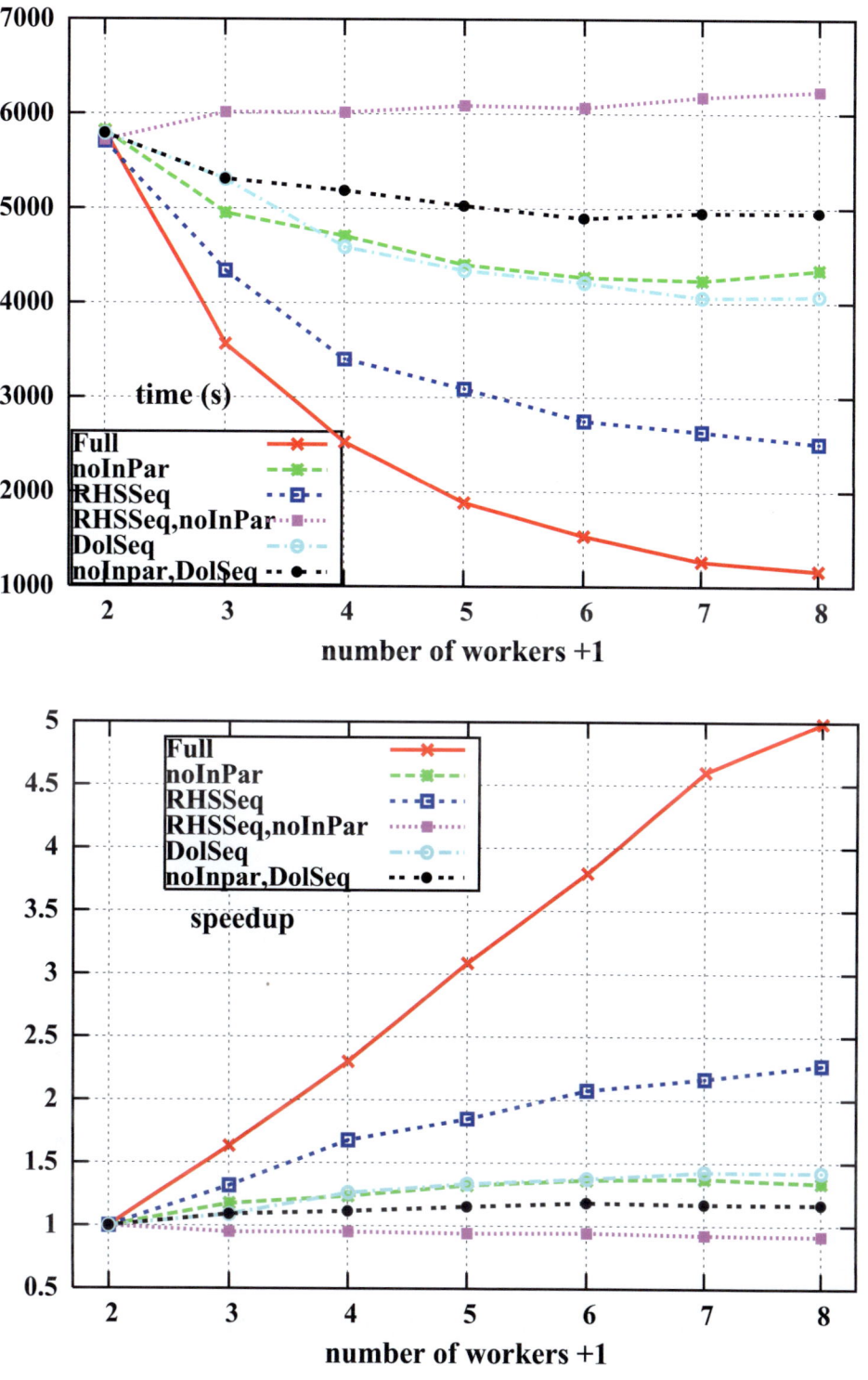

Fig. 2: `ParFORM` running the program `MZV` (with WEIGHT=16) where dollar variable module options, parallelized RHS expressions and `InParallel` statement are switched on or off.

Despite the less advantageous scalability we currently compute most of our tasks on the XC4000 since the individual processors are significantly faster than the one of the XC6000 cluster.

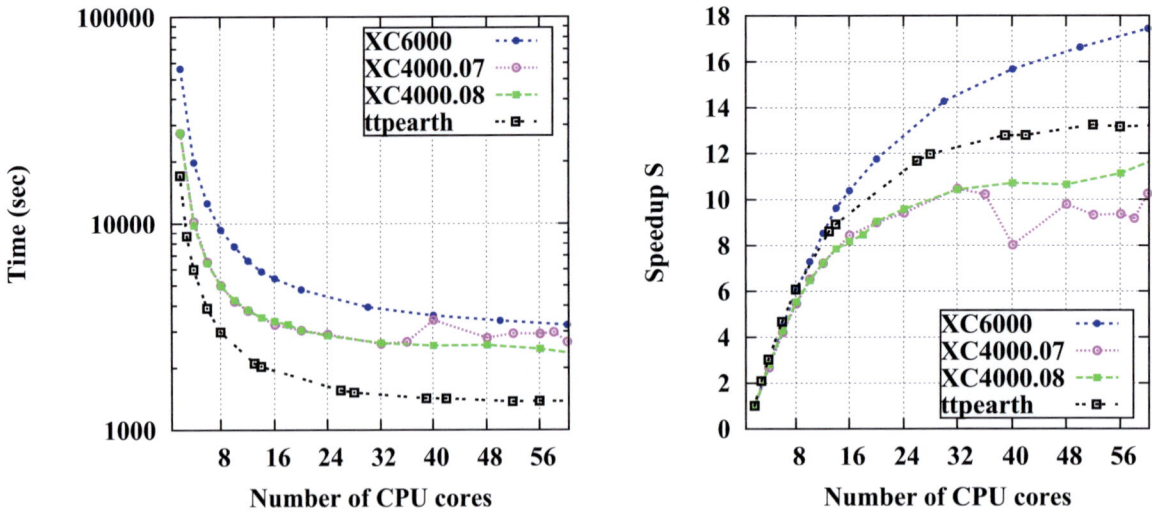

Fig. 3: CPU-time and speedup curve for a typical job on the XC6000 and XC4000 compared the Xeon cluster "ttpearth"(see text).

In Fig. 3 we also plot the result for the cluster "ttpearth" which consists of 24 nodes, 8-core Intel Xeon E5472 with 3.0 GHz, 32 GByte RAM, 4.5 TByte disk space each, and a InfiniBand interconnection. As one can see, both the absolute timings and scalability of ParFORM on this cluster are much better than the ones on XC4000.

3 Massless four-loop integrals

One important and clean place for precise tests of QCD and SM is the total cross section of electron positron annihilation (so-called R-ratio). This quantity together with the related semileptonic τ lepton decay rate provide us with invaluable information about the numerical value of the strong coupling constant α_s as well as its running from the τ lepton mass to that of Z boson. There is also a significant amount of purely theoretical interest to higher order contributions to this quantity related to renormalons, etc.

Due to the well-known "optical theorem" $R(s)$ is related to the absorptive part of the vector vacuum polarization function. As is well known, the absorptive part of the arbitrary (L+1)-loop p-integral (that is a massless Feynman integral depending on exactly one external momentum) is expressible in terms of the corresponding (L+1)-loop UV counterterm along with some L-loop p-integrals (the former have to be known *including* their non-divergent finite parts).

Thus, the order α_s^4 contribution to $R(s)$ is related to the absorptive part of the five-loop vector current correlator, whose calculation eventually boils down to the calculation of a huge number of four-loop p-integrals.

In order to cope with this problem a special package — BAICER — has been created. This is a FORM3 package capable of analytically computing p-integrals up to (and including) four loops. The package computes coefficients in decomposition of a given p-integral into the fixed basis of known ones. The coefficients are known to be rational functions of the space-time dimension D and are computed as expansion in $1/D$ as $D \to \infty$. From the knowledge of sufficiently many terms in the expansion one can reconstruct their exact form. The terms in the $1/D$ expansion are expressed in terms of simple Gaussian integrals. For a typical four-loop problem a few billion integrals occur. However, their calculation can be parallelized in a quite efficient way.

The order α_s^4 contribution to $R(s)$ was computed in 2008 [5] with the use of BAICER and on the basis of our local SGI multi-processor computer and the XC4000 cluster. The calculation has led to numerous updates of previous phenomenological analyses of the Z-boson and the τ-lepton decay rates into hadrons in NNNLO. As a net result one could say that two (of the four) most precise determinations of α_s as cited in [6] rely strongly on the result of this calculation.

4 Massive four-loop integrals

A second important class of diagrams are massive four-loop vacuum diagrams. These diagrams again only depend on a single scale, now the mass of a heavy quark. This class of diagrams appears in the low-energy expansion of the correlator of two heavy quark currents. The main application of the heavy-quark correlators is the extraction of the mass of the involved heavy quark from experimental data of the production cross section of hadrons at an electron-positron collider. As an alternative the experimental data can be substituted by a direct calculation of the correlators on the lattice.

The main software tool in this part of the project is the program TCrusher which implements the Laporta algorithm for the analytical solution of a system of linear equation generated by integration-by-parts identities. TCrusher is used to reduce the appearing several million integrals to a very small set of 13 master integrals, which are known analytically. In intermediate steps several hundred million integrals are generated which makes this step the most difficult part of the calculation.

Using the tool mentioned above we calculated the second and third physical moment of the vector, axial-vector and scalar correlator and up to fourth moment of the pseudo-scalar correlator [7, 8]. The new results for the moments of the vector correlator can be used to improve the determination of the masses of the charm and bottom quark from experimental data of the cross section $\sigma(e^+e^- \to hadrons)$ [9]. The results for the pseudo-scalar correlator can be used in combination with lattice simulations to obtain a precise value for the charm-quark mass

[10](updated in [8]). The determinations of the masses of the charm and bottom quark presented in these publications yield the most precise values currently available.

In combination with known results for the behaviour of the vacuum polarization function at threshold and in the high-energy region, the results for the low-energy moments can be used to reconstruct the behaviour of the vacuum polarization function over the whole energy range using a Padé approximation [11]. These approximations are important for contour improved methods which use the full information of the vacuum polarization function to determine e.g. quark masses.

Acknowledgements

Most of the computations presented in this contribution were performed on the Landeshöchstleistungsrechner XC4000.

References

[1] FORM version 3.0 is described in: J. A. M. Vermaseren, "New features of FORM", arXiv:math-ph/0010025;
for recent developments, see also: M. Tentyukov and J. A. M. Vermaseren, "Extension of the functionality of the symbolic program FORM by external software", arXiv:cs.sc/0604052;
FORM can be obtained from the distribution site at http://www.nikhef.nl/~form.

[2] M. Tentyukov, D. Fliegner, M. Frank, A. Onischenko, A. Retey, H. M. Staudenmaier and J. A. M. Vermaseren, "ParFORM: Parallel Version of the Symbolic Manipulation Program FORM", arXiv:cs.sc/0407066;

M. Tentyukov, H. M. Staudenmaier and J. A. M. Vermaseren, "ParFORM: Recent development", Nucl. Instrum. Meth. A **559** (2006) 224.
H. M. Staudenmaier, M. Steinhauser, M. Tentyukov, J. A. M. Vermaseren, "ParFORM", Computeralgebra Rundbriefe **39** (2006) 19.

See also http://www-ttp.physik.uni-karlsruhe.de/~parform.

[3] M. Tentyukov and J. A. M. Vermaseren, "The multithreaded version of FORM", arXiv:hep-ph/0702279.

[4] J. Blumlein, D. J. Broadhurst and J. A. M. Vermaseren, "The Multiple Zeta Value Data Mine", Comput. Phys. Commun. **181** (2010) 582 [arXiv:0907.2557 [math-ph]].

[5] P. A. Baikov, K. G. Chetyrkin and J. H. Kühn, Phys. Rev. Lett. **101** (2008) 012002 [arXiv:0801.1821 [hep-ph]].

[6] S. Bethke, "The 2009 World Average of $\alpha_s(M_Z)$", Eur. Phys. J. C **64** (2009) 689 [arXiv:0908.1135 [hep-ph]].

[7] A. Maier, P. Maierhofer and P. Marqaurd, Phys. Lett. B **669** (2008) 88.

[8] A. Maier, P. Maierhofer, P. Marquard and A. V. Smirnov, Nucl. Phys. B **824** (2010) 1.

[9] K. G. Chetyrkin, J. H. Kühn, A. Maier, P. Maierhofer, P. Marquard, M. Steinhauser and C. Sturm, Phys. Rev. D **80** (2009) 074010.

[10] I. Allison *et al.* [HPQCD Collaboration], Phys. Rev. D **78** (2008) 054513.

[11] Y. Kiyo, A. Maier, P. Maierhofer and P. Marquard, Nucl. Phys. B **823** (2009) 269.

Simulation Laboratory Earth and Environment

Ole Kirner[1], Lars Hoffmann[2], Stefan Versick[1], and Inge Bischoff-Gauß[1]

[1]Steinbuch Centre for Computing, Karlsruhe Institute of Technology
[2]Jülich Supercomputing Centre, Forschungszentrum Jülich

Abstract

The Simulation Laboratory (SimLab) `Earth and Environment' is a new community-oriented research and support infrastructure founded in 2010. It is a joint SimLab for climate and Earth system modelling with teams at the Steinbuch Centre for Computing (SCC) and the Jülich Supercomputing Centre (JSC). It supports atmospheric and environmental model systems using the facilities of supercomputing centres especially at JSC and SCC. The focus of our SimLab is in the range of High Performance Computing. But it also performs own research together with the atmospheric and earth science community.

1 Introduction

High-Performance Computing (HPC) is currently at a turning point. Achieving exascale performance in Earth system modelling in ten years time will cause substantial challenges for hardware and software development. Hardware vendors aim for a large increase in the number of cores per chip and per node, massive increases in the number of threads of execution in the system and reduction in memory per core and especially in memory bandwidth per core. This requires a detailed understanding of the implications of future HPC developments.

To support the scientific community with this understanding the Steinbuch Centre for Computing and the Jülich Supercomputing Centre have established simulation laboratories (SimLabs) as a new community-oriented research and support infrastructure (Attig et al., 2007). The SimLabs are thereby an integrated part of the HGF program `Supercomputing' of the Karlsruhe Institute of Technology and Forschungszentrum Jülich.

The SimLabs act as an interface between the experts at the supercomputing centres and the members of different scientific communities. They support especially applications with a focus in the field of HPC or Data Intensive Computing (DIC) and provide high level support in utilizing the HPC facilities at JSC, SCC and other computing centres.

The SimLabs also perform their own research on scientific applications. This work is typically done in close cooperation with scientific institutes through common projects. Hence a SimLab consists of a core group located at the super-computing centre and a number of associated scientists outside.

Currently there are seven simulation labs together with supporting cross-sectional teams defined in the HGF program Supercomputing. They are located in Karlsruhe and Jülich (see Fig. 1).

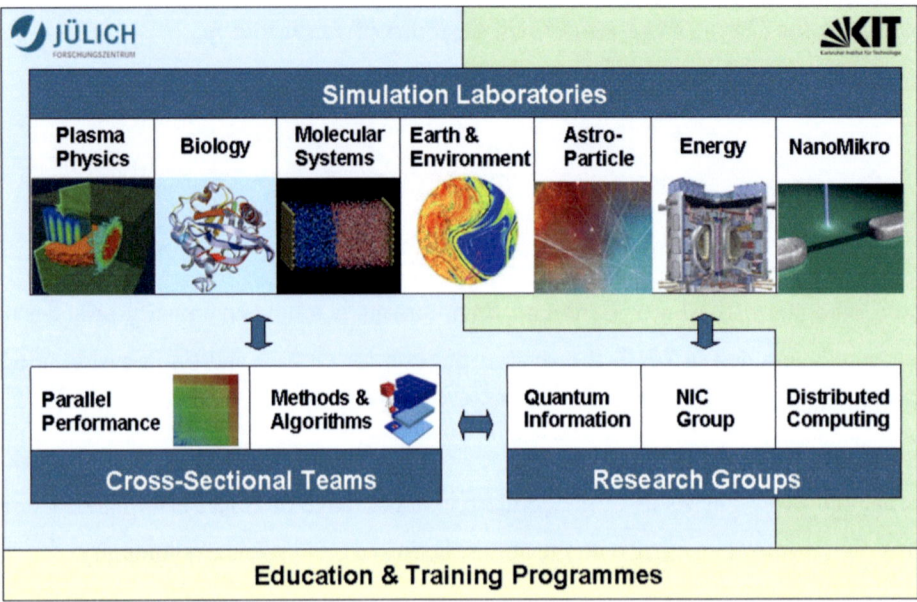

Fig. 1: Simulation Laboratories in the HGF program Supercomputing at Jülich Supercomputing Centre (JSC, FZJ) and Steinbuch Centre for Computing (SCC, KIT).

2 Simulation Lab Earth and Environment

The Simulation Laboratory Earth and Environment is a joint SimLab for climate and earth system modelling with teams at SCC ("SimLab Climate and Environment") and JSC ("SimLab Climate Science"). It provides a research and support infrastructure and acts as an interface between the atmospheric and earth science community and high-performance computing specialists at the supercomputing centres.

The mission of SimLab Earth and Environment is to provide high level support in utilizing the HPC facilities at JSC or SCC, first by porting global and regional climate earth system models to the supercomputers, and then in optimizing the performance of these models by enhancing their parallel scalability, load balancing and parallel in- and output. A major goal of the work is not only to improve the capability of the model systems to operate on various types of current HPC systems, but also to enable it to perform future simulation on peta- and exascales systems.

The SimLab also performs its own research on scientific applications, including the development of highly-scalable algorithms for climate and Earth system models, numerical weather prediction and data assimilation. This work is typically done in close cooperation with atmospheric and environmental institutes through common projects.

In the following there are some examples of current works and common projects by SimLab Earth and Environment:

1) Regular update of supported atmospheric regional and global model systems:

- Global chemistry-climate model ECHAM5/MESSy for Atmospheric Chemistry (EMAC, Jöckel et al., 2006; 2010).

- Global chemistry-transport model Karlsruhe Simulation Model of the Middle Atmosphere (KASIMA, Kouker et al., 1999).

- Global chemistry-transport model Chemical Lagrangian Model of the Stratosphere (CLAMS, McKenna, 2002a; 2002b).

- Mesoscale model Karlsruhe Atmospheric Mesoscale Model (KAMM, Adrian and Fiedler, 1991)

- Regional models of the Consortium for Small-scale Modelling (COSMO): COSMO-ART (Vogel et al., 2009) and COSMO-CLM (Rockel et al., 2008)

- Regional model Weather Research and Forecasting (WRF, Michalakes et al., 2001)

- Global and regional atmospheric data assimilation systems EURAD-IM and SACADA

- Radiative Transfer Model and Retrieval Algorithm SCIATRAN (Rozanov et al., 2005)

- Radiative Transfer Model and Retrieval Algorithm JURASSIC (Hoffmann, 2006)

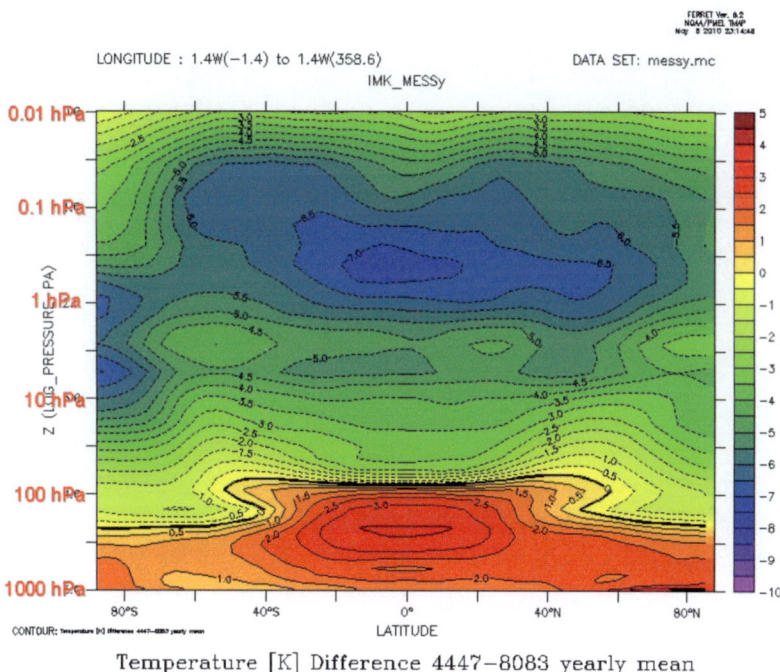

Fig. 2: Difference of mean temperatures in K of the averaged years 2044 to 2047 and 1980 to 1983 for the lower and middle atmosphere (up to 80 km). Data from a global long term simulation from 1960 to 2050 performed with the chemistry-climate-model EMAC.

2) Performing of test and standard simulations with these model systems and providing of model data for comparison with observations (Wetzel et al., 2010).

3) Performing of EMAC long-term simulations with boundary conditions of Intergovernmental Panel on Climate Change (IPCC, 2001) and World Meteorological Organization (WMO, 2007) together with Institute for Meteorology and Climate Research (IMK, Karlsruhe) in the project Chemistry-Climate Model Validation Activity for SPARC (CCMVal) (see Fig. 2).

4) Performing of KASIMA and EMAC simulations with respect to the influence of high energy particle precipitation together with IMK and Instituto de Astrofisica de Andalucia (IAA, Spain) in the project High Energy Particle Precipitation in the Atmosphere (HEPPA) (Funke et al., 2011, Jackmann et al., 2011).

5) High-resolution climate simulations with COSMO-CLM for Northern Africa together with IMK in the project Coordinated Regional climate Downscaling Experiment (CORDEX).

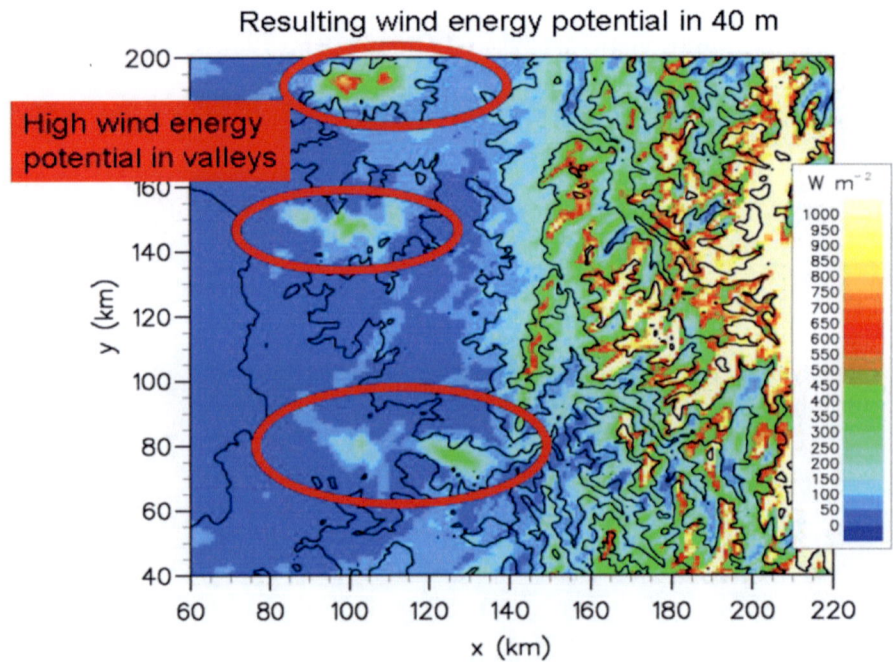

Fig.3: Evaluation of the wind energy potential in the heterogeneous area of Norte Chico, Chile (Region: Coquimbo and Atacama) in order to determine the location of wind power plants. Simulated wind energy potential in Wm^{-2} from a high-resolution simulation performed with the mesoscale model KAMM.

6) Simulations with KAMM for evaluation of the wind energy potential in Chile together with IMK and Uni de La Serena, Chile (see Fig. 3) (Bischoff-Gauß et al., 2008).

7) Simulations with KAMM for evaluation of the wind energy potential in Thailand together with IMK and Silpakorn Uni, Thailand.

8) KAMM Simulations of the „Meteor Crater" in Nevada and comparison with observations together with IMK and University of Utah, USA.

9) Development of a new parameterization of polar stratospheric clouds in EMAC together with IMK (Kirner et al., 2011).

10) Development of the EMAC submodel Age of Air together with IMK in the project Stratospheric Change and its Role for Climate Prediction (SHARP).

11) Extension of COSMO-ART into the stratosphere and merging with the COSMO/MESSy system (two way online nesting) together with IMK and Guttenberg University, Mainz in the project Modeling of Atmospheric Chemistry and Transport from the global to the local scales (MACCHIATO).

12) Update of the chemistry solver in CLaMS, together with the Institute for Energy and Climate Research (IEK, Jülich).

13) Development of a parallel template for stochastic atmospheric chemistry simulations, together with the University of Cologne.

14) Porting of the radiative transfer model SCIATRAN on the JuRoPA supercomputer to retrieve UT/LS water vapour data from SCIAMACHY measurements, together with the University of Bremen.

15) Porting of the radiative transfer model JURASSIC to the JuRoPA supercomputer to retrieve stratospheric temperature data from AIRS satellite measurements (Hoffmann and Alexander, 2009).

16) Performance assessment and data processing feasibility studies for the proposed ESA Earth Explorer mission PREMIER.

3   Conclusions and Outlook

SCC and JSC successfully established a joint SimLab for Climate Research as a new support and research infrastructure for the atmospheric science community. At JSC the support activities of the SimLab are coordinated by means of a `Call for SimLab Support` which was opened in summer 2010 for the first time. At SCC the SimLab will participate in a similar call in 2012.

References

[1]   Adrian, G. and Fiedler, F.: Simulation of Unstationary Wind and Temperature Fields over Complex Terrain and Comparison with Observations, Beitr. Phys. Atmosph. 64, 2748, 1991

[2]   Attig, N., Esser, R., and Gibbon P.: Simulation Laboratories: An Innovative Community-Oriented Research and Support Structure, Proceedings of the Cracow Grid Workshop (CGW'07), 16-18 October, 2007

[3] Bischoff-Gauß, I., Kalthoff, N., Khodayar, S., Fiebig-Wittmaack, M., and Montecinos, S.: Model Simulations of the Boundary-Layer Evolution over an Arid Andes Valley, Boundary-Layer Meteorol., 128, 357–379, 2008

[4] Funke, B., Baumgaertner, A., Calisto, M., Egorova, T., Jackman, C. H., Kieser, J., Krivolutsky, A., López-Puertas, M., Marsh, D. R., Reddmann, T., Rozanov, E., Salmi, S.-M., Sinnhuber, M., Stiller, G. P., Verronen, P. T., Versick, S., von Clarmann, T., Vyushkova, T. Y., Wieters, N., and Wissing, J. M.: Composition changes after the "Halloween" solar proton event: the High-Energy Particle Precipitation in the Atmosphere (HEPPA) model versus MIPAS data intercomparison study, Atmos. Chem. Phys. Discuss., 11, 9407-9514, 2011

[5] Hoffmann, L. and Alexander, M. J.: Retrieval of stratospheric temperatures from Atmospheric Infrared Sounder radiance measurements for gravity wave studies, J. Geophys. Res., 114, D07105, 2009

[6] Hoffmann, L.: Schnelle Spurengasretrieval für das Satellitenexperiment Envisat MIPAS, Forschungszentrum Jülich, Tech. Report JUEL-4207, Juelich, 2006.

[7] IPCC (Intergovernmental Panel on Climate Change): Climate Change 2001: Synthesis Report. A Contribution of Working Groups I, II and III to the Third Assessment Report of the Intergovernmental Panel on Climate Change (Watson, R. T. and the Core Writing Team (eds.)). Cambridge University Press, Cambridge, United Kingdom, and New York, USA, 2001

[8] Jackman, C. H., Marsh, D. R., Vitt, F. M., Roble, R. G., Randall, C. E., Bernath, P. F., Funke, B., López-Puertas, M., Versick, S., Stiller, G. P., Tylka, A. J., and Fleming, E. L.: Northern Hemisphere atmospheric influence of the solar proton events and ground level enhancement in January 2005, Atmos. Chem. Phys. Discuss., 11, 7715-7755, 2011

[9] Jöckel, P., Tost, H., Pozzer, A., Brühl, C., Buchholz, J., Ganzeveld, L., Hoor, P., Kerkweg, A., Lawrence, M. G., Sander, R., Steil, B., Stiller, G., Tanarhte, M., Taraborrelli, D., van Aardenne, J., and Lelieveld, J.: The atmospheric chemistry general circulation model ECHAM5/MESSy1: consistent simulation of ozone from the surface to the mesosphere, Atmos. Chem. Phys., 6, 5067-5104, 2006

[10] Jöckel, P., Kerkweg, A., Pozzer, A., Sander, R., Tost, H., Riede, H., Baumgaertner, A., Gromov, S., and Kern, B.: Development cycle 2 of the Modular Earth Submodel System (MESSy2), Geosci. Model Dev., 3, 717-752, 2010

[11] Kirner, O., Ruhnke, R., Buchholz-Dietsch, J., Jöckel, P., Brühl, C. and Steil, B.: Simulation of polar stratospheric clouds in the chemistry-climate-model EMAC via the submodel PSC, Geosci. Model Dev., 4, 169-182, 2011

[12] Kouker, W., Langbein, I., Reddmann, T. and Ruhnke, R.: The Karlsruhe Simulation Model of the Middle Atmosphere (KASIMA), Version 2, FZK 6278, Forschungszentrum Karlsruhe GmbH, Karlsruhe, 1999

[13] McKenna, D. S., Konopka, P., Grooß, J.-U., Günther, G., Müller, R., Spang, R., Offermann, D., and Orsolini, Y.: A new Chemical Lagrangian Model of the Stratosphere (CLaMS): Part I Formulation of advection and mixing, J. Geophys. Res., 107, 2002a

[14] McKenna, D. S., Grooß, J.-U., Günther, G., Konopka, P., Müller, R., Carver, G., and Sasano, Y.: A new Chemical Lagrangian Model of the Stratosphere (CLaMS): Part II Formulation of chemistry-scheme and initialisation, J. Geophys. Res., 107, 2002b

[15] Michalakes, J., Chen, S., Dudhia, J., Hart, L., Klemp, J., Middlecoff, J., and Skamarock, W.: Development of a next generation regional weather research and forecast model. Developments in Teracomputing. Proceedings of the Ninth ECMWF Workshop on the Use of High Performance Computing in Meteorology, W. Zwiehofer and N. Kreitz, Eds., World Scienti_c, 269276, 2001

[16] Rockel, B., Will, A., and Hense, A.: The Regional Climate Model COSMO-CLM (CCLM), Meteorol. Z. 17, 347348, 2008

[17] Rozanov, A., Rozanov, V., Buchwitz, M., Kokhanovsky, A., and Burrows, J. P.: SCIATRAN 2.0 - a new radiative transfer model for geophysical applications. Adv. Space Res. 36, 5, 1015–1019, 2005

[18] Vogel, B., Vogel, H., Bäumer, D., Bangert, M., Lundgren, K., Rinke, R., and Stanelle, T.: The comprehensive model system COSMO-ART - Radiative impact of aerosol on the state of the atmosphere on the regional scale, Atmos. Chem. Phys., 9, 8661-8680, 2009

[19] Wetzel, G., Oelhaf, H., Kirner, O., Ruhnke, R., Friedl-Vallon, F., Kleinert, A., Maucher, G., Fischer, H., Birk, M., Wagner, G., and Engel, A.: First remote sensing measurements of ClOOCl along with ClO and $ClONO_2$ in activated and deactivated Arctic vortex conditions using new ClOOCl IR absorption cross sections, Atmos. Chem. Phys., 10, 931-945, 2010

[20] WMO (World Meteorological Organization): Scientific Assessment of Ozone Depletion: 585 2006, Global Ozone Research and Monitoring Project - Report No. 50, 572 pp., Geneva, Switzerland, 2007

Compact and Stable Discontinuous Galerkin Methods with Application to Atmospheric Flows

S. Brdar[1], A. Dedner[2], R. Klöfkorn[1]

[1] *Section of Applied Mathematics, University of Freiburg, Freiburg i. Br. 79104, Germany.*
E-mail: slavko\robertk@mathematik.uni-freiburg.de

[2] *Mathematics Institute, University of Warwick, Coventry CV4 7AL UK.*
E-mail: A.S.Dedner@warwick.ac.uk

Abstract

In this work we formulate the Compact Discontinuous Galerkin 2 (CDG2) method introduced in [8] for advection-diffusion problems. We present a proof of stability for the linear heat equation. Numerical results are shown for the compressible Navier-Stokes equation. We compare our new method numerically with two other well-established methods: the Compact Discontinuous Galerkin (CDG) and the Local Discontinuous Galerkin (LDG) method. In contrast to the LDG method, the primal formulation of the CDG2 method only involves the direct neighbors, making it more suitable for execution on parallel computers. The CDG method also has this compactness property, but the performance of the method is not as good as for the CDG2 method in terms of L^2-error versus computation time.

1 Introduction

The CDG2 method uses the Discontinuous Galerkin (DG) approach to discretize diffusion fluxes for advection-diffusion problems. It was derived and analyzed for the first time in [8] for advection-diffusion problems.

In general the CDG2 method inherits all the properties of the DG method: it is highly efficient on parallel computers; higher accuracy is achieved by choosing higher polynomial degree locally in each cell; the implementation on unstructured grids is straightforward. At the same time, it has the potential to overcome some shortcomings of other DG methods, e.g., of the Interior Penalty (IP) and the Local Discontinuous Galerkin (LDG) method.

The IP method was proposed by Douglas and Dupont in 1975 in [4] and revised by Hartmann and Houston in 2008 for Navier-Stokes equations in [2]. In comparison to CDG2 the IP method, due to stability reasons, can not be used without the penalization of the jump of the numerical solution across the grid interfaces (see, for example, [2, 3]). In comparison to LDG the CDG2 method is *compact*, in the sense that updating the degrees of freedom (DOF) in one time step in one cell requires only data from the directly neighboring cells. This leads to a better sparsity pattern and allows for a more efficient parallelization of the method.

The paper is organized as follows. In Sec. 2 we formulate the CDG2 method for advection-diffusion problem. In Sec. 2.1 we give stability results and finally, in Sec. 3 we show some numerical experiments.

2 Primal formulation

We consider a general non-linear scalar advection-diffusion equation. A system of advection-diffusion equations can be treated by applying the same algorithm to each equation in the system. Consider

$$\partial_t u + \nabla \cdot (F(u) - A(u)\nabla u) = 0 \quad \text{in } \Omega \times [0, T] \tag{2.1}$$

equipped with Dirichlet boundary data g_D on $\Gamma = \partial \Omega$ and initial conditions u_0. For scalar case we have $u : \mathbb{R}^d \times [0, T] \to \mathbb{R}$, $F : \mathbb{R}^d \to \mathbb{R}^d$, $A : \mathbb{R} \times \mathbb{R}^d \to \mathbb{R}^d$. We start by rewriting (2.1) as a system of first order PDEs

$$\partial_t u + \nabla \cdot (F(u) - A(u)\sigma = 0, \tag{2.2a}$$

$$\sigma = \nabla u. \tag{2.2b}$$

Next, we employ a finite polygonal grid $\mathcal{T}_h = \{K\}$ which partitions Ω to define the following function spaces for some $l, k \in \mathbb{N}$

$$V_h^l = \{v \in L^\infty(\Omega, \mathbb{R}^l) \mid v|_K \in [\mathscr{P}_k(K)]^l\}.$$

Multiplication of (2.2a) with an arbitrary $\phi \in V_h^1$ and (2.2b) by $\psi \in V_h^d$, followed by integration (and one additional partial integration for (2.2b)) over Ω yields *the flux formulation* of the DG method

$$\int_\Omega \partial_t u = \int_\Omega (F(u) - A(u)\sigma) \cdot \nabla \varphi - \sum_{e \in \Gamma} \int_e (\hat{F}(u) - \hat{A}(u)) \cdot [\![\varphi]\!]_e,$$

$$\int_\Omega \psi \cdot \sigma = \int_\Omega \psi \cdot \nabla u - \sum_{e \in \Gamma_0} \int_e \{\!\{\psi\}\!\}_e \cdot [\![u]\!]_e - \sum_{e \in \Gamma} \int_e \{u - \hat{u}\}_e [\psi]_e. \tag{2.3}$$

where one still needs to specify the diffusion fluxes $(\hat{u}, \hat{A})$ and replace the advection flux $\hat{F}$ with one of the available numerical flux functions (Local Lax-Friedrichs, Roe, HLLC, Godunov, etc.).

In (2.3) we used the following notation: Γ is $\bigcup_{K \in \mathcal{T}_h} \partial K$, whereas $\Gamma_0 = \bigcup_{K \in \mathcal{T}_h} (\partial K \setminus \partial \Omega)$. For $e = K^+ \cap K^-$ and Hausdorff measure $\mathcal{H}_{d-1}(e) > 0$ we define operators $[\![\cdot]\!]_e$, $\{\cdot\}_e$ acting on $\phi \in V_h^1$ and $[\cdot]_e$, $\{\{\cdot\}\}_e$ on $\tau \in V_h^d$. When $e \cap \partial \Omega = 0$ we let

$$[\![\phi]\!]_e = \phi^- n^- + \phi^+ n^+, \qquad [\tau]_e = \tau^- \cdot n^- + \tau^+ \cdot n^+,$$
$$\{\phi\}_e = \phi^- + \phi^+, \qquad \{\{\tau\}\}_e = \tau^- + \tau^+,$$

otherwise if $e \subset \partial \Omega$

$$[\![\phi]\!]_e = (\phi - g'_D)n, \qquad [\tau]_e = \tau \cdot n,$$
$$\{\phi\}_e = \phi, \qquad \{\{\tau\}\}_e = \tau.$$

$n^\pm$ is outer outer normal on $K^\pm \in \mathcal{T}_h$ and n on Ω. g'_D is g_D only when ϕ is numerical solution u, otherwise 0.

In the following we derive the *primal formulation* of our new CDG2 method. To that end, we introduce the *lifting operators* $r_e : [L^2(\Gamma)]^d \to V_h^d$ and $l_e : L^2(\Gamma_0) \to V_h^d$ as

$$\int_\Omega r_e(\eta) \cdot \tau = - \int_e \eta \cdot \{\{\tau\}\}_e, \qquad \int_\Omega l_e(\phi) \cdot \tau = - \int_e \phi [\tau]_e.$$

We extend l_e for $e \subset \partial \Omega$ by setting $l_e(\cdot) \equiv 0$. Notice that the solution to the second equation in (2.3) can be expressed in the following way:

$$\sigma = \nabla u + \sum_{e \in \Gamma_0} r_e([\![u]\!]_e) + l_e([u - \hat{u}]_e).$$

In case of CDG2 the diffusion fluxes are

$$e \in \Gamma_0 : \quad \hat{A}(u) = \{\{A(u)\nabla u\}\}_e + \chi\left(\{\{A(u)L_e(u)\}\}_e + \beta_e[A(u)L_e(u)]_e\right)$$
$$\hat{u} = \{u\}_e,$$
$$e \notin \Gamma_0 : \quad \hat{A}(u) = A(u)\nabla u, \quad \hat{u} = g_D.$$

Here $\chi > 0$ is some stability constant which will be studied in detail in the next section. For convenience we define $L_e(u) := r_e([\![u]\!]_e) + l_e(\beta_e \cdot [\![u]\!]_e)$ on Γ. The *switch* function β_e is chosen to satisfy: $\beta_e = \frac{1}{2}\mathbf{n}_{K_e^1} = -\frac{1}{2}\mathbf{n}_{K_e^2}$, where $e = K_e^1 \cap K_e^2$ is an interior edge of the grid, on an edge $e \subset \partial \Omega$ we set $\beta_e = 0$. Here $\mathbf{n}_{K_e}$ is the outer unit normal of K_e on edge $e \subset \partial K$. We will discuss two definitions for β_e in the next section. In the following we denote with K_e^+ the element with $\beta_e \cdot \mathbf{n}_{K_e^+} = -\frac{1}{2}$ and with K_e^- the element with $\beta_e \cdot \mathbf{n}_{K_e^-} = \frac{1}{2}$. The edge e is called an *outflow* edge of K_e^- and an *inflow* edge of K_e^+.

2.1 Stability analysis

In this section we want to give L^2-stability conditions for the CDG2 method in the case of the linear heat equations. For LDG and CDG these stability results can be found in [5] and [7], respectively. The L^2-stability is defined as $\frac{d}{dt} \int_\Omega u^2 \, dt \leq 0$.

Theorem 2.1 (*L^2-stability*). *The CDG2 method is L^2-stable in case of the linear heat equation for homogeneous Dirichlet boundary conditions if one of the two following conditions is fulfilled*

$$\chi \geq \frac{\mathcal{N}(\mathcal{T}_h)}{4}\left(1 + C(\mathcal{T}_h)\right),$$

where $\mathcal{N}(\mathcal{T}_h)$ is maximal number of intersections with other elements that one grid element K in $\mathcal{T}_h$ can have and $C(\mathcal{T}_h) = \max_{e \in \Gamma_i}\{|K_e^-|/|K_e^+|\}$ and K_e^-, K_e^+ determined by β_e.

Proof. Let $u \in V_h$ be chosen arbitrary and $\mathbf{r}(u) = \sum_{e \in \Gamma} r_e(\llbracket u \rrbracket_e)$. Then the bilinear form $B(u,u)$ in the case of the CDG2 method can be rewritten as

$$B(u,u) = \|\nabla u + \mathbf{r}(u)\|_\Omega^2 - \|\mathbf{r}(u)\|_\Omega^2 + \chi \sum_{e \in \Gamma} \|L_e(u)\|_\Omega^2 + \sum_{e \in \Gamma} \frac{\xi}{|e|} \|\llbracket u \rrbracket_e\|_e^2. \qquad (2.4)$$

Note that $r_e(\cdot) \equiv 0$ in grid elements not having e as one edge. From that fact we derive the inequality

$$\|\mathbf{r}(u)\|_\Omega^2 \leq \mathcal{N}(\mathcal{T}_h) \sum_{e \in \Gamma} \|r_e(\llbracket u \rrbracket_e)\|_\Omega^2. \qquad (2.5)$$

We further notice that $\operatorname{supp} L_e(u) = K$ if $n_{K,e} \cdot \beta_e > 0$ and $e \subset \partial K$, and denote from now on $L_e(u)$, simply with L_e and $r_e(\llbracket u \rrbracket_e)$ with r_e. Since $L_e|_K \equiv 0$ when e is an inflow face for K ($n_{K,e} \cdot \beta_e = -\frac{1}{2}$), we deduce the following equality

$$\|L_e\|_\Omega^2 = \int_{K_e^-} L_e \cdot L_e = 2 \int_{K_e^-} r_e \cdot L_e = 2 \int_\Omega r_e \cdot L_e. \qquad (2.6)$$

Also, it is possible to prove that

$$\alpha_e \|r_e\|_{K_e^-}^2 = \|r_e\|_{K_e^+}^2, \qquad \text{with } \alpha_e = |K_e^-|/|K_e^+|. \qquad (2.7)$$

A detailed proof of this statement can be found [8]. This allows us to express $\|r_e\|_{K_e^-}^2$ in terms of $\|r_e\|_\Omega^2$ as $\|r_e\|_{K_e^-}^2 = \frac{1}{1+\alpha_e}\|r_e\|_\Omega^2$. Making use of equation (2.6) yields the following equality

$$\|L_e\|_\Omega^2 = 2 \int_\Omega r_e \cdot L_e = 2\left(\int_{K_{e-}} + \int_{K_e^+}\right) r_e \cdot L_e = 4\|r_e\|_{K_e^-}^2,$$

which in the combination with the previous one leaves us with

$$\|L_e\|_\Omega^2 = \sum_{e \in \Gamma} \frac{4}{1+\alpha_e}\|r_e\|_\Omega^2.$$

Inserting the previous result into equation (2.4) and applying inequality (2.5) we arrive at

$$B(u,u) \geq \|\nabla u + \mathbf{r}\|_\Omega^2 - \sum_{e \in \Gamma}\left(\mathcal{N}(\mathcal{T}_h) - \frac{4\chi_e}{1+\alpha_e}\right)\|r_e\|_\Omega^2 + \sum_{e \in \Gamma} \frac{\xi}{|e|}\|\llbracket u \rrbracket_e\|_e^2.$$

With $\chi_e \geq \frac{\mathcal{N}(\mathcal{T}_h)}{4}(1 + \alpha_e)$ we ensure $B(u,u)$ to be positive, and thus L^2-stable, which also holds if we choose $\chi \geq \max_e \frac{\mathcal{N}(\mathcal{T}_h)}{4}(1 + \alpha_e)$ as introduced in the theorem formulation. $\qquad \square$

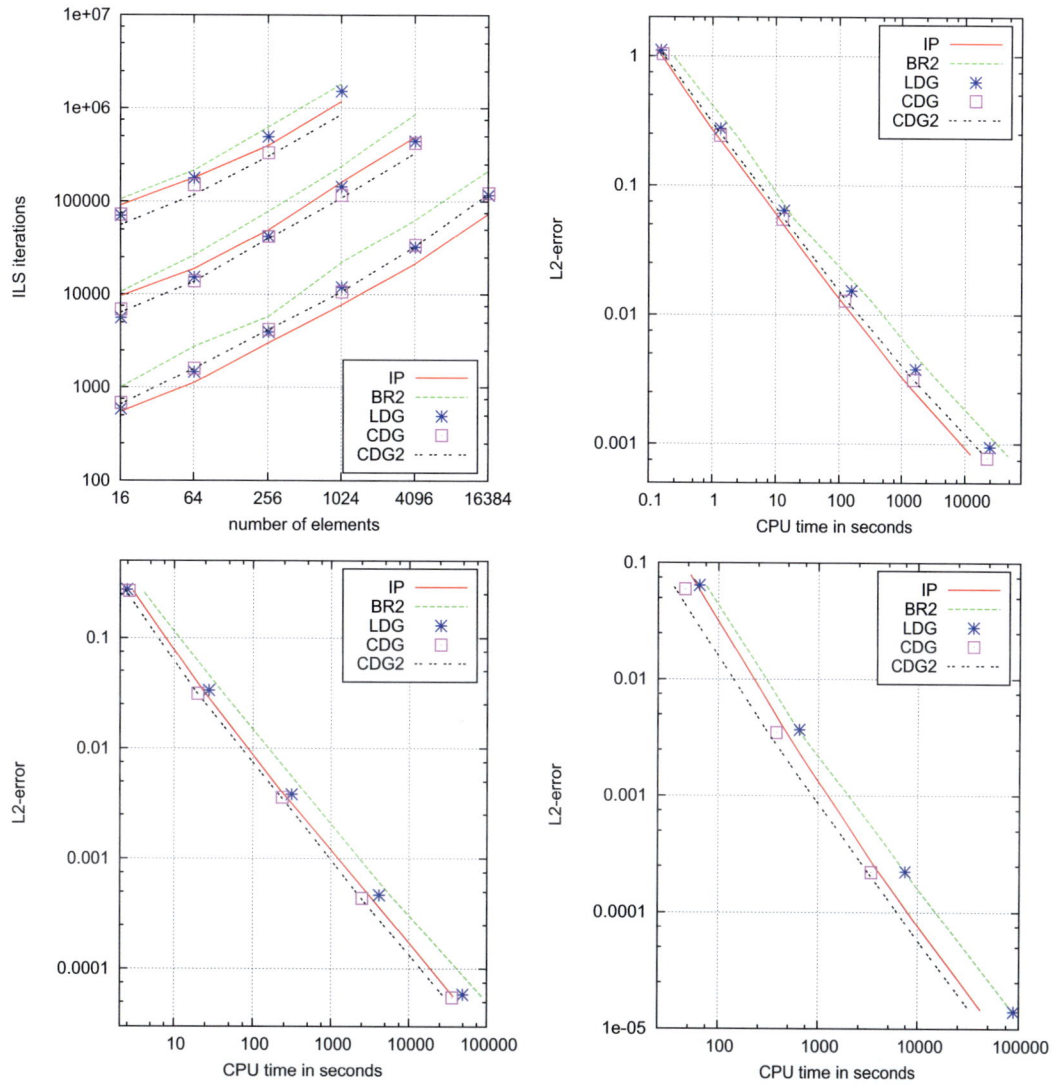

Figure 1: Navier-Stokes. ILS iteration(TL) and efficiency of the 2nd(TR), 3rd(BL), 4th(BR) order methods.

3 Numerical results

In this section we compare the CDG2 method with two other well established method, the LDG, and since recently, the CDG method. Most notable feature of the *compact* DG method is that in the case of second order PDEs the stencil only involves neighboring elements, thus reducing communications between the processes. But even though it is expected that the advantage of compact DG methods (CDG, CDG2) will become even more evident if the runs are executed on parallel machines, we will however carry out the tests on single core machine. The comparison will be performed on structured triangular grids to solve the Navier-Stokes equations. For Navier-Stokes equations we choose the analytical solution proposed in [6] with a homogeneous velocity field. As an application of the CDG2 method we choose a standard atmospheric test case in [9].

For all numerical examples we use the theoretical results for χ, for the CDG method given in [7] and for the CDG2 method given in Theorem 2.1. It remains to fix the switch β_e for each interior edge $e \in \Gamma_i$. For the CDG method we use the *upwind switch* $\beta_e = \frac{1}{2}\operatorname{sgn}(\mathbf{n}_{K_e} \cdot w)\mathbf{n}_{K_e}$. The *upwind* vector $w \in \mathbb{R}^d$ is chosen a priori (i.e. before each time step), such that $w \cdot \mathbf{n} \neq 0$ for any normal $\mathbf{n}$ to an interface of $K \in \mathscr{T}_h$. For the CDG2 method we use another switch which is motivated by the stability estimate for the method. In order to minimize the constant $C(\mathscr{T}_h)$ we introduce the *area switch* $\beta_e = \frac{1}{2}\mathbf{n}_{K_e^*}$, where K_e^* is the element adjacent to e with the smaller area. Thus $|K_e^-| \leq |K_e^+|$ and consequently $C(\mathscr{T}_h) \leq 1$.

p	Method	256	1024		4096		16384	
	LDG	6.39e-2	1.52e-2	2.07	3.78e-3	2.01	9.45e-4	2.00
1	CDG	5.46e-2	1.28e-2	2.09	3.12e-3	2.04	7.77e-4	2.01
	CDG2	5.69e-2	1.32e-2	2.11	3.21e-3	2.04	7.94e-4	2.02
p		64	256		1024		4096	
	LDG	3.33e-2	3.84e-3	3.11	4.67e-4	3.04	5.85e-5	3.00
2	CDG	3.11e-2	3.58e-3	3.12	4.38e-4	3.04	5.49e-5	3.00
	CDG2	3.26e-2	3.79e-3	3.10	4.58e-3	3.05	5.64e-5	3.02
p		16	64		256		1024	
	LDG	6.41e-2	3.69e-3	4.12	2.23e-4	4.05	1.40e-5	3.99
3	CDG	5.95e-2	3.49e-3	4.10	2.21e-4	3.98	1.39e-5	3.99
	CDG2	6.19e-2	3.72e-3	4.06	2.25e-4	4.05	1.37e-5	4.04

Table 1: Different methods for Navier-Stokes equations on structured rectangular grid using IMEX-RK.

The LDG method is implemented in the flux formulation, meaning that one evaluation of the LDG spatial operator requires two iterations through grid, first one to compute σ and the second for u, where at each grid iteration one DG computation is applied. In this way computation of lifting operators is avoided. Nevertheless, for the Navier-Stokes equation the LDG spatial operator becomes less efficient to compute than other mention methods, as can be seen in Figure 1. As a time integrator we use implicit-explicit Runge-Kutta (IMEX-RK) methods of different orders, the reason being better resolve of the advection (treated explicitly) while avoiding severe time step restriction of the diffusion (treated implicitly), which one would have if a fully explicit RK method was used.

The L^2-error and convergence rate are shown in Table 1. One can see that all method perform equally well, with LDG being slightly less accurate. But, as shown in Figure 1 the LDG is

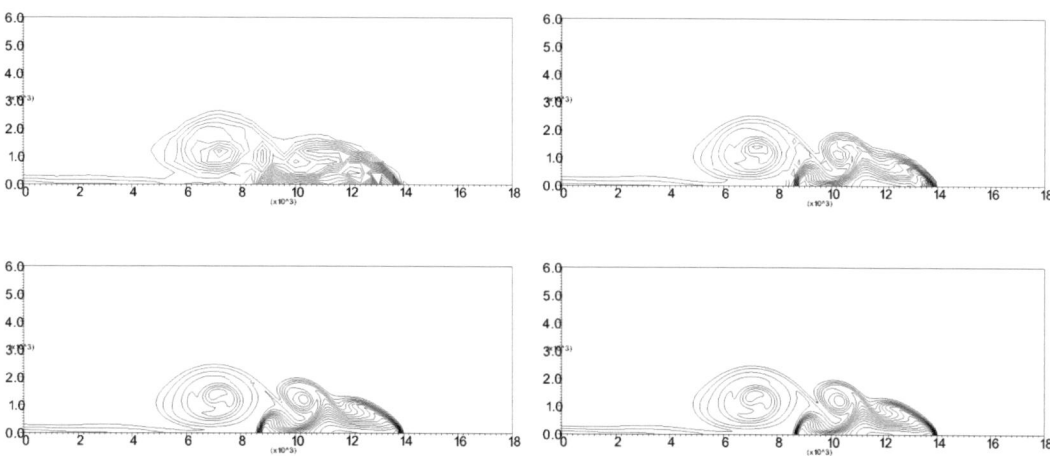

Figure 2: Potential temperature for the *density current* test case at resolutions $400m$, $200m$, $100m$, and $50m$ (from top left to bottom right) for the CDG2 method of 3rd order.

indeed the least efficient method under these settings, the best being one of the two compact methods. CDG2 is, despite being slightly less accurate, slightly more efficient than CDG.

In Figure 2 we apply the CDG2 method on the test case in [9] for an atmospheric flow. In comparison to the reference solution we observe the proper resolve of the flow formation, most evident on picture "100m,p=2" where all three rotors are fully developed. Due to projection of numerical solution onto the piecewise linear space the contours of the third and fourth order methods are somewhat unclear. Nevertheless, one can spot all rotors at 200m with the forth order method as well as for the third order at 100m, while for the second order method the flow is not yet resolved at 50m. On the other side the computational time for the second order method at 50m is 57%, and for third order at 100m 19% longer than the corresponding of the forth order method.

4 Conclusions

In this paper, we have formulated the higher order CDG2 method for advection-diffusion problems and in case of the linear heat equation we have proven the stability under certain conditions. The CDG2 method was computationally verified for the Navier-Stokes equations using known analytical solutions. The expected order of convergence was achieved. In comparisons for the Navier-Stokes system using IMEX Runge-Kutta methods as time integrator we conclude that the CDG2 method with χ as described in Theorem 2.1 is more efficient than other methods and works for realistic problems.

References

[1] J. Peraire, P.-O. Persson. The Compact Discontinuous Galerkin Method for Elliptic Problems, SIAM J. Sci. Comput., 30(4):18061824, 2008.

[2] R. Hartmann, P. Houston. An Optimal Order Penalty Discontinuous Galerkin Discretization of the Compressible Navier-Stokes Equations. J. Com- put. Phys., 22:96709685, 2008.

[3] H. Liu, J. Yan. The Direct Discontinuous Galerkin (DDG) Method for Diffusion with Interface Corrections, SIAM J. Numer. Anal., 47(1): 675-698, 2009.

[4] J. Douglas, T. Dupont. Interior Penalty Procedures for Elliptic and Parabolic Galerkin Methods, Lecture Notes in Phys. 58, Springer-Verlag, Berlin, 1976.

[5] F. Brezzi, G. Manzini, D. Marini, P. Pietra, and A. Russo. Discontinuous Galerkin Approximations for Elliptic Problems. Numer. Methods Partial Dffer. Equations, 16(4):365378, 2000.

[6] G. Gassner, F. Lörcher, and C.-D. Munz. A Discontinuous Galerkin Scheme Based on a Space-time Expansion ii. Viscous Fow Equations in Multidimensions. J. Sci. Comp., 34 (3):260286, 2008.

[7] S. Brdar, A. Dedner, R. Klöfkorn. The CDG Method for Navier-Stokes Equations. In: Proc. of Conference on Hyperbolic Problems: Theory, Numerics, Applications, 2010.

[8] S. Brdar, A. Dedner, R. Klöfkorn. Compact and stable Discontinuous Galerkin methods for convection-diffusion problems. Preprint, Mathematisches Institut, Universität Freiburg, 2010.

[9] J. M. Straka, R. B. Wilhelmson, L. J. Wicker, J. R. Anderson, K. K. Droegemeier. Numerical solutions of a non-linear density current: A benchmark solution and comparisons Int. J. Num. Meth. in Fluids, 17:1-22(1993).

Engineering State-of-the-Art Graph Partitioning Libraries @KIT

Vitaly Osipov, Peter Sanders, Christian Schulz, Manuel Holtgrewe

Karlsruhe Institute of Technology, Karlsruhe, Germany

E-mail: {osipov, sanders, christian.schulz}@kit.edu, manuel.holtgrewe@fu-berlin.de

Abstract

We describe two different approaches to multi-level graph partitioning (MGP). The first is an approach to parallel graph partitioning that scales to hundreds of processors. All components of this algorithm are implemented by scalable parallel algorithms. The second algorithm is based on the extreme idea to contract only a single edge on each level of the hierarchy. This obviates the need for a matching algorithm and promises very good partitioning quality since there are very few changes between two levels. Both algorithms produce a very high solution quality. Quality improvements compared to previous systems are due to better prioritization of edges to be contracted, better approximation algorithms for identifying matchings and FM local search algorithms that work more locally than previous approaches.

1 Introduction

Graph partitioning is a common technique in computer science, engineering, and related fields. Good partitionings of unstructured and irregular graphs are very valuable in the area of *high performance computing*. An important example are *partial differential equations*. These equations are usually solved numerically using a parallel computer, e.g. using a CG method. To effectively balance the load we need a graph model of computation and communication. Roughly speaking, vertices in the graph represent computation units and edges denote communication. Now this graph needs to be partitioned such that there are few edges between the blocks (pieces). In particular, when we want to solve the partial differential equation in parallel on k PEs (processing elements) we want to partition the graph into k blocks of about equal size. In this paper we focus on a version of the problem that constrains the maximum block size to $(1 + \varepsilon)$ times the average block size and tries to minimize the total cut size, i.e., the number of edges that run between blocks.[1]

---

[1] It is well known that there are more realistic (and more complicated) objective functions involving also the block that is worst and the number of its neighboring nodes [1] but minimizing the cut size has been adopted

A successful heuristic for partitioning large graphs is the *multilevel* approach depicted in Figure 1 where the graph is recursively *contracted* to achieve a smaller graph with the same basic structure. After applying an *initial partitioning* algorithm to this small graph, the contraction is undone and, at each level, a *local refinement* method is used to improve the partitioning induces by the coarser level. In this paper we present two algorithms: a scalable approach to parallel graph partitioning and the n-Level approach to graph partitioning. Somewhat astonishingly, we indeed found several opportunities for improvement with significant impact on partitioning quality and scalability.

After introducing basic concepts in Section 2, we present both algorithms in Section 3. This is followed by the evaluation of both algorithms and comparisons with other state-of-the-art graph partitioners in Section 4. Related work can be found in Section 5.

2 Preliminaries

Consider an undirected graph $G = (V, E, c, \omega)$ with edge weights $\omega : E \to \mathbb{R}_{>0}$, node weights $c : V \to \mathbb{R}_{\geq 0}$, $n = |V|$, and $m = |E|$. We extend c and ω to sets, i.e., $c(V') := \sum_{v \in V'} c(v)$ and $\omega(E') := \sum_{e \in E'} \omega(e)$. $\Gamma(v) := \{u : \{v, u\} \in E\}$ denotes the neighbors of v.

We are looking for *blocks* of nodes $V_1, \ldots, V_k$ that partition V, i.e., $V_1 \cup \cdots \cup V_k = V$ and $V_i \cap V_j = \emptyset$ for $i \neq j$. The *balancing constraint* demands that $\forall i \in 1..k : c(V_i) \leq L_{\max} := (1 + \varepsilon)c(V)/k + \max_{v \in V} c(v)$ for some parameter ε. The last term in this equation arises because each node is atomic and therefore a deviation of the heaviest node has to be allowed. The objective is to minimize the total *cut* $\sum_{i<j} w(E_{ij})$ where $E_{ij} := \{\{u, v\} \in E : u \in V_i, v \in V_j\}$. By default, our initial inputs will have unit edge and node weights. However, even those will be translated into weighted problems in the course of the algorithm.

A matching $M \subseteq E$ is a set of edges that do not share any common nodes, i.e., the graph (V, M) has maximum degree one. An edge coloring $\mathscr{C}$ assigns a color (a number) to each edge of a graph such that no two incident edges have the same color. Note that the edges with a particular color define a matching, i.e., $\mathscr{C}$ partitions the edges into matchings. We will be interested in colorings with a small number of different colors used.

Contracting an edge $\{u, v\}$ means to replace the nodes u and v by a new node x connected to the former neighbors of u and v. We set $c(x) = c(u) + c(v)$ so the weight of a node at each

---

as a kind of standard since it is usually highly correlated with the other formulations. We believe that the results presented here will be adaptable to other objective functions and also to other setting such as graph clustering where k and the block sizes are not necessarily fixed.

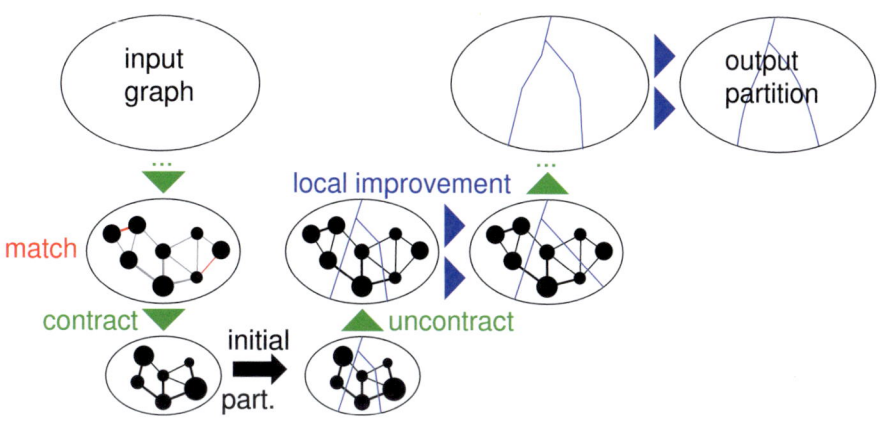

Figure 1: Multilevel graph partitioning.

level is the number of nodes it is representing in the original graph. If replacing edges of the form $\{u,w\}, \{v,w\}$ would generate two parallel edges $\{x,w\}$, we insert a single edge with $\omega(\{x,w\}) = \omega(\{u,w\}) + \omega(\{v,w\})$.

Uncontracting an edge e undos its contraction. In order to avoid tedious notation, G will denote the current state of the graph before and after a (un)contraction unless we explicitly want to refer to different states of the graph.

The multilevel approach to graph partitioning consists of three main phases. In the *contraction* (coarsening) phase, we iteratively identify matchings $M \subseteq E$ and contract the edges in M. This is repeated until $|V|$ falls below some threshold. Contraction should quickly reduce the size of the input and each computed level should reflect the global structure of the input network. In particular, nodes should represent densely connected subgraphs.

Contraction is stopped when the graph is small enough to be directly partitioned in the *initial partitioning phase* using some other algorithm. We could use a trivial initial partitioning algorithm if we contract until exactly k nodes are left. However, if $|V| \gg k$ we can afford to run some expensive algorithm for initial partitioning.

In the *refinement* (or uncoarsening) phase, the matchings are iteratively uncontracted. After uncontracting a matching, the refinement algorithm moves nodes between blocks in order to improve the cut size or balance. The nodes to move are often found using some kind of local search. The intuition behind this approach is that a good partition at one level of the hierarchy will also be a good partition on the next finer level so that refinement will quickly find a good solution.

3 Two approaches to graph partitioning

3.1 The parallel approach

We now present our approach to parallel graph partitioning. First of all the graph is distributed among all k PEs. This is done by computing a preliminary partition of the graph, e.g., using coordinate information. Currently we have implemented a recursive bisection algorithm for nodes with 2D coordinates that alternately splits the data by the x-coordinate and the y-coordinate [2, 3]. We can also use the initial numbering of the nodes.

Now we have to compute matchings to create coarser versions of the graph. We combine a sequential matching algorithm running on each PE and a parallel matching algorithm running on the *gap graph*. The gap graph consists of those edges $\{u, v\}$ where u and v reside on different PEs and $\omega(\{u, v\})$ exceeds the weight of the edges that may have been matched by the local matching algorithms to u and v.

In [4] we proposed to make contraction more systematic by separating two issues: A *rating function* indicates how much sense it makes to contract an edge based on *local* information. A *matching* algorithm tries to maximize the sum of the ratings of the contracted edges looking at the *global* structure of the graph. While the rating functions allows us a flexible characterization of what a "good" contracted graph is, the simple, standard definition of the matching problem allows us to reuse previously developed algorithms for weighted matching (see also Section 5). Matchings are contracted until the graph is "small enough". In most previous work, the edge weight $\omega(e)$ itself is used as a rating function (see Section 5 for more details). In [4] we have shown that the rating function expansion$^{*2}(\{u, v\}) := \frac{\omega(\{u,v\})^2}{c(u)c(v)}$ works best among other edge rating functions.

We employed the *Global Path Algorithm (GPA)* as sequential matching algorithm. It was proposed in [5] as a synthesis of the Greedy algorithm and the Path Growing Algorithm [6]. This algorithm achieves a half-approximation in the worst case, but empirically, GPA gives considerably better results than Sorted Heavy Edge Matching and Greedy (for more details look into [4]). The GPA scans the edges in order of decreasing weight but rather than immediately building a matching, it first constructs a collection of paths and even cycles. Afterwards, optimal solutions are computed for each of these paths and cycles using dynamic programming. Our implementation of the parallel matching algorithm proposed in [7] iteratively matches edges $\{u, v\}$ that are locally heaviest both at u and v until no more edges can be matched.

The contraction is stopped when the number of remaining nodes on some PE is below $\max(20, n/(\alpha k^2))$ for some tuning parameter α. The graph is then small enough to be par-

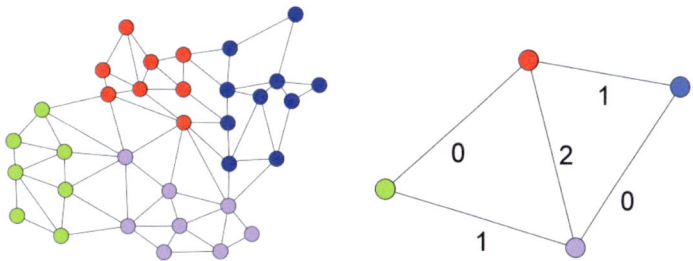

Figure 2: A graph which is partitioned into four blocks and its corresponding quotient graph $\mathcal{Q}$. The quotient graph has an edge coloring indicated by the numbers and each edge set induced by edges with the same color form a matching $\mathcal{M}(c)$. Pairs of blocks with the same color can be refined in parallel.

titioned on a single PE. We employ Scotch as an initial partitioner since it empirically performs better than Metis. This algorithm is then run simultaneously on all PEs, each with a different seed for the random number generator. The best solution is then broadcast to all PEs.

Recall that the refinement phase iteratively uncontracts the matchings contracted during the contraction phase. After a matching is uncontracted, local search based refinement algorithms move nodes between block boundaries in order to reduce the cut while maintaining the balancing constraint. As most other current systems, we adopt the basic approach from [8] which runs in linear time. The main difference of our approach to previous systems is that at any time, each PE may work on only one pair of neighboring blocks performing a local search constrained to moving nodes between these two blocks. Thus, we need parallel algorithms for deciding which processors work on which pairs of blocks.

For this purpose, we use the *quotient graph Q* whose nodes are blocks of the current partition and whose edges indicate that there are edges between these blocks in the underlying graph G. Since we have the same number of PEs and blocks, each PE will work on the block assigned to it and at one of its neighbors in Q. From now on, we will therefore identify blocks and PEs. Figure 2 gives an example.

We use matchings of Q to define with which neighbor in Q a PE is working at a particular point in time. If $\{u, v\}$ is in the matching, both corresponding PEs will refine the partitions u and v using different seeds for their random number generator. See below for more details. After the local search is finished, the better partitioning of the two blocks is adopted.

We employ the following strategy to find pairs of blocks for refinement: we step through the colors of an edge coloring of the quotient graph Q. Our coloring algorithm is a parallelization of a well known sequential greedy edge coloring algorithm. It can be shown that this algorithm

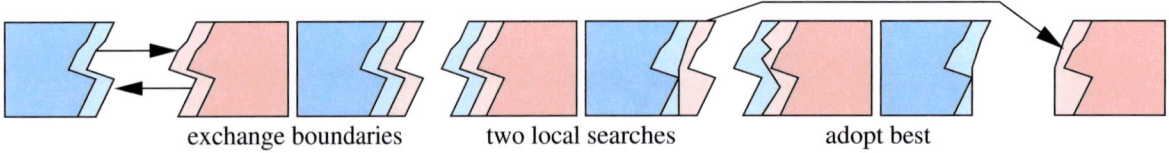

Figure 3: Refinement between two blocks using boundary exchange.

needs at most twice as many colors as an optimal edge coloring. For more details look into [4, 9]. We now describe the refinement between two blocks. Before a local search operation, we perform a bounded breadth first search starting from the boundary of each block, and send copies of this boundary array to the partner PE in the local search. The local search is then limited to this boundary area. This way, for large graphs, only a small fraction of each block has to be communicated. If it should really happen that the local search would profit from going beyond the boundary area, this will be possible in the next iteration of some of the outer loops. Figure 3 shows this schematically.

The local search algorithm itself is basically the FM-algorithm [8]: For each of the two blocks A, B under consideration, a PE keeps a priority queue of nodes eligible to move. The priority is based on the *gain*, i.e., the decrease in edge cut when the node is moved to the other side. Each node is moved at most once within a single local search. The queues are initialized in random order with the nodes at the partition boundary. We have tried several queue selection strategies: *Alternating* between A and B [8], *MaxLoad* where always the heavier block gives a node, and *TopGain*, where the queue promising larger gain is used. While MaxLoad yields partitions which are very balanced, TopGain produces partitions with higher quality within the balance constraint.

The search is broken when more than $\alpha \min\{|A|, |B|\}$ nodes have been moved without yielding an improvement. When the search stops, search is rolled back to the state with the lexicographically best value of the tuple (*imbalance, cutValue*). Where *imbalance* is $\max(0, \max(c(A) - L_{\max}, c(B) - L_{\max}))$.

3.2 The n-Level approach

We now describe our approach to sequential graph partitioning. Here our central idea is to get even better partitions by making subsequent levels as similar as possible – we (un)contract only a *single* edge between two levels. We call this *n*-GP since we have (almost) *n* levels of hierarchy. Figure 4 gives a high-level recursive summary of *n*-GP. Again we use Scotch as a base case

Function n-GP(G, k, ε)

    if G is small **then return** initialPartition(G, k, ε)

    pick the edge $e = \{u, v\}$ with the highest rating

    contract e; $\mathscr{P} := n{-}GP(G, k, \varepsilon)$;   uncontract e

    activate(u);   activate(v);   localSearch()

    return $\mathscr{P}$

Figure 4: n-GP.

partitioner when the graph is sufficiently small. In KaSPar, contraction is stopped when either only $20k$ nodes remain, no further nodes are eligible for contraction, or there are less edges than nodes left. The latter happens when the graph consists of many independent components. The edges to be contracted are chosen according to an edge rating function. KaSPar also adopts the rating function expansion$^{*2}(\{u, v\})$. Additionally, in order to avoid unbalanced inputs to the initial partitioner, KaSPar never allows a node v to participate in a contraction if the weight of v exceeds $1.5n/(20k)$. Selecting contracted edges can be implemented efficiently by keeping the contractable *nodes* in a priority queue sorted by the rating of their most highly rated incident edge.

In order to make contraction and uncontraction efficient, we use a "semidynamic" graph data structure: When contracting an edge $\{u, v\}$, we mark both u and v as deleted, introduce a new node w, and redirect the edges incident to u and v to w. The advantage of this implementation is that edges adjacent to a node are still stored in adjacency arrays which are more efficient than linked lists needed for a full fledged dynamic graph data structure. A disadvantages of our approach is a certain space overhead. However, it is relatively easy to show that this space overhead is bounded by a logarithmic factor even if we contract edges in some random fashion (see [10]). Overall, with respect to asymptotic memory overhead, n-GP is no worse than methods with a logarithmic number of levels.

The local search strategy is similar to the FM-algorithm [8]. We now outline our variant and then discuss differences. Originally, all nodes are unmarked. Only unmarked nodes are allowed to be activated or moved from one block to another. Activating a node $v \in B'$ means that for blocks $\{B \neq B' : \exists \{v, u\} \in E \wedge u \in B\}$ we compute the gain

$$g_B(v) = \sum \{\omega(\{v, u\}) : \{v, u\} \in E, v \in B\} - \sum \{\omega(\{v, u\}) : \{v, u\} \in E, v \in B'\}$$

of moving v to block B for blocks where v can be moved. Note that gains are allowed to be negative. Node v is then inserted into the priority queue P_B using $g_B(v)$ as the priority. We call a queue P_B eligible if the highest gain node in P_B can be moved to block B without violating the balance constraint for block B. Local search repeatedly looks for the highest gain node v in any eligible priority queue P_B and moves v to block B. When this happens, node v becomes nonactive and marked, the unmarked neighbors of v get activated and the gains of the active neighbors are updated. The local search is stopped if either no eligible nonempty queues remain, or one of the stopping criteria described below applies. After the local search stops, it is rolled back to the lowest cut state reached during the search (which is the starting state if no improvement was achieved). Subsequently all previously marked nodes are unmarked. The local search is repeated until no improvement is achieved.

The main difference to the usual FM-algorithm is that our routine performs a highly localized search starting just at the uncontracted edge. Indeed, our local search does nothing if none of the uncontracted nodes is a *border node*, i.e., has a neighbor in another block. Other FM-algorithms initialize the search with all border nodes. In n-GP the local search may find an improvement quickly after moving a small number of nodes. However, in order to exploit this case, we need a way to stop the search much earlier than previous algorithms which limit the number of steps to a constant fraction of the current number of nodes $|V|$.

Stopping Using a Random Walk Model. It makes sense to make a stopping rule more adaptive by making it dependent on the past history of the search, e.g., on the difference between the current cut and the best cut achieved before.

We model the gain values in each step as identically distributed, independent random variables whose expectation μ and Variance σ^2 is obtained from the previously observed p steps. In [11] we show how from these assumptions we can (heuristically) derive that it is unlikely that the local search will produce a better cut if

$$p\mu^2 > \alpha\sigma^2 + \beta \tag{1}$$

where α and β are tuning parameters and μ is the average gain since the last improvement. For the variance σ^2, we can also use the variance observed throughout the current local search. Parameter β is a base value that avoids stopping just after a small constant number of steps that happen to have small variance. Currently we set it to $\ln n$.

4 Experiments

Implementation   We have implemented the algorithm described above using C++ and MPI. Hash tables use the library (extended STL) provided with the GCC compiler. For the following comparisons we used Scotch 5.1, Metis 4.0 and ParMetis 3.1.1.

System   We have run our code on a cluster with 200 nodes each equipped with two Quad-core Intel Xeon processors (X5355) which run at a clock speed of 2.667 GHz, have 2x4 MB of level 2 cache each and run Suse Linux Enterprise 10 SP 1. All nodes are attached to an InfiniBand 4X DDR interconnect which is characterized by its very low latency of below 2 microseconds and a point to point bandwidth between two nodes of more than 1300 MB/s. Our program was compiled using GCC Version 4.3.1 and optimization level 3 using OpenMPI 1.2.8. Henceforth, a PE is one core of this machine.

Large instances		
graph	n	m
rgg20	2^{20}	13 783 240
Delaunay20	2^{20}	12 582 744
fetooth	78 136	905 182
598a	110 971	1 483 868
ocean	143 437	819 186
144	144 649	2 148 786
wave	156 317	2 118 662
m14b	214 765	3 358 036
auto	448 695	6 629 222
deu	4 378 446	10 967 174
eur	18 029 721	44 435 372
af_shell10	1 508 065	51 164 260

algorithm	large graphs		
	best	avg.	t[s]
KaSPar strong	12 450	12 584	87.12
KaPPa strong	13 323	+8%	28.16
Scotch	14 475	+19%	3.83
kMetis	15 540	+32%	0.71

Table 1: On the left hand side: Basic properties of the graphs from our benchmark set. On the right hand side the geometric means (times, cut values) over all instances.

Instances   We report experiments on two suites of instances summarized in Table 1. *rggX* is a *random geometric graph* with 2^X nodes where nodes represent random points in the unit square and edges connect nodes whose Euclidean distance is below $0.55\sqrt{\ln n/n}$. This threshold was choosen in order to ensure that the graph is almost connected. *DelaunayX* is the Delaunay triangulation of 2^X random points in the unit square. Graphs *fetooth..auto* come from Chris Walshaw's benchmark archive [12]. Graphs *deu* and *eur* are undirected versions of the road networks of Germany, and Western Europe respectively, used in [13]. Instance *af_shell10* comes from the Florida Sparse Matrix Collection [14]. For the number of partitions k we choose the values used in [12]: 2, 4, 8, 16, 32, 64. Our default value for the allowed inbalance is 3 % since this one is the default value in Metis. When not otherwise mentioned, we perform 10 repetitions of each run and report the average result. When averaging over multiple instances, we use the geometric mean in order to give every instance the same influence on the final figure. [2]

4.1 Comparison with other Partitioners

We now use our suite of larger graphs to compare our algorithm variants KaPPa Strong and KaSPar Strong (see [4, 11] for more details and configuration of the algorithms) with Scotch, Metis. Table 1 compares the performances of these algorithms. For kMetis the differences are 32 % for the strong variant of KaSPar and 22 % for the strong variant of KaPPa. For Scotch, we get 19 % and 10 % respectively. Note that these differences are much larger than what can be obtained by just repeated runs, which gives only about 3 % improvement for 10 repetitions. Comparing average execution times of parallel KaPPa with the sequential algorithms makes little sense because this depends a lot on the number of PEs used.

For the largest graphs available to us, we have scaled the number of processors further up to 1024. In Figure 5 we see that KaPPa[3] scales well all the way to the largest number of processors, while parMetis reaches its limit of scalability at around 100 PEs. Eventually, parMetis is slower than the fastest variant of KaPPa.

5 Related Work

This paper is a summary of [4] and [11]. There has been a huge amount of research on graph partitioning so that we refer to introductory and overview papers such as [15–18] for a general overview. Well-known software packages based on MGP are Chaco [19], DiBaP [20], Jostle [18, 21], Metis [22], Party [23, 24], and Scotch [25, 26].

---

[2]Because we have multiple repetitions for each instance, we compute the geometric mean of the average (avg.) edge cut values for each instance or the geometric mean of the best (best.) edge cut value occurred.

[3]The minimal variant scales up to 512 PEs but this could be repaired by breaking the contraction later.

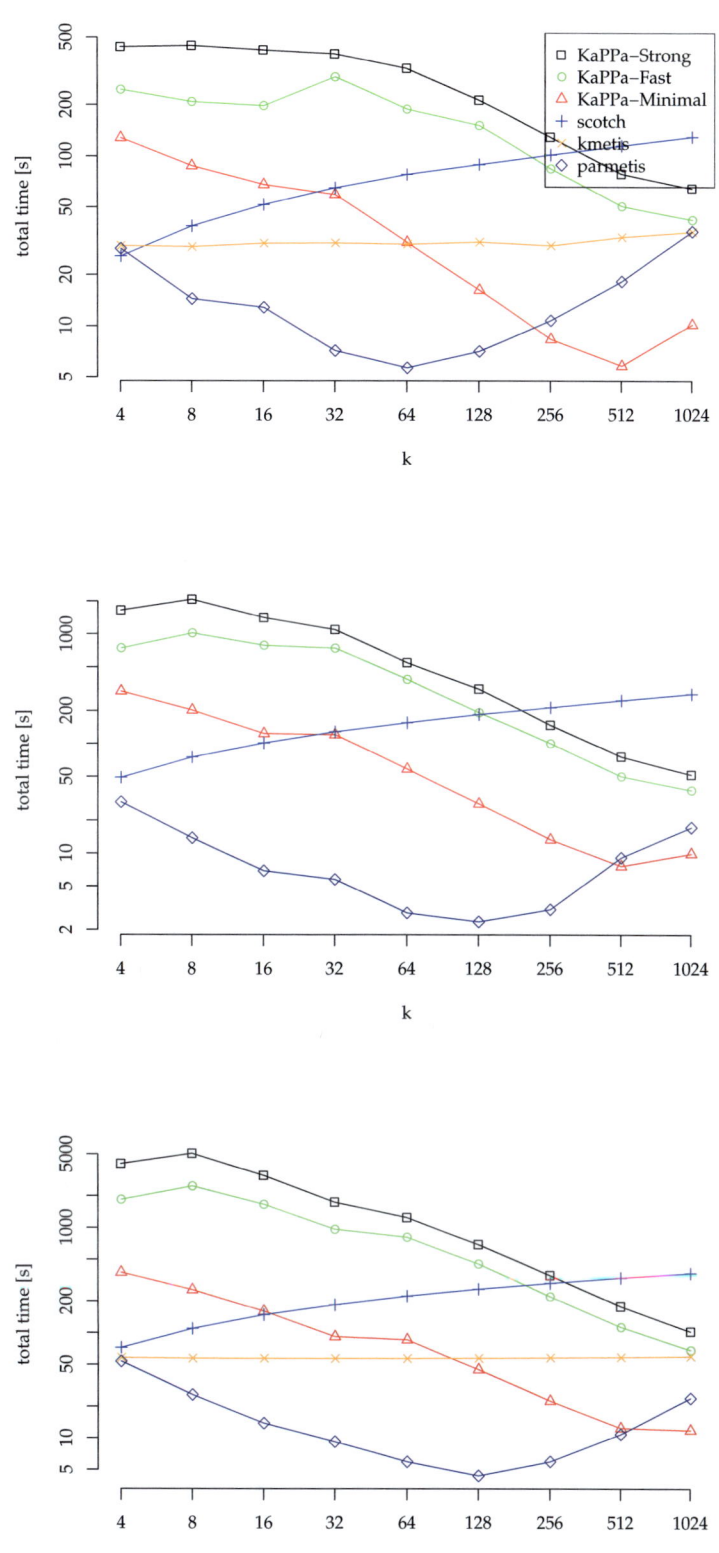

Figure 5: Scalability of KaPPa variants for graphs eur, rgg25, and delaunay25.

There is a long tradition of n-level algorithms in geometric data structures based on randomized incremental construction (e.g, [27, 28]). Our motivation for studying n-level are *contraction hierarchies* [29], a preprocessing technique for route planning that is at the same time simpler and an order of magnitude more efficient than previous techniques using a small number of levels.

The parallel version of Jostle [18] is similar to our approach since it applies local search to pairs of neighboring partitions. However, this parallelization has problems maintaining the balance of the partitions since at any particular time, it is difficult to say how many nodes are assigned to a particular block. We solve this problems by performing concurrent local searches only on independent pairs of partitions.

PT-Scotch, the parallel version of Scotch is based on recursive bipartitioning. This is more difficult to parallelize than direct k-partitioning since in the initial bipartition, there is less parallelism available. The unused processor power is used by performing several independent attempts in parallel. The involved communication effort is reduced by considering only nodes close to boundary of the current partitioning (band-refinement). We also use band-refinement but using a different algorithm and with much less replication of work.

DiBaP [30] is a multi-level graph partitioning package based on diffusion. It previously yielded the best partitioning results for the biggest graphs in [31] but has no scalable parallelization.

References

[1] B. Hendrickson. Graph partitioning and parallel solvers: Has the emperor no clothes? (extended abstract). In *IRREGULAR*, pages 218–225, 1998.

[2] J. L. Bentley. Multidimensional binary search trees used for associative searching. *Commun. ACM*, 18(9):509–517, 1975.

[3] M. J. Berger and S. H. Bokhari. A partitioning strategy for pdes across multiprocessors. In *ICPP*, pages 166–170, 1985.

[4] M. Holtgrewe, P. Sanders, and C. Schulz. Engineering a scalable high quality graph partitioner. In *Parallel & Distributed Processing (IPDPS), 2010 IEEE International Symposium on*, pages 1–12. IEEE, 2010.

[5] J. Maue and P. Sanders. Engineering algorithms for approximate weighted matching. In *6th Workshop on Exp. Algorithms (WEA)*, volume 4525 of *LNCS*, pages 242–255. Springer, 2007.

[6] D. Drake and S. Hougardy. A simple approximation algorithm for the weighted matching problem. *Information Processing Letters*, 85:211–213, 2003.

[7] F. Manne and R. H. Bisseling. A parallel approximation algorithm for the weighted maximum matching problem. In *7th Int. Conf. on Parallel Processing and Applied Mathematics (PPAM)*, volume 4967 of *LNCS*, pages 708–717. Springer, 2007.

[8] C. M. Fiduccia and R. M. Mattheyses. A Linear-Time Heuristic for Improving Network Partitions. In *19th Conference on Design Automation*, pages 175–181, 1982.

[9] C. Schulz. Scalable parallel refinement of graph partitions. 2009.

[10] R. Dementiev, P. Sanders, D. Schultes, and J. Sibeyn. Engineering an external memory minimum spanning tree algorithm. In *IFIP TCS*, Toulouse, 2004.

[11] V. Osipov and P. Sanders. n-Level Graph Partitioning. *ESA 2010*, pages 278–289.

[12] C. Walshaw and M. Cross. Mesh Partitioning: A Multilevel Balancing and Refinement Algorithm. *SIAM Journal on Scientific Computing*, 22(1):63–80, 2000.

[13] D. Delling, P. Sanders, D. Schultes, and D. Wagner. Engineering route planning algorithms. In *Algorithmics of Large and Complex Networks*, volume 5515 of *LNCS State-of-the-Art Survey*, pages 117–139. Springer, 2009.

[14] T. Davis. The University of Florida Sparse Matrix Collection, http://www.cise.ufl.edu/research/sparse/matrices, 2008.

[15] P.O. Fjallstrom. Algorithms for graph partitioning: A survey. *Linkoping Electronic Articles in Computer and Information Science*, 3(10), 1998.

[16] V. Kumar G. Karypis. A fast and high quality multilevel scheme for partitioning irregular graphs. *SIAM JOURNAL ON SCIENTIFIC COMPUTING*, 20(1):359–392, 1998.

[17] K. Schloegel, G. Karypis, and V. Kumar. Graph partitioning for high performance scientific simulations. In J. Dongarra et al., editor, *CRPC Par. Comp. Handbook*. Morgan Kaufmann, 2000.

[18] C. Walshaw and M. Cross. JOSTLE: Parallel Multilevel Graph-Partitioning Software – An Overview. In F. Magoules, editor, *Mesh Partitioning Techniques and Domain Decomposition Techniques*, pages 27–58. Civil-Comp Ltd., 2007. (Invited chapter).

[19] B. Hendrickson. Chaco: Software for partitioning graphs. http://www.sandia.gov/~bahendr/chaco.html.

[20] Henning Meyerhenke, Burkhard Monien, and Thomas Sauerwald. A new diffusion-based multi-level algorithm for computing graph partitions. *Journal of Parallel and Distributed Computing*, 69(9):750–761, 2009.

[21] Chris Walshaw. JOSTLE –graph partitioning software, 2005. `http://staffweb.cms.gre.ac.uk/~wc06/jostle/`.

[22] George Karypis and Vipin Kumar. MeTiS, A Software Package for Partitioning Unstructured Graphs, Partitioning Meshes, and Computing Fill-Reducing Orderings of Sparse Matrices, Version 4.0, 1998.

[23] Robert Preis. PARTY Partitioning Library , 1996. `http://www2.cs.uni-paderborn.de/cs/robsy/party.html`.

[24] Robert Preis and Ralf Diekmann. The PARTY Partitioning Library, User Guide . Technical report, University of Paderborn, Germany, 1996. Tr-rsfb-96-02.

[25] Francois Pellegrini. SCOTCH: Static Mapping, Graph, Mesh and Hypergraph Partitioning, and Parallel and Sequential Sparse Matrix Ordering Package, 2007. `http://www.labri.fr/perso/pelegrin/scotch/`.

[26] Francois Pellegrini. SCOTCH 5.1 User's guide. Technical report, Laboratoire Bordelais de Recherche en Informatique, Bordeaux, France, 2008.

[27] L. J. Guibas, D. E. Knuth, and M. Sharir. Randomized incremental construction of Delaunay and Voronoi diagrams. *Algorithmica*, 7(4):381–413, 1992.

[28] M. Birn, M. Holtgrewe, P. Sanders, and J. Singler. Simple and fast nearest neighbor search. In *2010 Proceedings of the Twelfth Workshop on Algorithm Engineering and Experiments, January*, volume 16, pages 43–54, 2010.

[29] R. Geisberger, P. Sanders, D. Schultes, and D. Delling. Contraction hierarchies: Faster and simpler hierarchical routing in road networks. In *7th Workshop on Experimental Algorithms (WEA)*, volume 5038 of *LNCS*, pages 319–333. Springer, 2008.

[30] H. Meyerhenke, B. Monien, and T. Sauerwald. A new diffusion-based multilevel algorithm for computing graph partitions of very high quality. In *IEEE International Symposium on Parallel and Distributed Processing, 2008. IPDPS 2008.*, pages 1–13, 2008.

[31] C. Walshaw. The Graph Partitioning Archive, `http://staffweb.cms.gre.ac.uk/~c.walshaw/partition/`, 2008.

SimLab Energy

Olaf Schneider

Karlsruhe Institute of Technology, Steinbuch Centre for Computing /SCC),
76128 Karlsruhe, Germany, olaf.schneider@kit.edu

Abstract

SimLab Energy, as one of the four simulation laboratories at the KIT, is concerned with community-oriented research and support in the area of scientific high-performance computing related to energy research and technology. We give a short survey over the current state and activities of the SimLab. Moreover, we briefly introduce EnSoC, the Energy Solution Center pursuing a similar agenda of research and dissemination with orientation toward energy industry.

1   Introduction

Computational methods of various kinds are wide-spread in the area of energy research and technology. Even, if we restrict us to high-performance computing (HPC) applications, there are numerous (potentially) computational demanding problems: bio-fuel synthesis, geo-thermal reservoirs, fossil oil and gas exploration, material behavior and radiation transport in nuclear facilities, long-term risk analysis for nuclear waste repositories, power plant operation planning and power grid control, energy market analysis and power trading – just to name some of them.

The Karlsruhe Institute of Technology has bundled research activities relating to these and other topics in the KIT Energy Center. This center was the first founded and is the largest one of the currently existing four KIT centers which serve as the major organizational units for research. Inside, the energy center is structured into seven topic fields: energy conversion, renewable energies, energy storage and distribution, efficient energy use, fusion technology, nuclear energy and safety, and energy systems analysis.

To establish the connection of the KIT center and the simulation laboratory, representatives of SCC attend the co-ordination and control bodies of the topics and the whole center. It is envisioned, that major decisions on the direction of work in the simulation laboratory are made jointly with the KIT center. At the daily work layer we have to combine the expertise inside the SimLab with complementary know-how on computational modeling and simulations that already exists in the application research groups. Therefore, close collaborations with those groups, possibly fostered by shared staff positions and PhD projects, are a key for the success of the Simulation Lab Energy.

The present paper provides a short survey on the Simulation Laboratory Energy. In the following section we report briefly on its organizational structures and current research activities. The Energy Solution Center (EnSoC) is presented in Section 3, followed by a section with final conclusions.

2   SimLab Energy at a glance

In the introduction we listed energy related research topics. Some of the computational models and methods used in applications include fluid dynamics (CFD), finite element method (FEM), discrete solvers for ordinary differential equations (ODE), many-body systems (MBS), optimization problems and linear programming. The length and the broad range of these lists suggest that we need to focus on selected topics and methods.

Regarding human resources it is worth to mention, that Simulation Lab Energy team is distributed between two KIT departments – the Steinbuch Centre for Computing (SCC), which is the central IT service and research unit, and the Institute for Applied Computer Science (IAI), which is concerned with application-oriented research and development in the field of information, automation, and systems technologies. This construction is a unique feature compared to the other simulation laboratories at the KIT, where the core teams are completely dedicated to SCC.

The IAI group is mainly concerned with modeling and simulation of electrical power grids with the aim to exploit the capabilities of smart grids. The development target is a dynamic and scalable model of an energy system, featuring a modular concept for different types of simulations, such as grid control and load balancing, optimization, and disasters. At the same time the model has to be flexible enough to scale with increasing granularity and complexity. The chosen modeling approach is a topological grid integrated with a real-time database of all energy generators and consumers.

Further research and development activities in the simulation laboratory are performed by the SCC in collaboration with energy related research groups at the KIT. Partly, these co-operations exist longer than the SimLab itself. In the reminder of this section we mention all of them briefly. Further details can be found in other contributions of the present proceedings.

In a co-operation with the Chemical Technology group of Prof. Olaf Deutschmann we aim at coupling fluid dynamics with chemical reaction kinetics. The envisioned application is the numerical study of reactive gas-liquid flows in mini-channels of monolithic reactors. In future, this type of chemical reactors could be used for the Fischer-Tropsch synthesis as part of the bio-fuel production process. The simulation codes to be coupled are TURBIT-VOF and DETCHEM [1].

Numerical experiments for hydrogen technology and nuclear reactor safety analysis are the application areas of GASFLOW [2] and other codes jointly developed by SCC and a group at the Institute of Nuclear and Energy Technology headed by Thomas Jordan.

The SimLab team is also integrated in the user support activities at SCC. For example, it takes care for the Monte-Carlo N-Particle Transport code MCNP5, which is used by the group of Ulrich Fischer at the Institute of Nuclear Physics and Reactor Technology (INR).

Recently we start a new co-operation with the geophysical institute. The group of Prof. Thomas Bohlen is concerned with seismic prediction using finite-difference wave models. The aim is to find fault zones or layer interfaces ahead of a borehole or a tunnel. Those predictions during the ongoing drilling or tunnel construction are essential to avoid accidents or damage at the tunnel cutter or drilling tool. Conventional methods places wave sources directly at the tunnel face. Other approaches use the drilling noise as seismic wave source. In our project we use tunnel surface waves generated away from the tunnel face, which are converted into body waves when arriving at the front face. The reflected body waves are converted back into surface waves and detected by receivers behind the cutter head. The computational task is to find structures in the solid, where given input values are the wave sources and the measurements at the detectors. The simulation package FDMPI [3] contains finite-difference wave models (Cartesian 2D and 3D, cylindrical 2.5D) and solves elastic and visco-elastic wave equations for stress and velocity in the time domain. The code is parallelized with MPI by means of spatial domain decomposition. Our benchmarks on bwGRiD and the JUROPA cluster of the Juelich Supercomputing Center shows, that the code is already impressively scalable. However, more detailed performance studies are needed. Based on this analysis we plan to improve the serial performance using compiler capabilities. The main target is to implement a new communication behavior in order to hide the communication times behind calculations. Since our final concern is an inverse problem, many simulations with FDMPI have to be performed in order to compute a seismic prediction. Therefore, a great effort to improve the performance and scalability of FDMPI is worthwhile.

3 Energy Solution Center (EnSoC)

Transferring the outcome of academic research to industrial and business applications is an integral activity of the KIT. To accelerate innovations in the area of energy research and high-performance computing (HPC), the KIT and six industry partners founded a non-profit association called Energy Solution Center [4].

Already three years ago, the state government of Baden-Württemberg initiated establishing HPC Solution Centers. The aim is to disseminate high-performance computing methods to industry. HPC is seen as an innovation driver whose wider use would generate enormous economic benefits, especially for small and medium enterprises.

In 2008 the Automotive Simulation Center Stuttgart [5] was founded. In 2009 it was followed by the Energy Solution Center in Karlsruhe. There are plans for similar organizations covering the business branches Chemistry & Pharmacy and Life Science & Medicine at the sites Ulm and Heidelberg, respectively. The centers shall be active in a nation-wide manner and bundle competencies in the selected areas in order to cope with the challenges with the help of high-performance computing.

As a non-profit organization it is the task of EnSoC to conceive and implement research projects at own facilities or in co-operation with other institutions, to bring together research and practice, to disseminate scientific results by publications and events, and to promote scientific education and advanced training. As main advantages over applied research in academia or classical industry-academic partnerships, EnSoC focuses on practical problems directly relating to industry and pools the competencies of partners from industry and science, which makes it easier to identify cross-connections and other synergies.

Currently, the first EnSoC projects are in the startup-period. They are concerned with the use of HPC and Cloud Computing for industrial CFD simulations and computations related to energy market and power trading. Moreover, the influence of e-mobile charge cycles on the electrical network will be investigated.

4   Conclusion

At the time of writing this, the simulation laboratories have passed their first anniversary. Regarding SimLab energy, the basic organizational setup including the connection with the KIT center is established. We reported about current support and development activities, which are partly on-going co-operations of SCC with other institutes at the KIT. The rise of EnSoC bears the potential of fruitful synergies with industry-related research.

References

[1]   DETCHEM – Detailed Chemistry, www.detchem.com

[2]   GASFLOW, www.gasflow.net

[3]   FDMPI, www.gpi.kit.edu/FDMPI.php

[4]   EnSoC – Energy Solution Center, www.ensoc.de

[5]   asc(s – Automotive Simulation Center Stuttgart, www.asc-s.de

High Performance Computations of Monte Carlo Radiation Transport for ITER Fusion Neutronics

Arkady Serikov[*], Ulrich Fischer, Dennis Grosse, Dieter Leichtle, Dirk Strauss

*Karlsruhe Institute of Technology (KIT), Hermann-von-Helmholtz-Platz 1,
76344 Eggenstein-Leopoldshafen, Germany*

Abstract

High performance computations are required to support design activities for the ITER fusion reactor which is currently in phase of construction in Cadarache, France (its web-site: www.iter.org). In the ITER tokamak geometry, the Monte Carlo (MC) method is the preferred one for radiation transport calculations. This method allows describing neutrons interactions with matter by tracking individual particle histories. The precision of the MC method depends on number of sampled particles according to statistical laws and on systematic uncertainties introduced by modeling assumptions. Due to the independence of particle histories, their tracks can be processed in parallel. Parallel computations on high performance cluster computers substantially increase number of sampled particles and therefore allow reaching the desired statistical precision of the MC results. Use of CAD-based approach with high spatial resolution improves systematic adequacy of the MC geometry modeling. These achievements are demonstrated on radiation transport calculations for designing the Blanket Shield Module and Auxiliary Shield of the ITER Electron Cyclotron Heating (ECH) upper launcher.

1 Introduction

The Monte Carlo (MC) method is most suitable computational technique of radiation transport for fusion neutronics applications. Using the MC method and continuous energy representation of nuclear cross-section data, complex fusion devices can be modeled in 3D geometry without major geometry approximations. Inherently feature of the MC method is its calculation accuracy which is limited only by its statistics and nuclear data uncertainties. Radiation transport simulation in the MC method is performed by sampling of independent random pathways on microscopic level, by tracking of individual particle histories from their "birth" to "death". Because the particle histories are tracking independently, the simulation can be computed on parallel multiprocessor systems, simulating each particle on the individual processor. The use of parallel computation can

---

*Corresponding Author, E-mail: arkady.serikov@kit.edu

substantially increase of number of sampling histories, improve by this way the MC statistics, and finally - increase calculation accuracy of the MC method. In this paper, the benefits of parallel MC computations running on the High Performance Computers (HPC) have been demonstrated on the example of fusion neutronics calculations performed for one component of the International Thermonuclear Experimental Reactor (ITER). Particularly, these challenging neutronic calculations are performed for designing the Electron Cyclotron Heating (ECH) launcher, the important components of the ITER to be installed in its upper port. The calculations have been performed by employing the Monte Carlo MCNP5 code [1] running in Message Passing Interface (MPI) parallel mode on high performance computer clusters. Three clusters have been considered in this paper to demonstrate the outstanding MCNP5 parallel performance: one at JSC-FZJ in Juelich, JUROPA/HPC-FF parallel supercomputer and two systems at Steinbuch Centre for Computing (SCC), KIT, Karlsruhe: HP XC3000 (HC3) and Opus[IB].

The methodological approach employed to tackle the neutronic analyses was based on the use of both standard MCNP5 variance reduction techniques (VRTs) and mesh-tally mapping of the results, as well as newly developed at KIT (former FZK) program interface McCad[2] allowing automatic conversion of CAD models into the MCNP geometry representation and vice versa. The McCad interface has been successfully applied for modeling of several fusion neutronics applications.[3] In designing of the ITER components, this CAD-based modeling and MCNP5 mesh tally capability are inevitable for resolving heterogeneous neutronic effects. The ITER-specific fusion neutronics is characterized by radiation deep-penetration with total neutron flux attenuation by 8 orders of magnitude from the plasma to the cryostat. The ECH launcher to be inserted in the ITER upper port extends by 5 m from the plasma first wall (FW) to the vacuum vessel connective flange at the rear side close to cryostat. The current design of the Quasi-Optical (QO) ECH launcher is shown in Fig. 1. Some aspects of its nuclear-safety-related and shielding

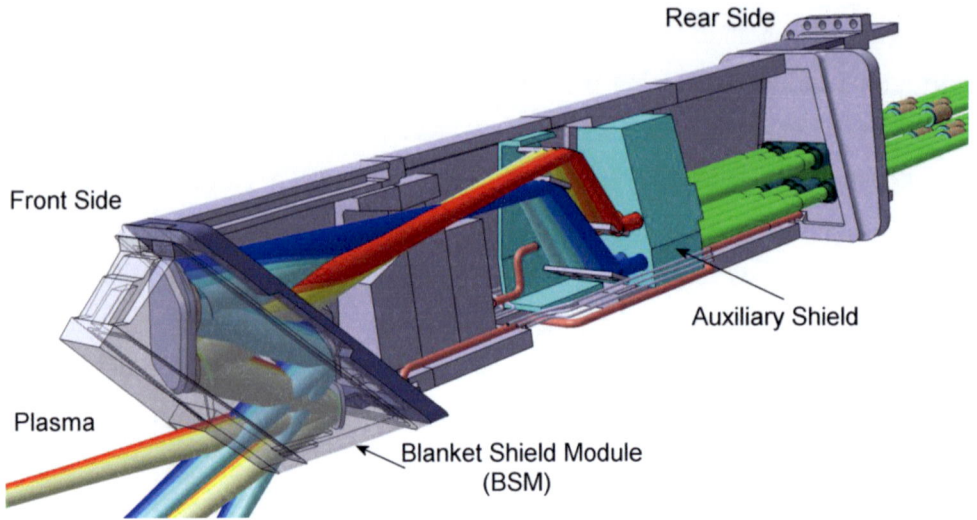

Fig. 1   CAD model of the Quasi-Optical (QO) design of the ECH launcher to be installed in ITER upper

analyses have been considered in Ref. [4]. This paper addresses the problems which require heterogeneous calculations utilizing high performance computational resources. The parts of the ECH launcher are analyzed in this work include Blanket Shield Module (BSM) and Auxiliary Shield shown in Fig. 1 together with its other structures which serve for realization of the launcher' aim. It is aiming to control Magneto-Hydro-Dynamic (MHD) instabilities in the ITER plasma. This is fulfilled by precisely focusing of millimeter waves (mm-waves) at 170 GHz and injecting them onto the plasma magnetic surfaces by means of the launcher's Quasi-Optical (QO) mm-wave system.[5] To provide the mm-wave beam injection shown in Fig. 1, the launcher has to have an opening to plasma. This requires the arrangement of shielding blocks inside the launcher without interfering with the propagation of the mm-wave beams. The beams are directed from the launcher's back-end along rows of 8 wave-guide channels and void space of the QO system shown in Fig. 1.

In this work, the MC radiation transport computations were performed with the Alite standard ITER model[6] representing a 40^0 torus sector with all the ITER components inside, as shown in Fig. 2. It is a complex and large model, consisting of ~5000 cells defined with over 3050 surfaces. Its radius is 17 m and it has a height of 25.5 m. Geometry of the ECH launcher was converted from CAD files into the MCNP5 input deck using McCad. After that dummy shield plug inside the ITER upper port was replaced with the ECH launcher as depicted in Fig. 2. The challenges encountered with the integration of the ECH launcher into the Alite ITER model, as well as an

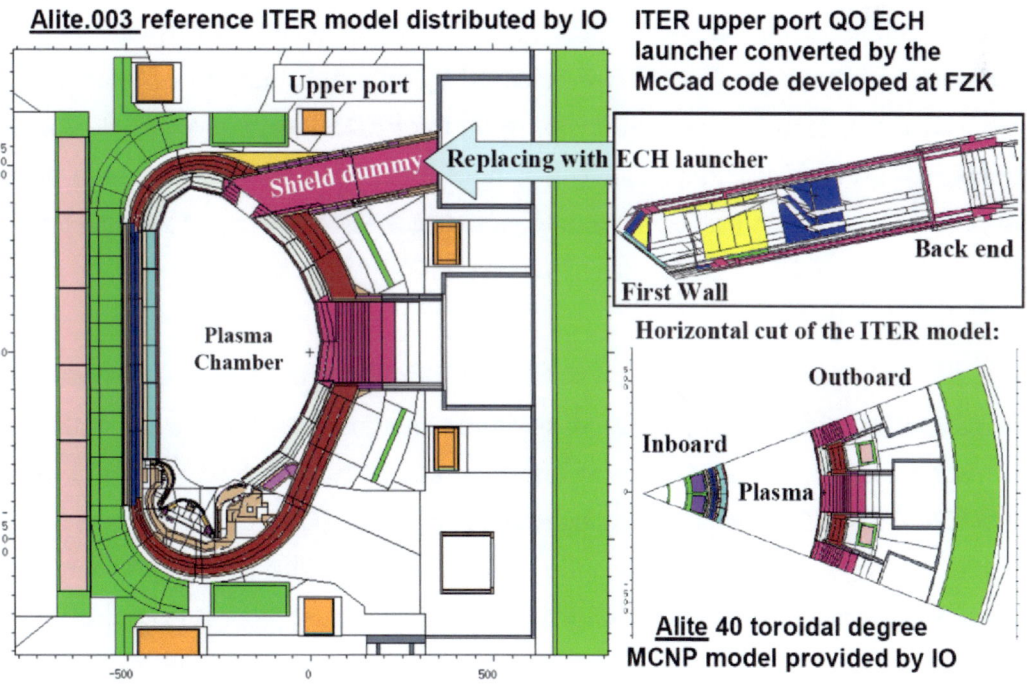

Fig. 2   Incorporation of the McCad converted Quasi Optical (QO) ECH launcher model inside the Alite.003 standard ITER model, with its vertical (on the left and right upper sides) and horizontal (right bottom side) cuts

overview of neutronic characteristics of the launcher and evolution of its shielding computations, have been addressed elsewhere.[7-9)] The need for detailed neutronic modeling of the QO design of the ECH launcher requires substantial computational resources which were satisfied by means of utilization of HPC-FF supercomputer described in Section II.

2   MCNP5 parallel performance

The MCNP5 code has been installed on the High Performance Computer dedicated For Fusion applications (HPC-FF). It is based on petaflop architectures of JUROPA/HPC-FF system currently in operation at Juelich Supercomputing Centre (JSC), Research Centre Juelich (FZJ) in Germany.[10)] Performance assessments of the MCNP5 code were carried out to find an efficient way to run the code in a parallel regime. The parallel version of the code has been compiled with the Intel Professional Fortran and C/C++ compilers, and uses the Message Passing Interface (MPI). In the computational scheme of the MPI-connected MCNP5 parallel job, the master processor sends the instructions to trace the nuclear reactions with each particle and to do the necessary computations to a selected number of slave CPUs. These instructions include the geometry definition and material composition. The MCNP5 parallel performance had been estimated previously [11)] on 32 slave CPUs on the CampusGrid Linux cluster at FZK, now reorganized into KIT Opus[IB]. The computational experience [11)] gained on the CampusGrid has been considered during the deployment of the MCNP5 parallel jobs on HPC-FF.[12)] Practice of MCNP5 MPI-parallel computations [11,12)] shows that it is important to keep the master-slave communication as little as possible. This is achieved by setting the number of intermediate data exchange, called "rendezvous", to a minimum using the PRDMP card of MCNP5. The optimal number of CPUs used in MCNP5 parallel calculations is dependent on complexity of the model, physical process involved in particle track and particle history longevity. As it was found, [11, 12)] the optimal number of CPUs is dependent on the MCNP5 job size expressed in number of histories (job-parameter NPS).

The results of the parallel performance and search for optimal number of CPUs are presented here in assumption of MCNP5 parallel run without intermediate rendezvous. Values in the PRDMP card are equal to total number of histories set by the NPS card. The batch system on JUROPA/ HPC-FF is MOAB with underlying resource manager TORQUE. When user sets certain number of CPUs in the MOAB script, then the NPS number is divided by this CPU number minus one. This is because in MPI-scheme one CPU is reserved for master process to control the MCNP job running on the slave CPUs. To do the MCNP5 parallel performance analysis, computational wall-clock time has been measured in dependence of number of used slave CPUs and size of the job. Results are presented in Figs. 3 and 4 in terms of speed-up and efficiency respectively.

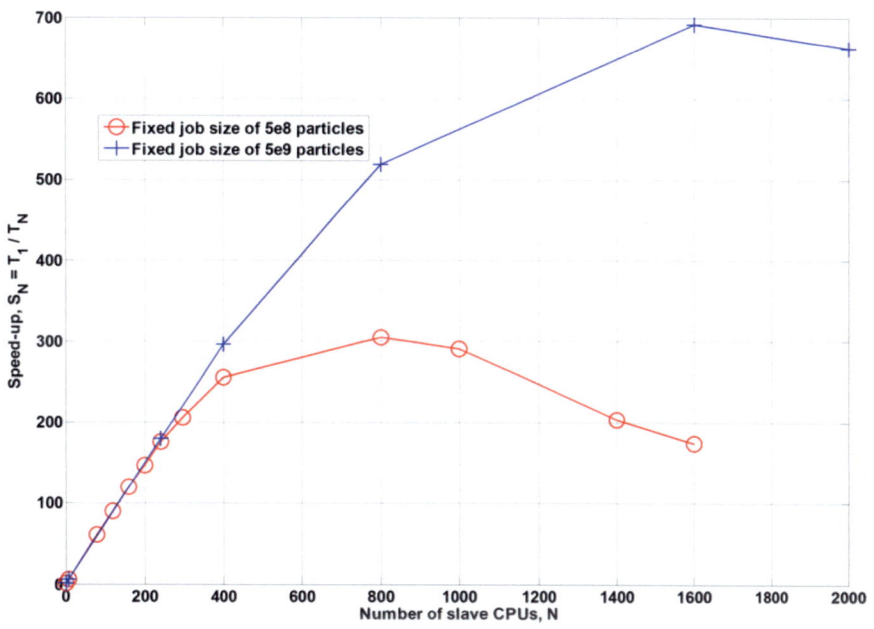

Fig. 3   Speed-up for two sizes of the MCNP parallel jobs with 5e8 and 5e9 particles

The speed-up (S_N) is defined as the ratio between the wall-time running on one processor (T_1) and the wall-time running on N slave processors (T_N), $S_N = T_1/T_N$. The efficiency (E_N) is estimated by the ratio between the speed-up (S_N) and the number of slave processors (N).

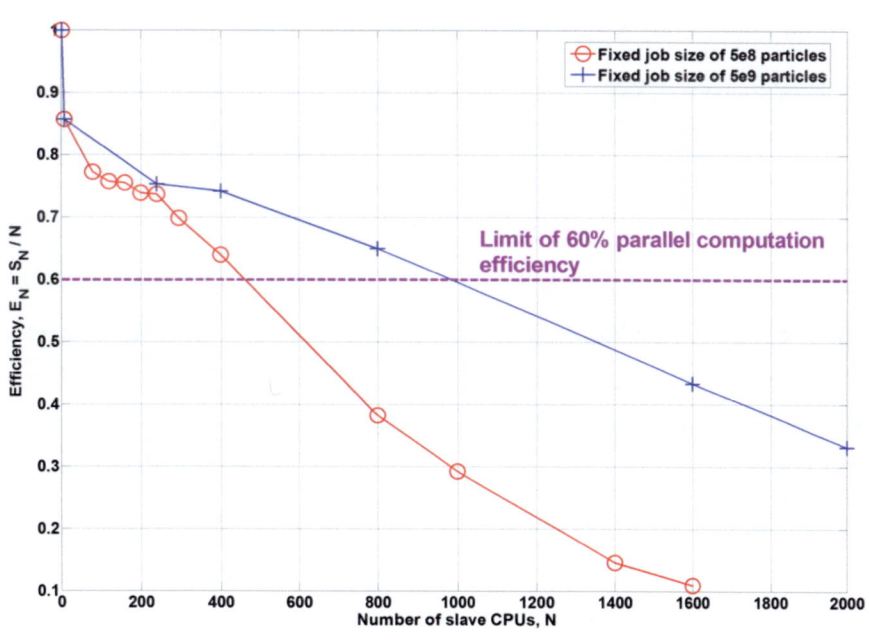

Fig. 4   Efficiency for two fixed MCNP5 parallel job sizes of 5e8 and 5e9 particles

The bigger the job-size, the bigger the chunks of information are which will be processed by a single slave CPU, and the less the communications are between the master and the slave CPUs. Following Fig. 3 the speed-up peak and the number of utilized CPUs are shifted to higher values when increasing the number of sampled particles from 5e8 to 5e9. The MCNP5 parallel efficiency, plotted in Fig. 4, shows the same positive tendency of the job size increasing if many hundreds of CPUs are available. This plot allows judging a job from the comparison with a computational efficiency limit. In this case a limit of 60% was chosen as a good compromise between performance and availability of CPUs. The job size of 5e9 particles falls below this efficiency limit at about 1000 slave CPUs. That is, using more CPUs is getting less effective, and according to Fig. 3 it even spends more time to run the job if more than 1600 CPUs are used.

3 Fusion neutronics applications in ITER Upper QO ECH Launcher

Here in Section III, we present new results of specific neutronic tasks of the design development of the ITER upper Electron Cyclotron Heating (ECH) launcher which are selected by the criterion of high power of the MCNP5 parallel computations required to resolve neutronic heterogeneous effects. Considering the methodological aspects of this work, the MCNP5 code inherent features such as its variance reduction techniques (VRTs), mesh tallies and use of MPI-parallelism have been enhanced and completed with the CAD-based radiation transport capabilities of the McCad geometry interface.

The neutronics results were normalized to 500 MW of DT fusion power, 80% of it is released in form of 14 MeV neutrons emitted from ITER plasma chamber depicted in Fig. 2, where cross-sections of the applied 3D Alite MCNP5 model are plotted.

As an example of success in the accomplishment of the highly demanding task, high-resolution mapping of the helium production distribution in the ITER location supposed to be re-welded was established using the MCNP mesh-tally.[9,12] It was important to calculate this mapping because the re-weldability of irradiated steel is limited by the content of generated helium. Use of the HPC-FF system gave the possibility to obtain the MCNP5 results with a high-resolution $2x2x2$ mm^3 mesh tally. The mesh tally grid superimposed over complex launcher geometry revealed neutronic heterogenic effects in helium gas production rate in the corner of Vacuum Vessel and ITER upper ECH launcher. The analysis of mesh-tally calculations has revealed the locations of an extensive helium production up to 19 appm per 0.63 full power year in the boron-doped ferromagnetic steel of SS304B4 grade, which exceeds the helium content allowed for re-weldability by a factor of 19. This outcome excludes the possibility to re-weld these ferromagnetic plates inserted in the structure of ITER Vacuum Vessel (VV) and influences the shielding arrangement.[9,12]

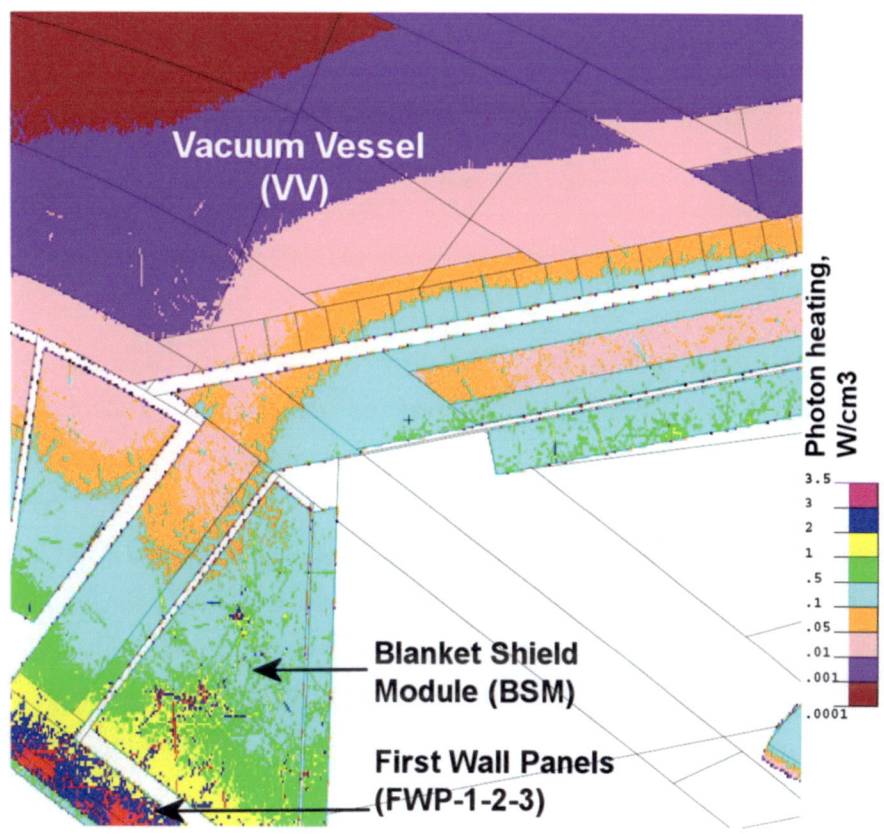

Fig. 5   Map of Photon heating distribution, W/cm^3

3.1 Nuclear Heating Distribution in Blanket Shield Module

Nuclear heating is a key input parameter for structural analyses of the launcher and adjacent components in ITER and it plays an important role in designing of the reactor components to be exposed to neutron radiation in ITER. Neutron radiation causes production of secondary photons which interact with matter, and these photons induce heat deposition which becomes predominant in heavy (high atomic mass) materials such as steel or copper used in structures of the series of First Wall Panels layers (FWP-1-2-3) of the Blanket Shield Module (BSM) at the front side of the ITER ECH launcher shown in Fig. 1. The spatial averaged nuclear heating results for BSM with separation of neutron and photon deposition are presented in Table 1. Obviously, neutron deposition dominates heating in light material (beryllium), and photon heating dominates in heavy materials, making maximum of 4.56 W/cm^3 in total heat on the second FWP2 layer of copper heat sink. The map of photon heating is depicted in Fig. 5 using fine 2x2x2 mm^3 mesh tally, and the results are consistent with Table 1.

Position	Neutron (n) heating, W/cm³	Photon (p) heating, W/cm³	Total n+p heating, W/cm³
FWP1: Be	2.47E+00	5.57E-01	3.03E+00
FWP2: Copper heat sink	1.09E+00	3.47E+00	4.56E+00
FWP3: Copper heat sink	9.24E-01	3.39E+00	4.31E+00
BSM - shield block	1.56E-01	8.11E-01	9.67E-01

Tab. 1   Cell-averaged total nuclear heating in First Wall Panel (FWP) and Blanket Shield Module (BSM)

Figure 6 shows a color map of the MCNP5 statistical relative error (R) given at one standard deviation (1σ) within 68% confidence interval of the helium production results. As recommended,[1] a result calculated with the track-length estimation tally of MCNP is generally reliable if the associated statistical error R is less than 0.10. This is true for most part of BSM and VV being analyzed. A tally result is questionable if 0.1<R<0.2, and it could differ by a factor of a few if 0.2<R<0.5. The error estimation indicates about general reliability for the results obtained around the critical location. Visual non-uniformity in Figs. 5 and 6 such as dash-lines similar to wormholes in BSM and Vacuum Vessel is explained by statistical fluctuation of particles, and it is found in particle low-populated locations in middle of BSM and in-depth of VV. At these non-uniformity locations errors are more than 20%-30%; hence, the results in these exceptional locations should be not used.

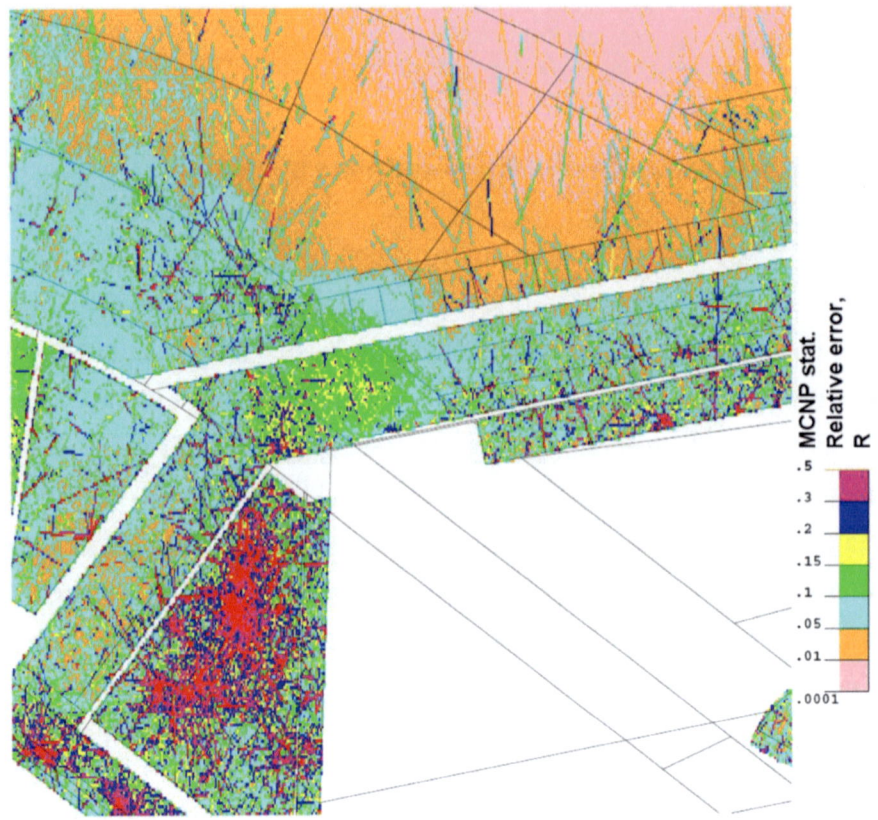

Fig. 6   MCNP5 statistical relative errors of photon heating

3.2 Nuclear Heating Analysis for Auxiliary Shield

The auxiliary shield blocks have been arranged in the center of the ECH QO launcher serving for radiation shielding and bearing structure support functions. They are positioned behind the mm-wave optics mirror system and composed with three shield blocks made of solid 100% SS 316L(N)-IG ITER grade steel without any cooling material such as water or void. The mass density of steel is 7.93 g/cm^3. The CATIA model of the auxiliary shield blocks was converted by the McCad geometry interface into the MCNP5 representation and then incorporated inside the upper port launcher of the Alite.003 standard ITER model as shown in Fig. 7. Then the MCNP5 3D mesh-tally was defined and superimposed over the auxiliary shield and upper port walls around it. The mesh-tally grid is plotted in Fig. 7 and the nuclear heating results calculated on it are mapped using the standard MCNP5 plotter in Figs. 8 and 9. The results are normalized on 500 MW of ITER fusion power. The heating has been calculated in the low-resolution mesh-tally with its cell size of 8x8x4 cm^3. This size was chosen because the estimations of spatial-averaged heating have shown very low values at ~2 m distance from the plasma.

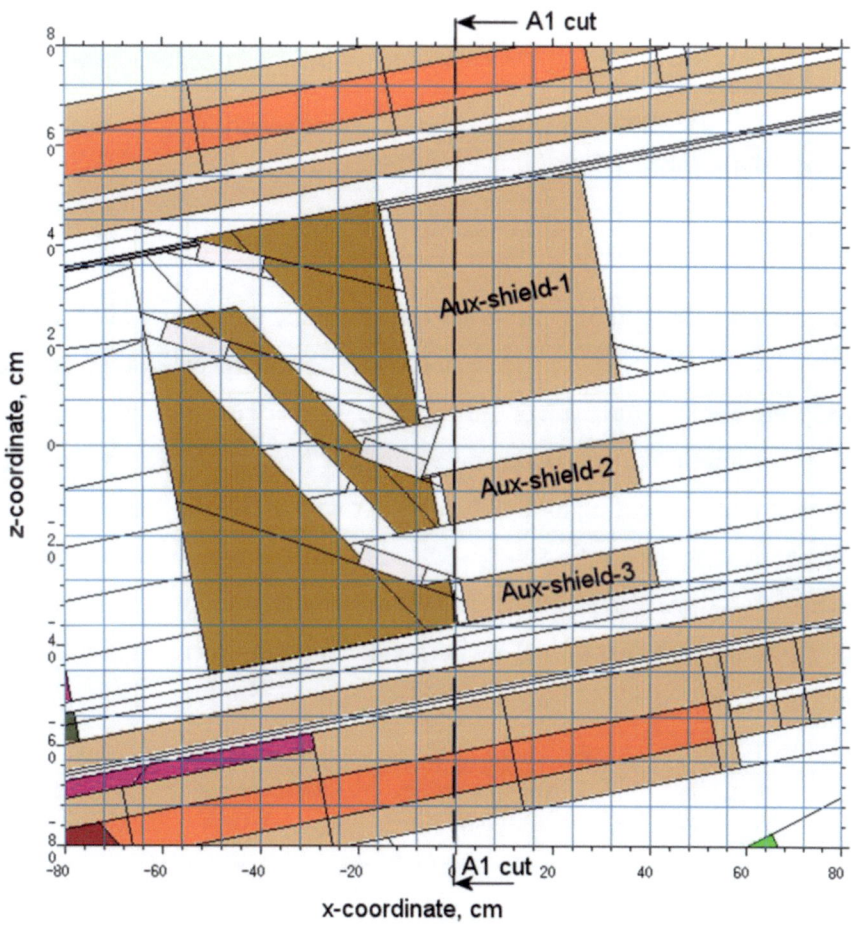

Fig. 7   Vertical radial-poloidal (x-z) cut by central plane at y=0 cm of the Alite.003 MCNP model with inserted ECH launcher. The mid-part of the launcher with superimposed mesh-tally is cut through the three auxiliary shield blocks (Aux-shield-1-2-3)

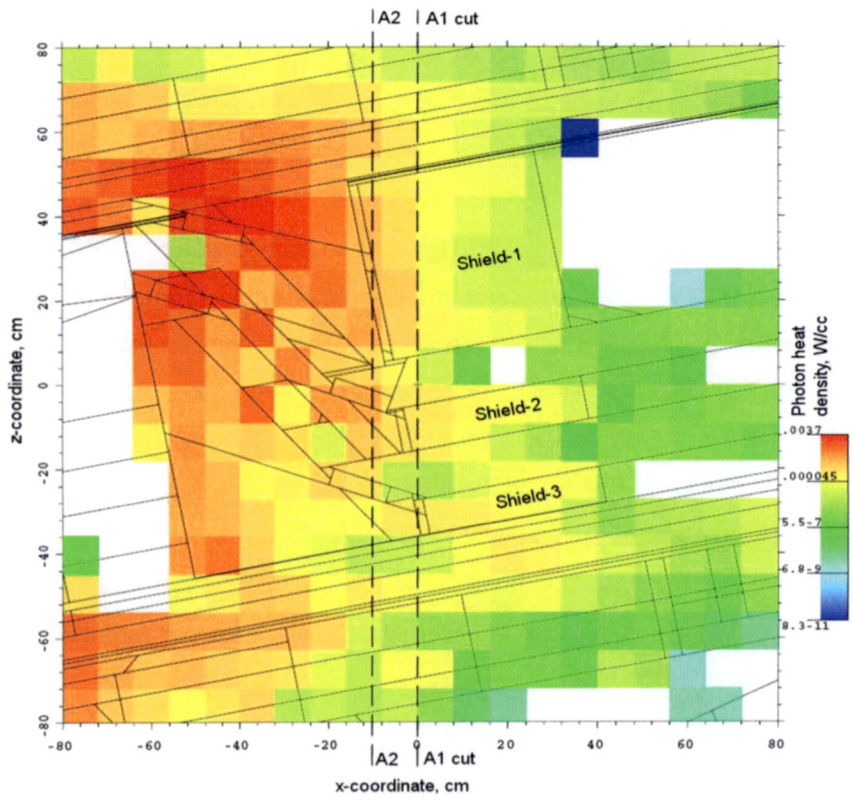

Fig. 8   Map of photon heat density (W/cm3) superimposed over the vertical radial-poloidal (x-z) cut of the MCNP mesh-tally depicted in Fig. 7

The space-averaged nuclear heating results calculated for the three blocks of the auxiliary shield are listed in Table 2, where photon and neutron heat deposits are presented separately and also as a sum. As followed from Table 2, the main contribution to nuclear heating is produced by the photon heat deposition. According to the spatial-averaged nuclear heating results of Table 2, the photon heating is higher than neutron heating by the factor in a range of 32-56, that means photon heating dominates in nuclear heating, generating 97% - 98% of total heating. For this reason, the maps of nuclear heating distribution are plotted mostly for photon heat deposition, e.g. in Fig. 8 photon map is shown on the 3D mesh-tally central cut by perpendicular to y-axis plane at y=0 cm. Figure 9 shows orthogonal to Fig. 8 map along its A2 cut pointed out in Fig. 8.

Auxiliary shield block	Shield block volume, cm^3	Photon heating, W/cm^3	Neutron heating, W/cm^3	Sum heating (photon + neutron), W/cm^3
Aux-shield-1	6.79E+04	7.60E-05	2.40E-06	7.84E-05
Aux-shield-2	1.67E+04	8.81E-05	1.58E-06	8.96E-05
Aux-shield-3	1.36E+04	8.87E-05	2.00E-06	9.07E-05

Tab. 2   Nuclear heat density (W/cm3) in spatially-averaged over the MCNP5 model cells of the auxiliary shield blocks

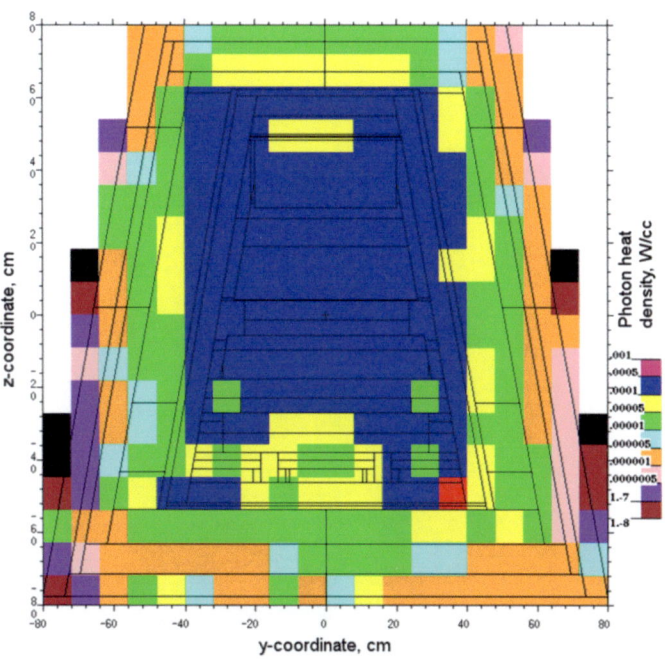

Fig. 9 Map of photon heat density (W/cm3) superimposed over the vertical toroidal-poloidal (y-z) A2 cut MCNP mesh-tally depicted in Fig. 8. Mosaic picture is caused by misalignment between the MCNP geometry and the regular mesh-tally cells

It is observed in Fig. 8 that heating reaches local maximal values at the upper part of the auxiliary shield block-1, and in order to find this maximum more precisely, additional cut A2 has been arranged. The resulting photon heating distribution along the A2 cut is presented in Fig. 9, where heating in the block-1 is limited by 5e-4 W/cm³. The location of heat-peaking area is confirmed by more sophisticated 3D maps getting available by means of using VisIt 2.0.2 graphics tool, which certainly could enhance capabilities of MCNP to plot mesh-tally results in 3D maps. The VisIt tool is software developed by the Department of Energy (DOE) Advanced Simulation and Computing Initiative (ASCI) to visualize and analyze the results of terascale simulations.[13] Figure 10 illustrates sum of photon and neutron heating distribution on 3D mesh-tally map with pseudo-color scale. The VisIt tool [13] allows plotting maps using only ASCII text format of mesh-tally results; hence, a variety of mathematical operations are allowed for post-processing of the heating results.

The fragmentation of heating distributions maps into multicolor mosaic on the edges of the materials is explained by the misalignment between the arbitrary oriented MCNP cells and the regular x-y-z rectangular cells of mesh-tally used for heating calculations. The heating is averaged inside the mesh cells. Therefore, if going along the border regions between material and void, the material-to-void ratio inside the mesh-tally elements is changing substantially, causing quite visible difference in averaged mesh-tally heating shown in Figs. 8-10. This difference can be diminished by reducing the size of mesh-tally cells.

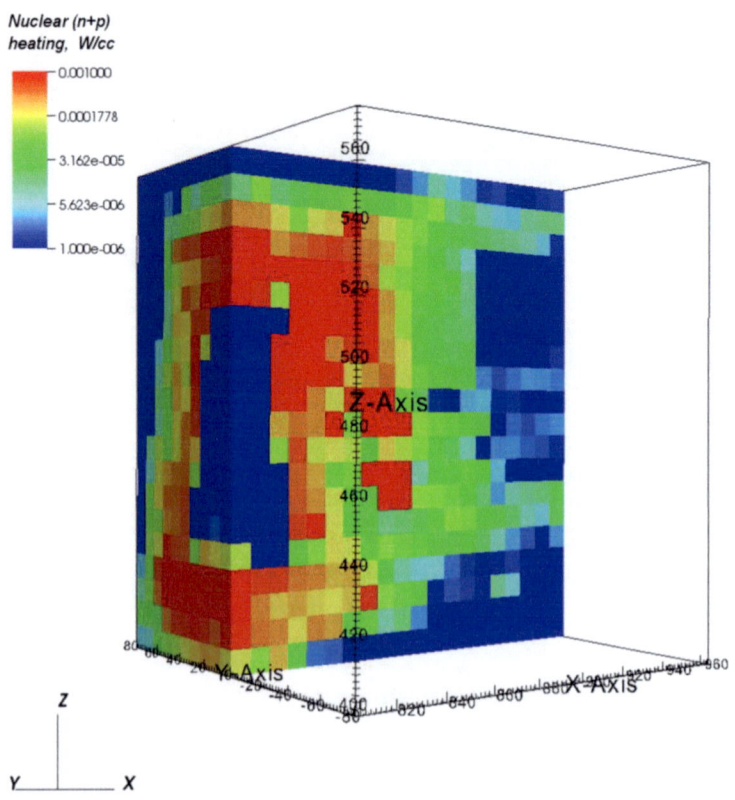

Fig. 10 3D map of total nuclear heating (W/cm3) with photon and neutron heat depositions, Mosaic picture is caused by misalignment between the MCNP geometry and the regular mesh-tally cells

4   General Summary

The High Performance Computation (HPC) resources allocated at HPC-FF@JSC in Juelich and Opus[IB] @SCC-KIT and HC3@SCC-KIT in Karlsruhe have been evaluated from the end-user's point of view applying to Monte Carlo radiation transport calculations. The calculations have been performed with MCNP5 code running in parallel mode. An extensive experience of neutronics analyses using MCNP5 parallel MPI-version on several Linux clusters provides proofs of order-of-magnitude speed-up, which scales with the number of processors. An important issue for scaling is keeping or increasing the calculation load on each processor: the higher ratio of computation per communication, the closer speed-up scaling to linear law. The short MCNP5 jobs assigned to parallel run have high overhead; hence, use of many processors is inefficient. Parallel performance is sensitive to number of intermediate message exchanges between master and slaves (rendezvous). The rendezvous number should be reduced in compromise with fault tolerance. The best performance is for only one rendezvous.

From the experience of the MCNP5 parallel runs for the ITER fusion neutronic applications, an optimal number of CPUs depends on size of the MCNP5 task and number of available processors on the cluster. In our practice, the averaged number of CPUs we have set on HPC-FF is ~800, while usual number of CPUs on HC3 and Opus[IB] is ~96. These are rough number of CPUs which can be used without a long task queuing. The maximum speed-up was found on HPC-FF equaled ~700 with 1600 CPUs, this means that wall-clock time to run the same job on 1 CPU was 700 times longer than on 1600 CPUs. A considerable increase of number of CPUs exploiting the resources of the HPC-FF supercomputer makes available to accomplish shielding tasks for the ITER design development much faster than ever before, e.g. a job for one month running on 27 CPUs on the Opus[IB] cluster with speed-up of 24, now can be finished in one day on HPC-FF with speed-up of ~700 on ~1600 CPUs. This is evident benefit of evolution in speed-up of MC radiation transport computations using HPC with parallel multiprocessing.

It is demonstrated in this paper that for the ITER heterogeneous models with a possibility of radiation streaming effects resulting in hot-spots, precise 3D mapping of the results obtained in geometry model close to the original CAD model is required. The statistical errors associated with the mesh-tally results were reduced by applying VRTs and by taking the advantages of the MCNP5 MPI parallel computations on HPC-FF. The complex heterogeneous neutronics effects in ITER could be investigated due to the powerful HPC-FF computational resources and effective MPI-parallelization of the MCNP5 code. The presented examples of the MCNP5 parallel calculations for the design support of the ECH upper launcher have proved that certain types of neutronic calculations could be done only on supercomputers. Such radiation transport implementation supported by CAD-based automatic model converters and 3D visualizing tools (e.g. McCad and VisIt) preserves geometry complexity, reduces error-prone human involvement in the MCNP5 geometry modeling, and speeds up iterative design process of the ITER components development.

High heating of the launcher Blanket Shield Module (BSM) reaching 4.56 W/cm^3 imposes essential requirement on the cooling system design with effective heat-removal. From the nuclear heating analysis in the auxiliary shield of the ITER upper QO ECH launcher, using the MCNP5 mesh-tally spatial distribution, it is possible to conclude that peak nuclear heating in the auxiliary shield blocks is limited by 5e-4 W/cm^3. This low value indicates that no additional active cooling is required. The cell size of the used mesh tally was defined by the structural designing needs requested for nuclear heating estimations. In case of high heating inside BSM the mesh tally resolution was very fine (on mm-scale), while low heating inside the auxiliary shield was calculated on low-resolution grid of 4-8 cm scale.

Acknowledgment

This work, supported by the European Communities under the contract of Association between EURATOM and Karlsruhe Institute of Technology, was carried out within the frameworks of the European Fusion

Development Agreement and the Fusion for Energy Joint Undertaking. Views and opinions expressed herein do not necessarily reflect those of the European Commission. This work was carried out using an adaptation of the Alite MCNP model which was developed as a collaborative effort between the FDS team of ASIPP China, ENEA Frascati, JAEA Naka, UKAEA Culham and the ITER Organization.

References

[1]   X-5 Monte Carlo Team, MCNP — *A General Monte Carlo N-Particle Transport Code, Version 5, Volume I, MCNP Overview and Theory,* Los Alamos National Laboratory Report, LA-UR-03-1987, April 24, 2003 (Revised 10/3/05).

[2]   D. Grosse, H. Tsige-Tamirat, "Current Status of the CAD Interface Program McCad for MC Particle Transport Calculations," Proc. M&C 2009, Saratoga Springs, New York, May 3-7, 2009, American Nuclear Society (2009) [CD-ROM].

[3]   A. Serikov et al., "Use of McCad for the generation of MCNP models in fusion neutronics," ibid.

[4]   A. Serikov, et al., "Nuclear-Safety-Related and Shielding Analyses of the ITER Quasi-Optical ECH Launcher," *IEEE Transactions on Plasma Science*, **38**[3], 224-231 (2010).

[5]   R. Heidinger et al., "Conceptual design of the ECH upper launcher system for ITER," *Fusion Engineering and Design,* **84**, 284-289 (2009).

[6]   M.J. Loughlin, et al., "ITER nuclear analysis strategy and requirements," *Fusion Science and Technology*, **56**[2], 566–572 (2009).

[7]   A. Serikov, U. Fischer, et al., "Nuclear analyses for the ITER ECH launcher," *Nuclear Fusion*, **48**, 054016 (2008).

[8]   A. Serikov et al., "Overview of recent nuclear analyses for the Upper ECH launcher in ITER," *Fusion Engineering and Design*, **85**, 1885-1895 (2010), doi:10.1016/j.fusengdes.2010.06.016

[9]   A. Serikov et al., "Evolution of shielding computations for the ITER upper ECH launcher," *Proc. of the ANS RPSD 2010 Joint Topical Meeting,* Las Vegas, NV, April 18-23 (2010).

[10] JUROPA/HPC-FF system: http://www.fz-juelich.de/jsc/juropa/.

[11] A. Serikov et al., "Performance assessments of the MCNP5 parallel computations for the ITER ECRH launcher," *Proc. German Annual Meeting on Nuclear Technology (Jahrestagung Kerntechnik JK-2008)*, May 27-29, 2008, Hamburg, Germany, (2008) [CD-ROM].

[12] A. Serikov et al., "MCNP5 parallel computations on JUROPA/HPC-FF supercomputer for ITER applications," *Proc. German Annual Meeting on Nuclear Technology (Jahrestagung Kerntechnik JK-2010)*, May 4-6, 2010, Berlin, Germany, (2010) [CD-ROM].

[13] VisIt Tool: https://wci.llnl.gov/codes/visit/home.html.

Recent Developments for the GASFLOW CFD Code: Real Gas Equations of State

J. Travis*, J. Xiao*, Z. Xu* and D. Piccioni Koch**

*Institut für Kern- und Energietechnik (IKET)
**Steinbuch Centre for Computing (SCC)
Karlsruher Institut für Technologie (KIT)
76021 Karlsruhe, Germany

Abstract

GASFLOW is a finite-volume computer code that solves the time-dependent compressible Navier-Stokes equations for multiple gas species in a dispersed liquid water two-phase medium with turbulence. The fluid-dynamics algorithm is coupled with conjugant heat and mass transfer models to represent walls, floors, ceilings, and other internal structures to describe complex geometries, such as those found in nuclear containments and facilities. Recent applications involve simulations of cryogenic hydrogen tanks at elevated pressures. These applications, which often have thermodynamic conditions near the critical point, require more accurate real-gas equations of state (EOS) and transport properties than the standard ideal gas EOS and classical kinetic-theory transport properties. The standard for real-gas modeling is provided by the National Institute for Standards and Technology (NIST) in Boulder, Colorado. We have implemented Leachman's NIST hydrogen EOS as well as a two simpler models: (1) a modified van der Waals EOS and (2) a modified Nobel-Abel EOS. Testing and verifying the real-gas EOS implementations is difficult, but most important to provide confidence in the new EOS model developments. A "numerically exact benchmark" problem has especially been developed to address these concerns. This report provides a rigorous development for the implementation of the generalized real-gas EOS into the GASFLOW CFD code, the specific implementation Leachman's NIST model, a modified van der Walls model, and a modified Nobel-Abel, plus a logical testing procedure based upon a numerically exact benchmark problem. An example GASFLOW simulation is presented for an ideal cryocompressed tank.

1 Introduction

The purpose of this report is to formulate the numerical procedure to implement generalized real gas equations of state for the GASFLOW[1] ICE'd-ALE CFD Code.

2 Simplified GASFLOW Equation Set

For this discussion, we simplify the GASFLOW Equation set with the assumptions: 1. Single fluid specie, 2. No phase change, 3. No heat and/or mass transfer, and 4. No chemical reactions to the following set of equations:

Volume Equation

$$\frac{\partial}{\partial t} V = V \nabla \cdot \mathbf{u} \tag{1}$$

Mixture Mass Equation

$$\frac{\partial}{\partial t} \rho = -\nabla \cdot (\rho \mathbf{u}) \tag{2}$$

Mixture Momentum Equations

$$\frac{\partial}{\partial t} (\rho \mathbf{u}) = -\nabla \cdot (\rho \mathbf{u} \mathbf{u}) - \nabla p + \nabla \cdot \tau + \rho \mathbf{g} \tag{3}$$

Mixture Internal Energy Equation

$$\frac{\partial}{\partial t} (\rho I) = -\nabla \cdot (\rho \mathbf{u} I) - p \nabla \cdot \mathbf{u} - \nabla \cdot \mathbf{q} \tag{4}$$

General Thermodynamic Equation of State

$$P = P(\rho, T) = Z(\rho, T) \rho \frac{R}{M} T \tag{5}$$

General Caloric Equation of State

$$I = I(\rho, T) \tag{6}$$

3 The ICE'd-ALE Numerical Methodology

We integrate the above equation set over regular finite volumes using a classical staggered-mesh with fluid scalars occupying control volume centroids while velocities are located at control volume edges. This method is time-split into three distinct phases: A. An explicit Lagrangian "physics" phase; B. An implicit Lagrangian pressure propagation phase; and C. An explicit rezone or advection phase.

Phase A: Explicit Lagrangian Phase

We determine all advanced variables with superscript "A" from the beginning of the time cycle values denoted "n".

Volume Equation

$$\frac{V^A - V^n}{\Delta t} = V^n \nabla \cdot \mathbf{u}^n \tag{7}$$

Mixture Mass Equation

$$\frac{\left(\rho V\right)^A - \left(\rho V\right)^n}{\Delta t} = 0 \tag{8}$$

Mixture Momentum Equations

$$\frac{\left(\rho V \mathbf{u}\right)_m^A - \left(\rho V \mathbf{u}\right)_m^A}{\Delta t} = -V_m^n \nabla p^n + V_m^n \nabla \cdot \tau_m^n + \rho_m^n V_m^n \mathbf{g} \tag{9}$$

Mixture Internal Energy Equation

$$\frac{\left(\rho V I\right)^A - \left(\rho V I\right)^n}{\Delta t} = -V^n p^n \nabla \cdot \mathbf{u}^n - V^n \nabla \cdot \mathbf{q}^n \tag{10}$$

General Thermodynamic Equation of State

$$p\left(\rho^A, T^A\right) = Z\left(\rho^A, T^A\right) \rho^A \frac{\mathrm{R}}{\mathrm{M}} T^A \tag{11}$$

General Caloric Equation of State

$$I^A = I\left(\rho^A, T^A\right) \tag{12}$$

Phase B: Implicit Lagrangian Pressure Iteration Phase

Volume Equation

$$\frac{V^B - V^A}{\Delta t} = V^n \nabla \cdot \left[\left(\mathbf{u}\right)^B - \left(\mathbf{u}\right)^n \right] \tag{13}$$

Mixture Mass Equation

$$\frac{\left(\rho V\right)^B - \left(\rho V\right)^A}{\Delta t} = 0 \tag{14}$$

Mixture Momentum Equations

$$\frac{\left(\rho V \mathbf{u}\right)_m^B - \left(\rho V \mathbf{u}\right)_m^A}{\Delta t} = -V_m^n \nabla \left(p^B - p^n\right) \tag{15}$$

Mixture Internal Energy Equation

$$\frac{\left(\rho V I\right)^B - \left(\rho V I\right)^A}{\Delta t} = -V^n p^n \nabla \cdot \left(\mathbf{u}^B - \mathbf{u}^n\right) \tag{16}$$

The General Thermodynamic Equation of State

$$p\left(\rho^B, T^B\right) = Z\left(\rho^B, T^B\right)\rho^B \frac{R}{M} T^B \tag{17}$$

The General Caloric Equation of State

$$I^B = I\left(\rho^B, T^B\right) \tag{18}$$

With considerable thermodynamic manipulation, algebra, and the assumption

$$\frac{\left(V^B - V^A\right)}{V^B} \cong \frac{\left(V^B - V^A\right)}{V^A}, \text{ provided } \frac{\left(V^B - V^A\right)}{V^A} << 1,$$

Equations (13)-(18) can be reduced to a single Poisson pressure change equation

$$\Delta t^2 \nabla \cdot \left[\frac{V_m^n}{\left(\rho_m V_m\right)^A} \nabla \delta p\right] - \frac{V^A}{V^n} \frac{(\delta p)}{\left(p^A + C^A\right)} = \frac{V^A}{V^n} \frac{\left(p^n - p^A\right)}{\left(p^A + C^A\right)} + \Delta t \nabla \cdot \left[\mathbf{u}^A - \mathbf{u}^n\right] \tag{19}$$

where

$$C^A = \frac{p^n + (\rho V)^A \left[c_v(T,\rho) \frac{\left[\rho^2 \left(\frac{R}{M}\right) T \left(\frac{\partial Z}{\partial \rho}\right)_T\right]}{\left[\left(\frac{pV}{T}\right) + (\rho V)\left(\frac{R}{M}\right) T \left(\frac{\partial Z}{\partial T}\right)_\rho\right]} - \left(\frac{\partial I}{\partial \rho}\right)_T \left(\frac{\rho}{V}\right)\right]^A}{\left[(\rho V) \frac{c_v(T,\rho)}{\left[\left(\frac{pV}{T}\right) + (\rho V)\left(\frac{R}{M}\right) T \left(\frac{\partial Z}{\partial T}\right)_\rho\right]}\right]^A}. \tag{20}$$

Equation (19) is 2nd order and linear in δp. After solving this equation, we can the back substitute δp into (15) to determine $\mathbf{u}^B$, $p^B = p^n + \delta p$, V^B from (13), ρ^B from (14), T^B from inverting (17), and I^B from either (16) or (18).

Phase C: Explicit Eulerian (Advection) Phase

We've determine all advanced variables with superscript "*B*" from the previous phase and now we complete the time cycle to values "*n+1*" by performing the convection phase.

Volume Equation

$$V^{n+1} = V^n \tag{21}$$

Mixture Mass Equation

$$\frac{\left(\rho V\right)^{n+1} - \left(\rho V\right)^{B}}{\Delta t} = -V^{n}\nabla \cdot \left(\rho \mathbf{u}\right)^{B} \tag{22}$$

Mixture Momentum Equations

$$\frac{\left(\rho_{m}V_{m}\mathbf{u}\right)^{n+1} - \left(\rho_{m}V_{m}\mathbf{u}\right)^{B}}{\Delta t} = -V_{m}^{n}\nabla \cdot \left(\rho \mathbf{u}\mathbf{u}\right)^{B} \tag{23}$$

Mixture Internal Energy Equation

$$\frac{\left(\rho VI\right)^{n+1} - \left(\rho VI\right)^{B}}{\Delta t} = -V^{n}\nabla \cdot \left(\rho \mathbf{u}I\right)^{B} \tag{24}$$

The General Thermodynamic Equation of State

$$p\left(\rho^{n+1}, T^{n+1}\right) = Z\left(\rho^{n+1}, T^{n+1}\right)\rho^{n+1}\frac{\text{R}}{\text{M}}T^{n+1} \tag{25}$$

The General Caloric Equation of State

$$I^{n+1} = I\left(\rho^{n+1}, T^{n+1}\right) \tag{26}$$

The summation of the complete computational cycle yields the following:

Mixture Mass Equation

$$\frac{\left(\rho V\right)^{n+1} - \left(\rho V\right)^{n}}{\Delta t} = -V^{n}\nabla \cdot \left(\rho \mathbf{u}\right)^{B} \tag{27}$$

Mixture Momentum Equations

$$\frac{\left(\rho_{m}V_{m}\mathbf{u}\right)^{n+1} - \left(\rho_{m}V_{m}\mathbf{u}\right)^{n}}{\Delta t} = -V_{m}^{n}\nabla \cdot \left(\rho \mathbf{u}\mathbf{u}\right)^{B} - V_{m}^{n}\nabla p^{B} + V_{m}^{n}\nabla \cdot \tau_{m}^{n} + \rho_{m}^{n}V_{m}^{n}\mathbf{g} \tag{28}$$

Mixture Internal Energy Equation

$$\frac{\left(\rho VI\right)^{n+1} - \left(\rho VI\right)^{n}}{\Delta t} = -V^{n}\nabla \cdot \left(\rho \mathbf{u}I\right)^{B} - V^{n}p^{n}\nabla \cdot \mathbf{u}^{B} - V^{n}\nabla \cdot \mathbf{q}^{n} \tag{29}$$

4   Some Example Equations of State for the above Analysis

Ideal Gas

$$p\left(\rho, T\right) = \rho\frac{\text{R}}{M}T \quad and \quad I\left(T\right) = I_{ig}\left(T\right)$$

$$\left(\frac{\partial Z}{\partial \rho}\right)_{T} = 0 \quad , \quad \left(\frac{\partial Z}{\partial T}\right)_{\rho} = 0 \quad , and \quad \left(\frac{\partial I}{\partial \rho}\right)_{T} = 0$$

Modified Nobel-Abel

$$p(\rho,T) = \frac{\rho \frac{R}{M} T}{c - b\rho} \quad and \quad I(T) = I_{ig}(T)$$

$$\left(\frac{\partial Z}{\partial \rho}\right)_T = \frac{b}{(c - b\rho)^2}, \left(\frac{\partial Z}{\partial T}\right)_\rho = 0, \text{ and } \left(\frac{\partial I}{\partial \rho}\right)_T = 0$$

The coefficients "b" and "c" in the above Modified Nobel-Abel EOS for the 2 thermodynamic states

(245 K, 2.5 MPa, 2.43277 kg/m^3),   and   (35 K, 2.5 MPa, 49.66182 kg/m^3)

can be found as:

$b = -0.040026142924481$ and $c = 0.886493850623252$.

The reason these 2 particular thermodynamic states were selected for fitting the 2 coefficients is demonstrated in Section 5 below.

Modified van der Waals

$$p(\rho,T) = \frac{\rho \frac{R}{M} T}{c - b\rho} - a\rho^2 \quad and \quad I(\rho,T) = I_{ig}(T) - a\rho$$

$$\left(\frac{\partial Z}{\partial \rho}\right)_T = \frac{b}{(c - b\rho)^2} - \frac{M}{R} \frac{a}{T}, \left(\frac{\partial Z}{\partial T}\right)_\rho = a\left(\frac{\rho}{T^2}\right)\left(\frac{M}{R}\right), \text{ and } \left(\frac{\partial I}{\partial \rho}\right)_T = -a$$

The coefficients "a", "b" and "c" in the above Modified van der Waals EOS for the 3 thermodynamic states:

(245 K, 2.5 MPa, 2.43277 kg/m^3),   (35 K, 2.5 MPa, 49.66182 kg/m^3), and

(61.5 K, 25 MPa, 64.2 kg/m^3),

can be found solution as:

$a = 4.70470053582692E+3$, $b = 9.81499353729889E-3$, and $c = 0.996969112920896$.

The reason these 3 thermodynamic states were selected for fitting the 3 coefficients is demonstrated in Section 5 and 6 below.

Leachman's NIST

Modern equations of state [2,3] are often formulated using the Helmholtz energy as the fundamental property with independent variables of temperature and density,

$$\alpha(T,\rho) = \alpha^0(T,\rho) + \alpha^r(T,\rho), \tag{30}$$

where α is the Helmholtz energy, $a^0(T,\rho)$ is the ideal gas contribution to the Helmholtz energy, and $a^r(T,\rho)$ is the residual Helmholtz energy, which corresponds to the influence of intermolecular forces. Thermodynamics properties can be calculated as derivatives of the Helmholtz energy. For example, the pressure is

$$p = \rho^2 \left(\frac{\partial \alpha}{\partial p} \right)_T. \tag{31}$$

In practical applications, the functional form is explicit in the dimensionless Helmholtz energy, α, using independent variables of dimensionless density and temperature. The form of this equation is

$$\frac{\alpha(T,\rho)}{RT} = \alpha(\tau,\delta) = \alpha^0(\tau,\delta) + \alpha^r(\tau,\delta), \tag{32}$$

where $\tau = T_c/T$, the inverse reduced temperature and $\delta = \rho/\rho_c$, the reduced density.

The ideal gas Helmholtz energy is represented in the computational convenient parameterized form

$$\alpha^0(\tau,\delta) = \ln\delta + 1.5\ln\tau + a_1 + a_2\tau + \sum_{k=3}^{N} a_k \ln\left[1 - \exp(b_k\tau)\right], \tag{33}$$

and the residual contribution to the Helmholtz free energy takes the form

$$\alpha^r(\tau,\delta) = \sum_{i=1}^{l} N_i\delta^{d_i}\tau^{t_i} + \sum_{i=l+1}^{m} N_i\delta^{d_i}\tau^{t_i} \exp\left(-\delta^{p_i}\right) + \\ \sum_{i=m+1}^{n} N_i\delta^{d_i}\tau^{t_i} \exp\left[+\varphi_i(\delta-D_i)^2 + \beta_i(\tau-\gamma_i)^2\right] \tag{34}$$

where the parameters and coefficients for parahydrogen and normal hydrogen are given by Leachman[1,2].

The advantages of this new explicit formulation in the Helmholtz free energy become apparent in the calculation of the various properties:

Pressure:
$$p(T,\rho) = \rho R T \left[1 + \delta \left(\frac{\partial \alpha^r}{\partial \delta} \right)_\tau \right], \tag{35}$$

Compressibility factor:
$$Z(T,\rho) = \frac{p}{\rho R T} = 1 + \delta \left(\frac{\partial \alpha^r}{\partial \delta} \right)_\tau, \tag{36}$$

Internal energy:
$$u(T,\rho) = R T \tau \left[\left(\frac{\partial \alpha^0}{\partial \tau} \right)_\delta + \left(\frac{\partial \alpha^r}{\partial \tau} \right)_\delta \right], \text{ and} \tag{37}$$

Isochoric heat capacity:
$$c_v(T,\rho) = -R \tau^2 \left[\left(\frac{\partial^2 \alpha^0}{\partial \tau^2} \right)_\delta + \left(\frac{\partial^2 \alpha^r}{\partial \tau^2} \right)_\delta \right]. \tag{38}$$

Some derivatives required for the GASFLOW real gas formulation Equations (19) and (20) are:

$$\left(\frac{\partial Z}{\partial \rho} \right)_T = \delta \left(\frac{\partial^2 \alpha^r}{\partial \delta^2} \right)_\tau \left(\frac{\partial \delta}{\partial \rho} \right) + \left(\frac{\partial \alpha^r}{\partial \delta} \right)_\tau \left(\frac{\partial \delta}{\partial \rho} \right) = \frac{1}{\rho_c} \left[\delta \left(\frac{\partial^2 \alpha^r}{\partial \delta^2} \right)_\tau + \left(\frac{\partial \alpha^r}{\partial \delta} \right)_\tau \right]$$

$$\left(\frac{\partial Z}{\partial T} \right)_\rho = \delta \left(\frac{\partial^2 \alpha^r}{\partial \delta \partial \tau} \right) \left(\frac{\partial \tau}{\partial T} \right) = -\frac{\delta \tau}{T} \left(\frac{\partial^2 \alpha^r}{\partial \delta \partial \tau} \right) = -\frac{\rho}{\rho_c} \frac{T_c}{T^2} \left(\frac{\partial^2 \alpha^r}{\partial \delta \partial \tau} \right)$$

$$\left(\frac{\partial I}{\partial \rho} \right)_T = \frac{R}{M} T_c \left[\left(\frac{\partial^2 \alpha^0}{\partial \tau \partial \delta} \right) \left(\frac{\partial \delta}{\partial \rho} \right) + \left(\frac{\partial^2 \alpha^r}{\partial \tau \partial \delta} \right) \left(\frac{\partial \delta}{\partial \rho} \right) \right] = -\frac{R}{M} \frac{T^2}{\rho} \left(\frac{\partial Z}{\partial T} \right)_\rho = \frac{R}{M} \frac{T_c}{\rho_c} \left(\frac{\partial^2 \alpha^r}{\partial \delta \partial \tau} \right)$$

5   A Numerically Exact Benchmark Problem

Implementing real gas equations of state in CFD codes is a difficult task. Testing and verifying the real gas EOS implementation is important to provide the code developers and users confidence that the required development and coding has been correctly accomplished. This section provides a numerically exact benchmark problem to help developers and users gain that confidence.

We describe a time-dependent, one-dimensional, filling problem. A schematic drawing of the problem is shown in Fig. 1. A short tube is filled with hydrogen at 2.5 MPa and 245 K. Initially there is a constant velocity from the bottom toward to top at a slow velocity of 1 cm/s exiting out the top at the same velocity. Magically we introduce cold hydrogen at 35 K and 25 MPa into the bottom of the tube with the same inflowing velocity of 1 cm/s. The problem is to compute the cold hydrogen pushing the warmer hydrogen out the tube top in a constant pressure process. Clearly, the cold hydrogen will completely fill the tube in 10 s, so we specify the problem time greater than 1 s, but less than 10 s.

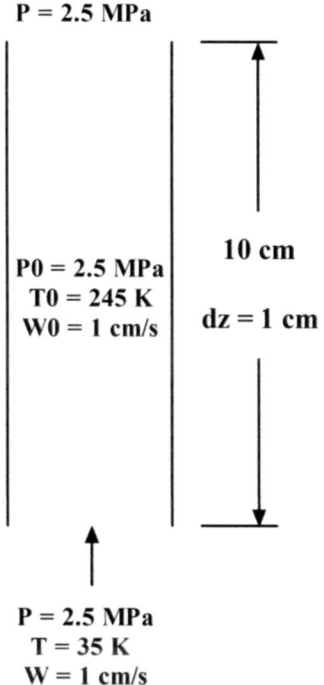

Fig. 1   A Schematic Drawing for the time-dependent, one-dimensional Benchmark Filling Problem

6   Analysis using a Real Gas Equation of State

An exact numerical solution can be found for the above stated benchmark problem from the following hyperbolic "system"; conservation of mass and energy plus the caloric and thermodynamic equations of state constraints (in further discussions, we refer simply to the *system*):

$$\frac{\partial}{\partial t}(\rho) + \frac{\partial}{\partial x}(\rho u) = 0 \tag{39}$$

$$\frac{\partial}{\partial t}(\rho h) + \frac{\partial}{\partial x}(\rho h u) = 0 \tag{40}$$

$$h(T,\rho) = RT\left\{\tau\left[\left(\frac{\partial \alpha^0}{\partial \tau}\right)_\delta + \left(\frac{\partial \alpha^r}{\partial \tau}\right)_\delta\right] + \delta\left(\frac{\partial \alpha^r}{\partial \delta}\right)_\tau + 1\right\} \tag{41}$$

$$p(T,\rho) = \rho RT\left[1 + \delta\left(\frac{\partial \alpha^r}{\partial \delta}\right)_\tau\right] \tag{42}$$

Note that there are 3 unknowns (ρ, T, and u), which must be iterated until the above *system* is satisfied.

7 Exact Numerical and GASFLOW Solutions for the Benchmark

In Fig. 2, we compare the temperature and density profile results between the exact numerical solution of the *system* and the GASFLOW solution for the inviscid gas dynamics equations (Euler Equations) using 1st order upwind differencing, 2nd order Lax-Wendroff, and 2nd order

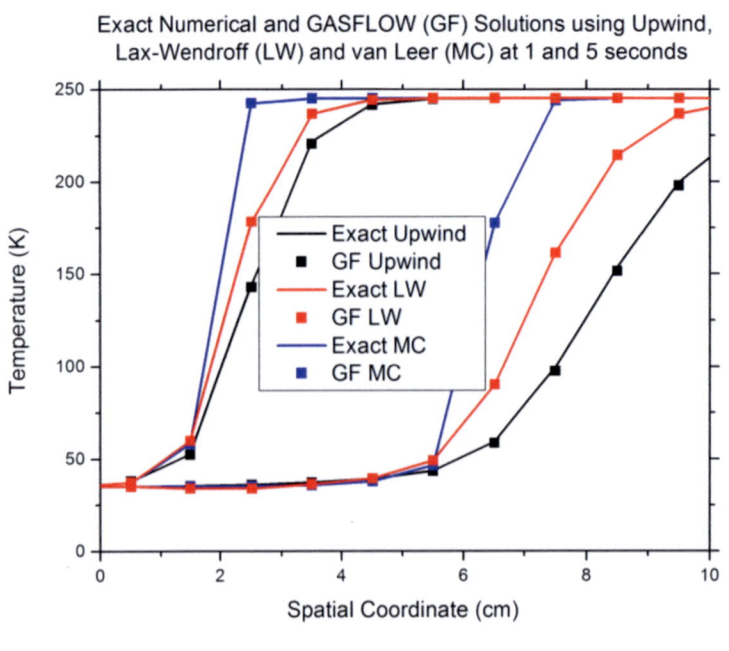

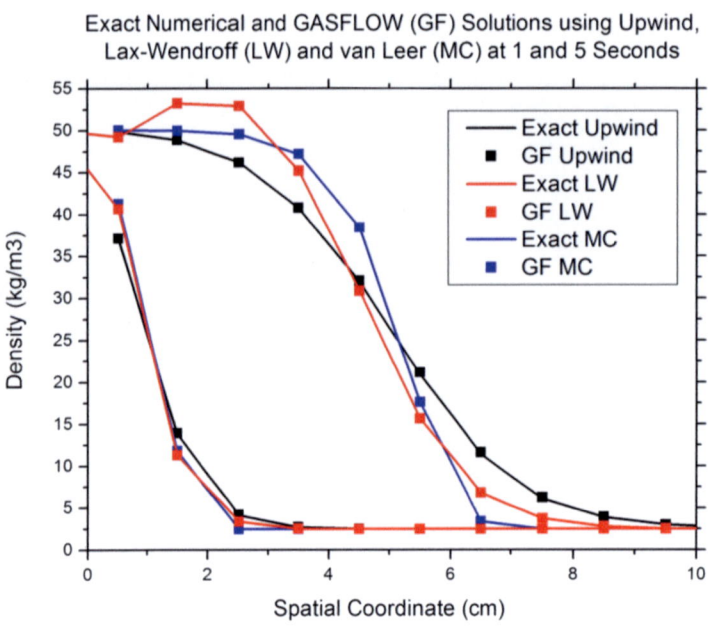

Fig. 2 Comparison of the Exact Numerical (System) and GASFLOW Solutions computed on a uniform 1 cm mesh showing the Temperature Distributions for Upwind differencing, Lax-Wendroff differencing and TVD MC (van Leer) limiter

TVD MC (van Leer [4]). These three convective schemes are implemented in GASFLOW, and this is the reason we carry the analysis forward focused around these schemes.

We are satisfied with these results; and consequently, we believe that we have implemented the real gas Equations of State correctly into the GASFLOW code.

8 Example of an Ideal (no structural heat transfer) Cryocompressed Tank Filling Simulation

A Cryocompressed Tank, shown schematically shown in Figure 4, can be filled with 35 K hydrogen from initial to final conditions, see Table 1: Stage 0. Decompressing the tank from the initial conditions to 2.5 MPa, Stage 1. Cooling the tank by filling to 35 K hydrogen with constant pressure 2.5 MPa, and Stage 2. Charging the tank with a 35 K hydrogen to 25 MPa. The thermodynamic paths are presented in Figure 5. Table 2 gives the GASFLOW computed process times for two filling rates 20 and 100 kg/hr, respectively. The simulations exactly follow the thermodynamic paths in Figure 5.

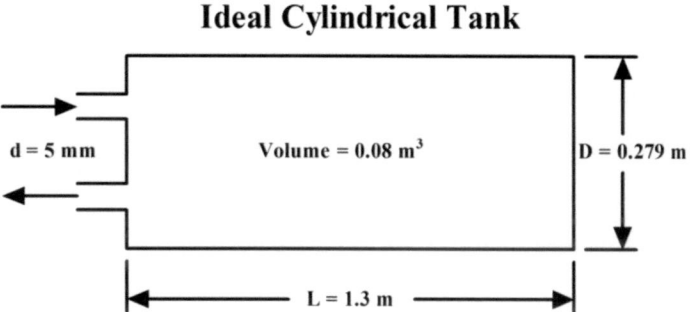

Ideal Cylindrical Tank

d = 5 mm Volume = 0.08 m³ D = 0.279 m

L = 1.3 m

Fig. 3   Simple Schematic Model of a Cryocompressed Tank

Conditions	Pressure (MPa)	Temperature (K)	Density (kg/m³)
Initial	5	300	3.9
Final	25	61.5	64.2

Tab. 1   Initial and Final Conditions for an Ideal Filling a Cryocompressed Tank with Hydrogen

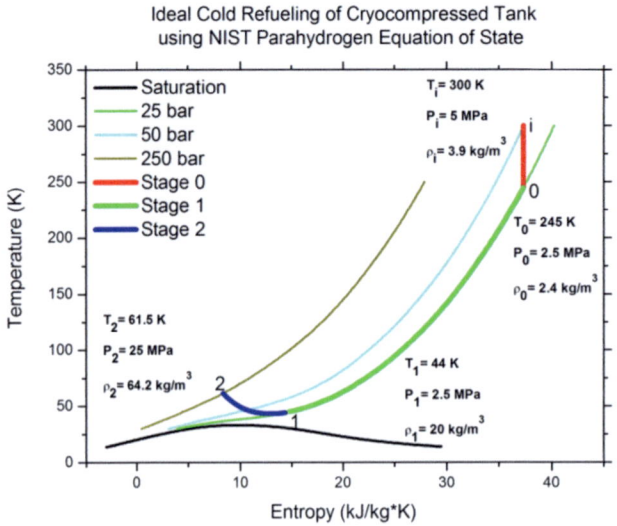

Fig. 4   The Thermodynamics of Filling a Cryocompressed Tank with Hydrogen

Filling Rates (kg/hr)	Stage 0 Time (s)	Stage 1 Time (s)	Stage 2 Time (s)	Total Time (s)
20	5	270	630	905
100	5	55	125	185

Tab. 2   Ideal GASFLOW Results for two Cryocompressed Tank Filling Rates

References

[1]   Travis, J.R., et al., "GASFLOW: A Computational Fluid Dynamics Code for Gases, Aerosols, and Combustion, Vols. 1, 2 and 3", LA-13357-M and FZKA-5994, 1998.

[2]   Leachman, Jacob, "Fundamental Equations of State for Parahydrogen, Normal Hydrogen, and Orthohydrogen, Masters of Science Thesis", *University of Idaho*, 2007.

[3]   Leachman, J.W.; Jacobsen, R.T.; Lemmon, E.W., "Fundamental Equations of State for Parahydrogen, Normal Hydrogen, and Orthohydrogen", *J. Phys. Chem. Ref. Data*, 38, pp721 (2009).

[4]   van Leer, B., "Towards the ultimate conservative difference scheme III: Upstream-centered finite-difference schemes for ideal compressible flow", *J. Comp. Phys.*, 23, pp263 (1977).

Numerical investigations of gas-liquid flows in mini-channels for applications in chemical process engineering

Martin Wörner

Karlsruher Institut für Technologie (KIT), Institut für Kern- und Energietechnik (IKET)

Hermann-von-Helmholtz-Platz 1, 76344 Eggenstein-Leopoldshafen, Germany

E-mail: martin.woerner@kit.edu, Phone: +49 7247 82 4477

Abstract

In order to perform detailed numerical investigations of gas-liquid flows with deformable interfaces the in-house computer code TURBIT-VOF is developed at KIT. This contribution gives a concise overview about the mathematical and numerical foundation of the code and provides illustrations of its application in the field of chemical process engineering, where the flow of elongated gas bubbles moving within a continuous liquid phase through narrow channels is finding increasing technological and scientific interest. In the second part of the paper the performance of the TURBIT-VOF code on different hardware platforms available at KIT (NEC SX-8R, NEC SX-9, HP XC3000) is analyzed and conclusions for promising optimization and parallelization strategies are drawn.

1 Introduction

Operations in chemical process engineering that involve multiple phases (e.g. a gas and a liquid or two immiscible liquids) are traditionally performed in large devices (with typical dimension of one or several meters) such as stirred tank reactors, bubble columns or air lift reactors. Micro process engineering aims to perform these operations, where appropriate, in miniaturized devices (with typical dimension of 1 mm or below). The underlying goal is to achieve a "process intensification" by taking advantage of the large surface area to volume ratio and enhanced heat/mass transfer rates. In this context, ceramic monolith reactors (a block with hundreds of straight millimeter-sized rectangular channels) are a promising option for production of liquid fuels from syngas (a mixture of H_2 and CO) by Fischer-Tropsch synthesis [1]. To foster the understanding of the relevant flow phenomena and transport processes, here detailed numerical investigations of the flow of a regular sequence of elongated gas bubbles (Taylor bubbles) embedded in a continuous liquid phase within a single square mini-channel are performed.

2   Numerical method

The time-dependent three-dimensional computations are performed with the in-house computer code TURBIT-VOF developed at KIT. The code is written in Fortran and solves the Navier-Stokes equations with surface tension term in non-dimensional single field formulation for two incompressible Newtonian fluids with constant viscosity and coefficient of surface tension on a regular staggered Cartesian grid by a finite volume method. All spatial derivatives are approximated by central differences. Time integration is performed by an explicit third order Runge-Kutta method. A divergence free velocity field at the end of each time step is enforced by a projection method; the resulting Poisson equation is iteratively solved by the linear solver package LINSOL [2] developed at KIT. The dynamic evolution of the deformable gas-liquid interface is computed by a volume-of-fluid method with piecewise planar interface reconstruction. Thus, in each mesh cell where both phases coexist at a certain time step, the interface is locally approximated by a plane (whose location and orientation is "reconstructed"). For details about the governing equations and the numerical method we refer to [3].

3   Typical results

In performing a numerical simulation for a certain case, the transient evolution from the initial velocity field and bubble shape towards the fully developed flow of a bubble translating with constant velocity and steady shape (corresponding to a certain prescribed axial pressure drop) is computed in a sequence of jobs. Fig. 1 a) shows a sketch of the computational set-up. We consider a so-called unit cell, which consists of one gas bubble and one liquid slug. In axial (vertical) direction we apply periodic boundary conditions to mimic the influence of the trailing and leading bubbles. No-slip boundary conditions are used at the four lateral walls of the channel. As a result of a simulation, detailed data about the full three-dimensional and time-dependent phase distribution, velocity field and pressure field within both phases are obtained; see Fig. 1 b).

In a series of TURBIT-VOF simulations, the co-current downward flow of nitrogen bubbles in viscous squalane (which is a good solvent for Fischer-Tropsch products) within a vertical mini-channel was investigated. The inner dimensions of the square channel are 1 mm × 1 mm, which allows a direct comparison and validation with available experimental results. The axial length of the unit cell L_{uc} is up to 6 mm. In this case the (uniform) grid consists of $80 \times 480 \times 80$ cubic mesh cells (about $3 \cdot 10^6$ mesh cells in total). In Fig. 2 the computed steady bubble shape is displayed for five different values of the capillary number $Ca = \mu_L U_B / \sigma$ and Reynolds number $Re = \rho_L D_h U_B / \mu_L$. Here, U_B is the bubble velocity, D_h the channel hydraulic diameter, σ the coefficient of surface tension, and μ_L and ρ_L are the liquid viscosity and density, respectively. Fig. 2 shows that with increase of Ca the rear and front meniscus of the bubble become more flat and pointed, respectively, in agreement with experiments [4].

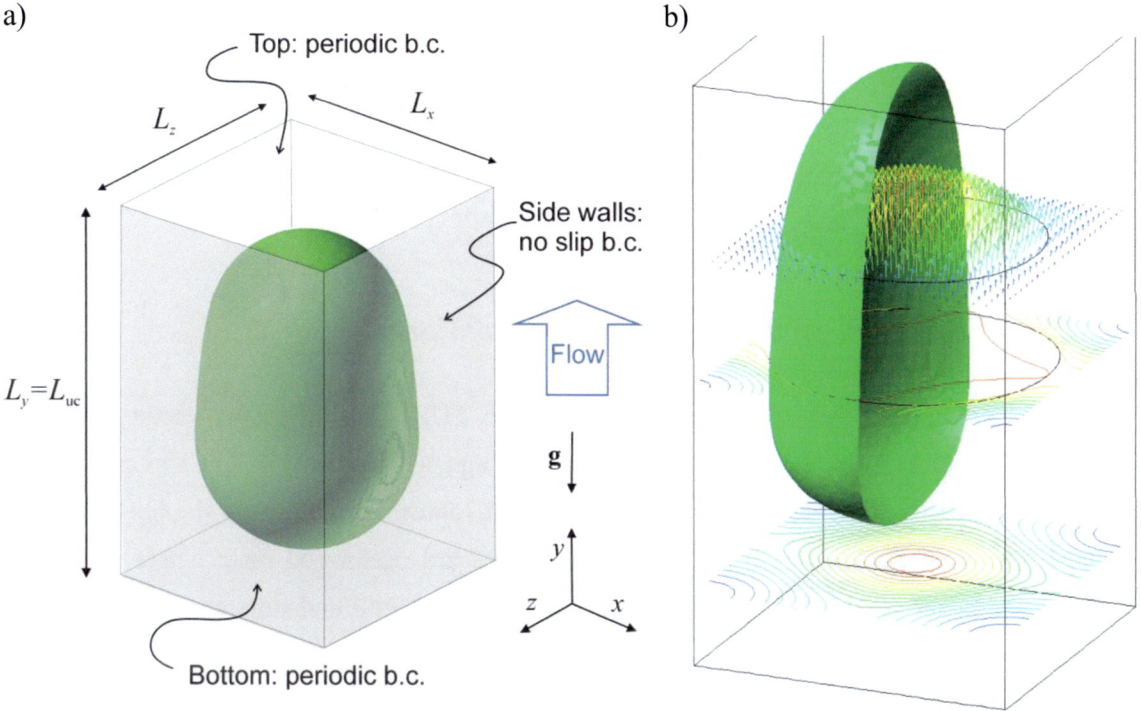

Fig. 1: a) Sketch of computational domain and coordinate system. b) Visualization of computed bubble shape (only half of the bubble is displayed). Also shown are the local velocity field (vectors) and the concentration field (contour lines) of a chemical species (which is transferred from the gas into the liquid phase) in different axial cross-sections

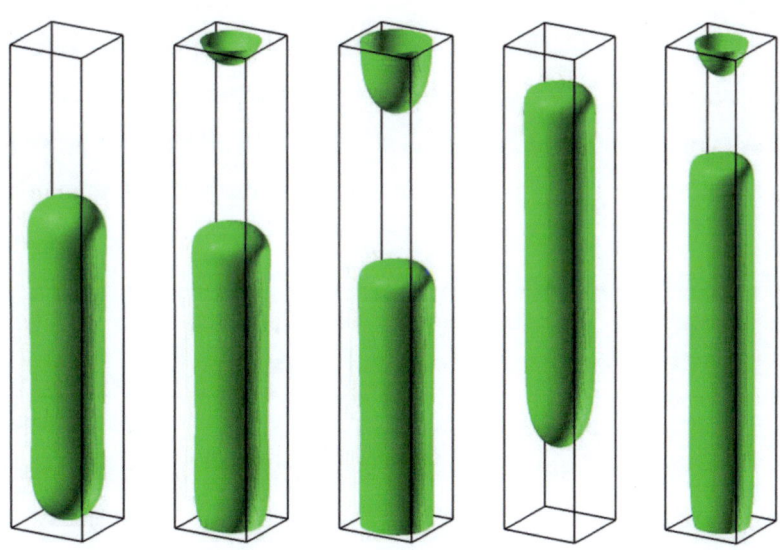

Fig. 2: Perspective view of computed steady bubble shape for L_{uc} = 6 mm for five different values of the capillary number. From left to right, the values of (*Ca; Re*) are (0.045; 1.22), (0.117; 3.19), (0.17; 4.64), (0.25; 6.81), (0.491; 13.4). The solid lines indicate the size of the computational domain. For further details about the simulations we refer to [4,7]

Additionally to the hydrodynamics, the transient interfacial mass transfer of a (passive) chemical species (initially dissolved in the gas phase only) into the continuous liquid phase can be simulated starting from hydrodynamically fully developed flow. Optionally, this mass transfer can be combined with a chemical reaction, which can be homogenous (i.e. occur in the liquid bulk phase) or heterogeneous (i.e. occur at the channel walls) [5,6].

4   Code performance on different hardware platforms

The current hardware platform for production jobs with TURBIT-VOF is the vector computer system NEC SX-8R at the Steinbuch Center for Computing (SCC) located at KIT Campus North. The code is compiled with the sxf90 compiler and an option that ensures double precision representation of all REAL variables. The computations are performed on a single processor since the code is not yet parallelized. The CPU time per mesh cell and time step for running a certain case is typically in the range 60 − 100 µs. In a transient simulation usually a few 10 000 time steps are computed; this corresponds to a total CPU time of one or several month. As a first step toward the intended optimization of the code, a flow trace analysis is performed by running one of the cases displayed in Fig. 2 for 10 time steps. The results of the flow trace analysis are listed in Table 1. Only those subroutines are included in Table 1 who require at least 1% of the total CPU time. As can be seen, about 75.1 % of the CPU time is consumed by program unit linin2, which includes the calls to the LINSOL solver package for solution of the pressure Poisson equation. The column "Vectorization Optimization Ratio" in Table 1 shows a value close to 100 % for this program unit, indicating excellent vectorization. The other five program units listed in Table 1 belong to the interface reconstruction algorithm EPIRA (exact plane interface reconstruction algorithm) [3,8]. The intersection between the plane which represents the interface and the cubical mesh cell is a polygon, with either 3, 4, 5 or 6 edges. The procedure to determine the number of edges and the location and orientation of each polygon involves a distinction

Program unit	Frequency	Exclusive time		Vect. Opt. Ratio	Remark
	[-]	[s]	[%]	[%]	
linin2	10	2499.7	75.1	99.37	Solution of Poisson equation
volume	13165932	181.1	5.4	47.16	Interface reconstruction
wsepbe	103814562	168.5	5.1	0.00	Interface reconstruction
wsepir	415258248	160.7	4.8	0.00	Interface reconstruction
wsbkor	10802207	39.0	1.2	0.00	Interface reconstruction
wsepia	1590	34.4	1.0	0.00	Interface reconstruction

Table 1: Results of flow trace analysis on NEC SX-8 for 10 time steps

between a large number of different cases. As a consequence, the EPIRA algorithm includes many IF statements and is thus hard to vectorize. Therefore, for most of these subroutines (with exception of the function volume) the Vectorization Optimization Ratio is zero. Overall, the code reaches a performance of about 4 GFLOPS on SX-8.

Recently the installation at SCC was upgraded by a SX-9, NECs most recent vector system. Since the LINSOL package is not available yet on SX-9, first test runs of TURBIT-VOF on SX-9 are performed using the LINSOL binary compiled on SX-8. The total CPU time for 10 time steps on a $80 \times 480 \times 80$ mesh is reduced from 3327.4 s on SX-8 to 2422.6 s on SX-9, i.e. is about 27.2 % lower on SX-9 than on SX-8. The CPU time of the six program units listed in Table 1 on SX-8 and SX-9 is compared in Fig. 3 a). As can be seen, the vector code (i.e. linin2) is about 65 % faster on SX-9 than on SX-8. On the other hand, scalar code (the program units corresponding to the interface reconstruction) is more than 100 % slower on SX-9 than on SX-8. As a consequence, LINSOL requires only about 35.8 % of the total CPU time on SX-9 instead of the 75.1 % on SX-8, see Fig. 3 b).

The SCC at KIT Campus South operates the distributed memory parallel computer HP XC3000 (abbreviated hc3) which consists of SMP nodes with 64 bit Xeon processors from Intel. On hc3, the TURBIT-VOF code is compiled with the Intel compiler (version 10.1.022) with three different optimization options (-g = no optimization, -O2, and -O3). In Fig. 4 the CPU time on a single hc3 node is compared to that on SX-8 and SX-9. It is evident that the CPU time on hc3 is more than three times larger than on SX-8. Interestingly, the optimization level has only a very small effect on the overall CPU time. The reason is that on hc3 about 97 % of the CPU time is needed by the LINSOL library, which is not affected by the optimization option.

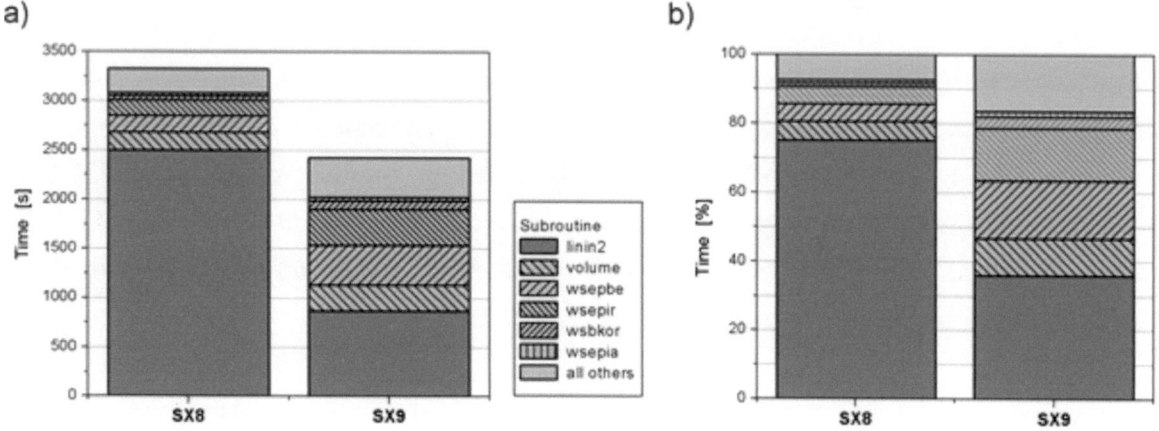

Fig. 3: Comparison of CPU time of different program units on SX-8 and SX-9: a) absolute CPU time (seconds); b) relative CPU time in percent of total CPU time

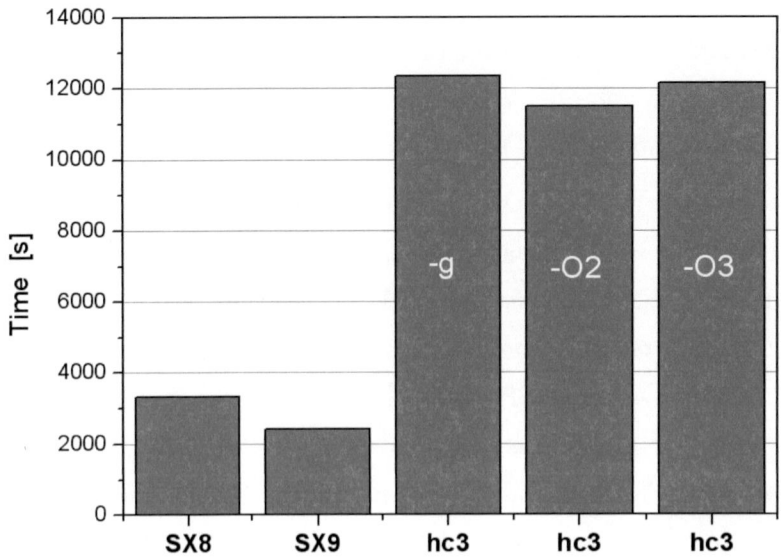

Fig. 4: Comparison of CPU time on SX-8, SX-9 and hc3 (with three different optimization options).

5 Conclusions

The analysis of the performance of the TURBIT-VOF code on different hardware platforms allows the identification of different strategies for possible optimization and parallelization. As on SX-8 about 75 % of the CPU time is required by LINSOL, the most meaningful optimization is to speed up the solution of the pressure Poisson equation. In this context, testing of three measures is suggested by SCC (H. Häfner): i) testing of different solvers available within the LINSOL package, ii) testing of a weaker residuum criterion (currently 10^{-8}), and iii) pre-conditioning. To improve the performance of the code on SX-9, an optimization and (if possible) vectorization of the yet not vectorizable interface reconstruction subroutines is mandatory. As concerns the hc3 machine, running the TURBIT-VOF code on a single node is not meaningful due to the very large CPU time of such a job. The wall clock time can probably drastically be reduced by running a parallel version of LINSOL on a certain number of processors. A promising strategy could thus be to run the unparallelized TURBIT-VOF code on a single hc3 node, but branch to multiple processors when LINSOL is called (a parallel version of LINSOL is available). After solution of the pressure Poisson equation the execution of the TURBIT-VOF code is continued on a single node again. In the near future we intend to test several of the mentioned optimization steps in cooperation with SCC SimLab Energy.

Acknowledgement

The author thanks Daniela Piccioni Koch and Harmut Häfner from SCC for their support in implementing the TURBIT-VOF code on NEC SX-9 and hc3 and in performing the CPU time measurements.

References

[1] Guettel R, Knochen J, Kunz U, Kassing M, Turek T. Preparation and catalytic evaluation of cobalt based monolithic and powder catalysts for Fischer-Tropsch synthesis. Ind. Eng. Chem. Res. **47** (2008) 6589–6597.

[2] Häfner H, Schönauer W, Weiss R. The program package LINSOL – Basic concepts and realization. Appl. Num. Meth. **30** (1999) 213–224.

[3] Öztaskin MC, Wörner M, Soyhan HS. Numerical investigation of the stability of bubble train flow in a square minichannel. Phys. Fluids **21** (2009) 042108.

[4] Keskin Ö, Wörner M, Soyhan HS, Bauer T, Deutschmann O, Lange R. Viscous co-current downward Taylor flow in a square mini-channel. AIChE J. **56** (2010) 1693–1702.

[5] Onea A, Wörner M, Cacuci, DG. A qualitative computational study of mass transfer in upward bubble train flow through square and rectangular mini-channels. Chem. Eng. Sci. **64** (2009) 1416–1435.

[6] Kececi S, Wörner M, Onea A, Soyhan HS. Recirculation time and liquid slug mass transfer in co-current upward and downward Taylor flow. Catalysis Today **147S** (2009) S125–S131.

[7] Wörner M. Numerical evidence for a novel non-axisymmetric bubble shape regime in square channel Taylor flow. 7th Int. Conf. Multiphase Flow, Tampa, Fl., May 30 - June 4, 2010 CD-ROM.

[8] Sabisch W, Wörner M, Grötzbach G, Cacuci DG. 3D volume-of-fluid simulation of a wobbling bubble in a gas-liquid system of low Morton number. 4th Int. Conf. Multiphase Flow, New Orleans, La., May 27 - June 1, 2001 CD-ROM.

Towards Large Scale Adaptive Turbulence Simulations

Christoph Altmann[*], Christian Engfer[†], Gregor Gassner[*], Florian Hindenlang[*], Thorsten Lutz[*], Claus-Dieter Munz[*]

[*] Institut für Aerodynamik und Gasdynamik, Universität Stuttgart, Pfaffenwaldring 21, 70569 Stuttgart,
E-mail: altmann/gassner/hindenlang/lutz/munz@iag.uni-stuttgart.de
[†] Deutsches SOFIA Institut, Universität Stuttgart, Pfaffenwaldring 31, 70569 Stuttgart,
E-mail: engfer@dsi.uni-stuttgart.de

1 Introduction

The computational fluid dynamics community is still one of the main applicants of high performance computing. This is due to the fact that almost all industrial flow problems are turbulent and are determined by the interaction of phenomena on multiple scales. The state of the art in industry is such that many problems can be solved with acceptable accuracy as a steady solution of the time averaged equations which are closed by a turbulence model named Reynolds Averaged Navier Stokes (RANS) equations. Nevertheless, the simulation of unsteady solutions for problems which are inherently unsteady or for which the turbulence models fail or contain a large amount of uncertainty today is still a challenge. Improved numerical methods as well as today's and future large scale massively parallel computer architectures with well adopted numerical algorithms more and more enable the simulation of these challenging unsteady problems.

Two activities towards these goals are described in this paper: The first one is a large scale simulation of the unsteady flow field around the Stratospheric Observatory For Infrared Astronomy (SOFIA), a reflecting telescope carried inside an open port of a Boeing 747SP aircraft. Here, the finite volume RANS-solver TAU ([3]) was used for detached eddy simulations (DES). The objective is to characterize the unsteady pressure fluctuations in the cavity and to reduce their impact on the telescope through passive flow control devices [6]. The second topic is the development of a new generation of numerical methods specialized for unsteady compressible flow with high fidelity turbulence models. These so called discontinuous Galerkin schemes combine the advantageous features of high order schemes with an enormous flexibility, making them an ideal candidate for modern large scale parallel calculations. A highly efficient time discretization strategy [2], [1] is described, which allows local grid refinement and local order-of-accuracy increase in space and time. Here, first results of the simulation of turbulent fluid flow are shown.

2 Motivation

Today, the solution to many industrial problems is found with acceptable accuracy by solving time averaged equations, closed by a turbulence model. These Reynolds averaged Navier-Stokes (RANS) calculations can handle mostly stationary flows. A lot more difficulties arise when unsteady phenomena have to be resolved. Here, current tools may likely fail, especially for complex problems involving extremely different flow scales. An efficient simulation of turbulence is one of the key points of HPC. Hereby, the class of discontinuous Galerkin (DG) high order schemes gained significantly in popularity, since it combines the advantageous features of a high order scheme with an enormous flexibility, making it an ideal candidate for modern large scale parallel calculations. This is a result of the element-local structure of DG schemes. Similar to finite element schemes, the DG approximate solution is defined as a polynomial expansion, where the time dependent polynomial coefficients are the degrees of freedom (DoF). This polynomial approximation is inserted into a variational formulation of the governing equations to determine the DoF. The difference to the classical finite elements is that the approximation as well as the test functions may be discontinuous at the interface between grid cells similar to the finite volume framework. At the Institute of Aerodynamics and Gas Dynamics, Universität Stuttgart, the research focus in numerical flow simulation lies on the construction of high order schemes which are optimized for space-time approximations rather than a simple extension of steady state schemes to the transient case. Explicit and implicit DG schemes have been developed for Maxwell, Euler, Navier-Stokes, MHD and multiphase flows. The goal is to develop reliable and efficient simulation tools for turbulent flows, especially in the context of Direct Numerical Simulations (DNS) and Large Eddy Simulations (LES). Since complex turbulent problems are often still too large to be directly simulated on today's computers, LES models help to reduce the problem to a suitable size for efficient simulation. Due to their yet large computational needs, LES calculations are still not widely used in commercial applications.

3 State of the Art in Adaptive Turbulence Modeling

Per definition, resolution in a LES is still coarse with respect to the small scales. Thus, convergence statements and error estimations which typically rely on small h, i.e. $h \to 0$, are not necessarily valid in such computations. This problematic is further intensified due to the non-linearity of the Navier-Stokes equations, as the non-resolved scales could have a massive impact on the resolved scales and thus a massive impact on the overall solution accuracy. In coarse resolution computations of 3D flow simulations it is even possible to get physical wrong results, e.g. laminar solutions to actual turbulent setups. If such a computation is combined with spatial adaptation, where, for instance, flow quantities of interest as (error) indicator variables are used, it is not guaranteed that the overall accuracy of the approximation improves, as an initial (too) coarse resolution could prevent the flow from developing necessary turbulent features over time. A mechanism to account for the multiscale behavior of turbulent flow is necessary and desirable. A proposed remedy to those problems is the implementation of a turbulence model, which is designed to appropriately account for the non-linear interaction of unresolved and resolved scales. Those LES models are either implicitly built into the numerical discretization or are explicitly added to the Navier-Stokes equations. They are typically dependent on (at least) one model parameter, which itself often depends on the local spatial resolution. Derivation of LES models often assumes homogenous distribution of the spatial resolution, which is not valid in practical simulations when stretched, curved or unstructured grids are used. Thus, if spatial adaptation is used in a LES, the model has to be adopted for an inhomogeneous, locally strongly varying distribution of the resolution. To evaluate the effect of the used turbulence model, the added artificial sub grid scale viscosity is monitored and used as an indication of the resolution of the actual computation. Another practical quantity to judge the effect of the LES model is the turbulent kinetic energy, which can be determined either by postprocessing of the instantaneous solution or is already part of the explicitly added turbulence model. If such quantities are used to trigger adaptation, a successful application would imply that spatial resolution is effectively used to control the influence of the turbulence model and consequently would result in a more accurate simulation, as spatial resolution could be used to homogenize the influence of the LES model over the whole domain. This is especially the case when a time accurate local time-stepping mechanism can be used in combination with spatial adaptation, as this results in an space and time adaptive algorithm. Section 4 shows results from a calculation with an implicit LES model and the corresponding speedup factors compared to a global time stepping calculation.

4 Natural Gas Injection

Due to the sustainable growth of natural gas vehicles in automotive industries, valves and nozzles used for gas injection at medium and high pressure begin do play an increasing role. Being able to describe the noise generation of such devices at high pressure and therefore high Mach numbers is of great importance. Figure 1 shows a typical setup within a vehicle equipped with a natural gas engine. Commercial flow solvers used in industry cannot provide reliable statements or predictions, since their numerical methods are no match for such complex problems. Here, we need to simulate the injection flow with the generation of sound waves as well as the interaction of flow and acoustic with the geometry and its reaction onto the injection flow. Primal goal is a low-noise construction of valves and nozzles already during the design process with the help of numerical simulation tools. In a first simulation step, the noise generation of the injection nozzle (see keyword "gas stream" in Figure 1) itself has to be understood. A fourth order calculation with the unstructured DG research code HALO was set up. The HALO code uses an explicit discontinuous Galerkin method of arbitrary order and is capable of performing an explicit time accurate local time stepping to speed up calculations. As an unstructured code, several element types (e.g. hexahedra, tetrahedra, prisms and pyramids) are implemented and can be used side-by-side. One main advantage of explicit DG schemes is that they are able to scale optimally for a very high number of processors, which makes them suitable for very large computations. An essential element achieving this scalability is a dynamic load balancing, as the computational load strongly varies during the computation due to the local time stepping feature and the automatic hp adaptation. The scheme has already proven its large-scale capabilities with computations on more than 4000 processors on the HLRB II supercomputer. In addition, calculations on up to now 1000 processors were performed to test all code components and to determine parts that do not scale. The calculation itself consists

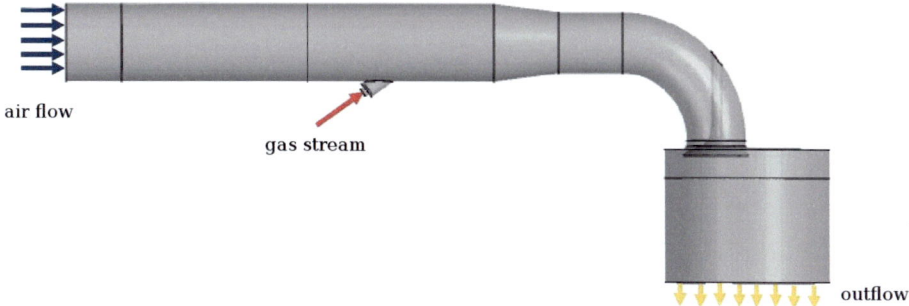

air flow

gas stream

outflow

Fig. 1: Inlet manifold with natural gas injection device.

if of 552,712 hybrid elements with a polynomial degree of $p = 3$, resulting in approx. 11 Mio. DoF, and was run at the HLRB in Munich on 1000 ALTIX II processors. The gas is injected at supersonic speed and the jet expands to ambient condition. At the injector outlet, fine shock structures have to be captured thus high spatial and temporal resolution is needed. Inside the jet, a medium resolution is used which is coarsened towards the outflow boundaries. For the shock capturing, artificial viscosity is applied locally to the troubled grid cells. The smallest time step in this example is $\Delta t_{min} = 1.12 \times 10^{-11} s$, which is due to the small grid size and high velocities as well as the artificial viscosity. The total number of time steps for all grid cells performed for $\Delta T = 1\mu s$ is 1.8×10^8. Having $n_{elems} = 552,712$ elements, the total number of time steps for a global time-stepping would be $n_{elems} \Delta T / \Delta t_{min} = 4.9 \times 10^{10}$. Comparing this two numbers reveal, that the speed up due to the local time stepping compared to the global time stepping variant of the scheme is a factor of ~ 274. Figure 2 shows iso-contours as well as a slice plane of the density of the free stream injection process at $t = 0.8$ to demonstrate the complex flow field, while Figure 3 gives an impression of the grid being used for calculation.

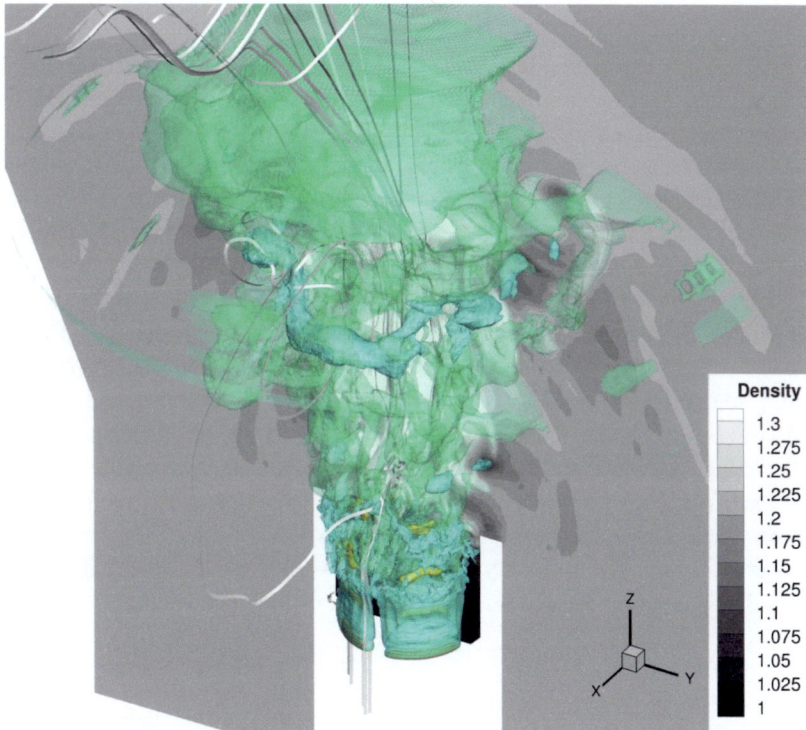

Density
1.3
1.275
1.25
1.225
1.2
1.175
1.15
1.125
1.1
1.075
1.05
1.025
1

Fig. 2: 3D simulation of a supersonic free stream injection nozzle at $t = 0.8$. Density slice plane and iso-contours are shown.

In addition, Figure 4 shows visualization of the density gradients as well as the Mach number distribution at a cutting plane across the injector, demonstrating the multi-scale character of this flow.

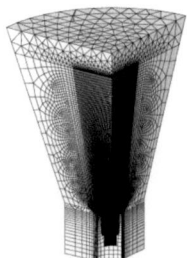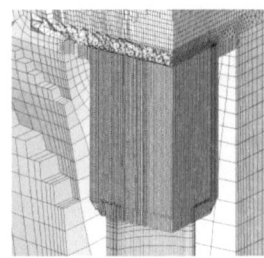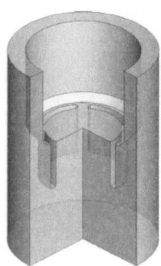

Fig. 3: Unstructured grid and nozzle geometry. One can see the structured grid blocks that couple onto tetrahedra as well as the kidney-shaped ejection nozzles.

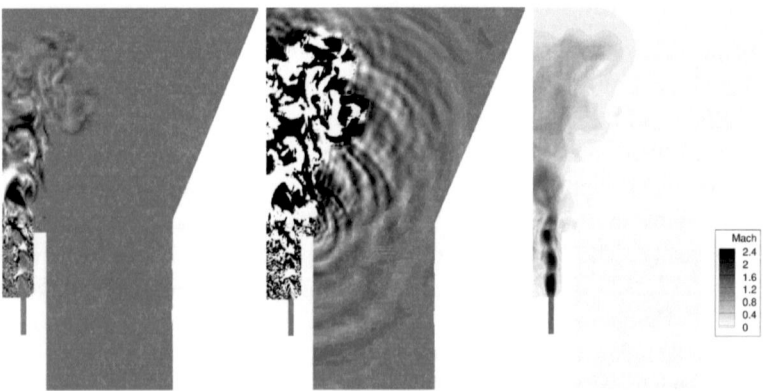

Fig. 4: Diagonal cutting plane: Density gradient inside and outside of the jet and Mach number.

Since this large-scale calculation need a numerical code optimized for several thousands of processor cores, additional effort was put into developing efficient parallelization strategies. In conjunction with the local time stepping mechanism or adaptation mechanisms, this task is challenging, yet has to be handled very careful. Depending on the flow, computationally intense regions may vary in time, leading to load imbalances that can cause a significant drop in efficiency. In an intermediate step, elements are therefore redistributed onto the different processors to adjust their load. The current and predicted computing time of the element hereby acts as a weight, put into the distribution tool ParMETIS that calculates the new element partitioning.

For testing and benchmarking the scaling capabilities of the HALO code, we chose an example where a perfect load balance was to achieve. We were using the so-called manufactured solution technique for the 3D compressible instationary Navier-Stokes equations: When forcing an exact solution, this results in an inhomogeneous source term on the right hand side of the Navier-Stokes equations that is then put into the code. The problem was set up with periodic boundaries so that boundary communication will not differ from the inter-processor communications. The size of the computational problem was then increased exactly the same way as the number of processors for calculation was increased. This way, we kept a constant load in computation as well as in communication between neighboring processors. Table 1 shows the good scale-up efficiency of the code for up to 4080 ALTIX processors with a constant load per processor. The efficiency when running with N processors is calculated as the calculation time on one processor divided by the time needed for a calculation on N processors.

Number of processors	1	1000	2197	4080
Efficiency [%]	-	99.1	97.8	98.8

Tab. 1: Scale-up efficiency of the HALO code.

The massive amount of high order data from the described simulations gives rise to another problem: data analysis and visualization. Since current state-of the art visualization tools can only display data up to second

172

order of accuracy, high order data currently must be sub-sampled to visualize all information. This procedure even tightens the problem of large data amounts and file sizes. Parallel visualization tools can help that spread the data over several processors. With the help of suitable indicators, an a posteriori data reduction is also possible. We are currently investigating another way to handle large data sets without sub-sampling: In cooperation with the Institute of Visualization and Interactive Systems (VIS), Universität Stuttgart, tools are being developed that are able to directly visualize high order information.

5 SOFIA

The Stratospheric Observatory For Infrared Astronomy SOFIA is a 2.5m reflecting telescope housed in an open cavity on board of a Boeing 747SP aircraft as shown in Figure 5. The observatory, a joint project between NASA and DLR, operates in the stratosphere at an altitude above 13km to study the universe in the infrared spectrum [4]. The flow over the open port during the observation flights at transonic Mach numbers presents some challenging

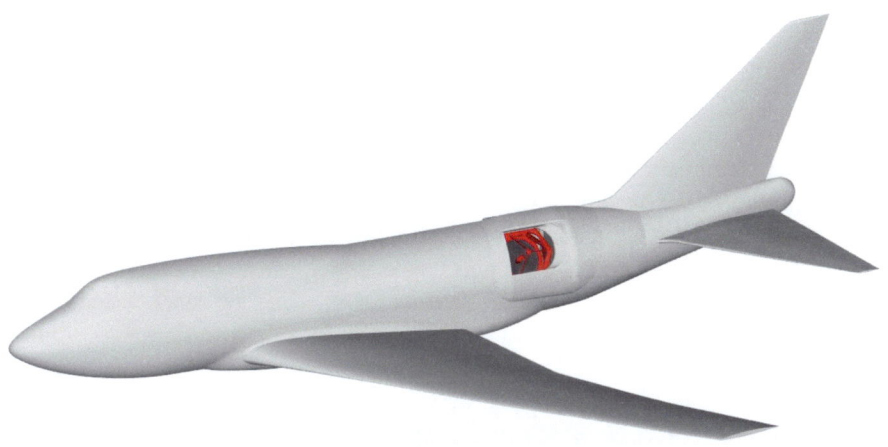

Fig. 5: Half model of SOFIA aircraft with open door.

aerodynamic and aero-acoustic problems. For high Reynolds numbers, the flow over cavities such as the SOFIA telescope port is characterized by unsteady flow phenomena associated with prominent pressure fluctuations caused by amplified acoustic resonances. This phenomenon causes unwanted vibrations of the telescope structure and deteriorates the image stability[6]. To investigate the unsteady pressure fluctuations inside the cavity and to assess the impact of the shear layer and acoustic waves on the telescope CFD simulations are performed with the Finite-Volume RANS-solver TAU that was developed by the Institute of Aerodynamics and Flow Technology of DLR [3]. The cell vertex based code solves the unsteady, compressible, three-dimensional Reynolds-averaged Navier-Stokes equations on unstructured and hybrid grids. For the CFD simulations, the URANS (Unsteady Reynolds Averaged Navier Stokes Equations) and DES (Detached Eddy Simulation) turbulence approach was applied. In URANS simulations turbulence is modeled statistically whereas DES resolves the dominant turbulent structures in space and time. The computational model consists of the left hand side of the SOFIA aircraft (application of symmetry boundary conditions), including the whole cavity, the telescope structure, the fuselage with wings and control surfaces as shown in Figure 5.

First of all, CPU efficient URANS simulations were performed. The URANS grid size for the SOFIA configuration is about 20E+6 cells. For parallelization the grid was decomposed into 510 sub-domains to utilize 510 processors in parallel. A typical CFD computation using the URANS turbulence model consisted of 6000 physical time steps with 180 inner iterations per step. One physical time step consumed about 56s of wallclock time, yielding an overall time consumption of about 48000CPUh for one run. The physical time step was chosen to 16.4ms, resulting in a computational period of 0.1s under wind-tunnel conditions (1.6s under flight conditions). This time interval is necessary for the evaluation of the considered frequency spectrum between 0-200 Hz. Supplementary DES simulations were conducted with the URANS results used to determine the length scale and grid size in the LES zone. The LES zone (highlighted in Figure 6) encloses the shear layer region and is discretized by 15E+06

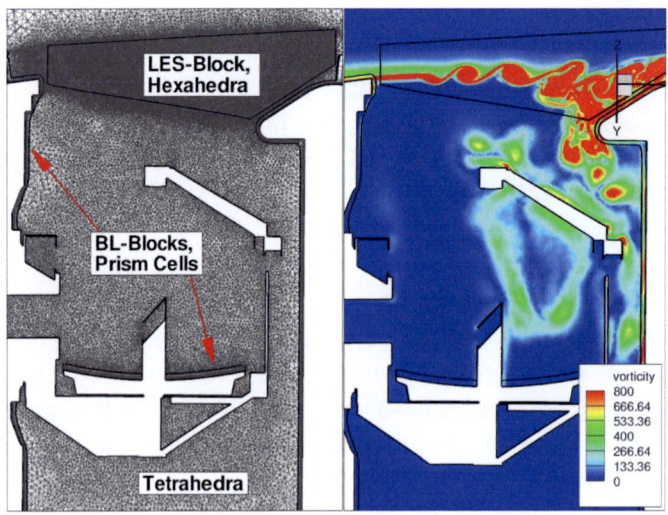

Fig. 6: Cut through the SOFIA cavity: DES grid (left), shear-layer visualization (right).

hexahedra, highly isotropic cells necessary to resolve the shear layer vortices that are visualized on the right of Figure 6. The DES grid size of the baseline configuration consists of 46E+06 cells in total. The central-scheme according to Jameson was used for the spatial discretization in combination with the implicit LUSGS-scheme. Turbulence was modeled by the Spalart Almaras subgrid scale model, whereas the transition from the LES mode is based on the wall distance and the local mesh size (natural DES). The time dependent solution was gained by employing the dual-time stepping scheme with 40 inner iterations per physical time step. About 8500 physical time steps were run to initialize the computation until transient pressure fluctuations disappeared. After this initial period approximately 7000 time steps were computed with a physical time step size of 1E-04. The DES simulation was performed on 1020 processors on the HLRB II supercomputer. The computational cost for one DES run was about 65000CPUh. For the SOFIA configuration the TAU solver has proven good large scale capabilities. By using multiple of 1020 processors further speed up of the computation can be achieved as shown in Figure 7.

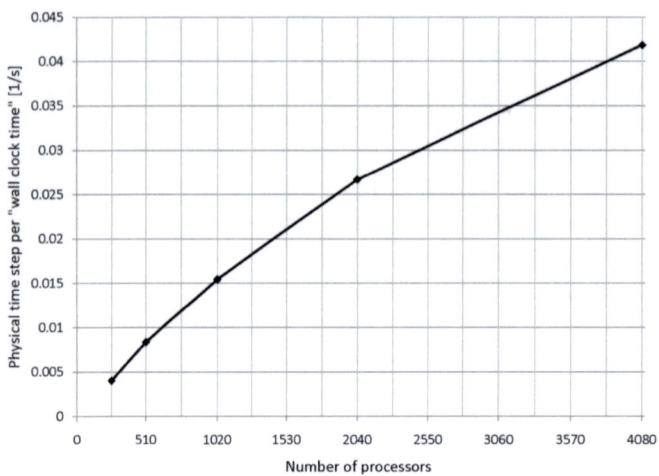

Fig. 7: Scalability of the TAU solver on the HLRB II supercomputer

After an assessment of the spatial and temporal discretization error the objective of the CFD simulations is to improve the telescope's performance by mitigating the amplitudes and changing the characteristic frequencies of the pressure fluctuations inside the cavity. This can be reached by using passive flow control device upstream and downstream the cavity port. One approach is to install a porous fence upstream the cavity leading edge [5].

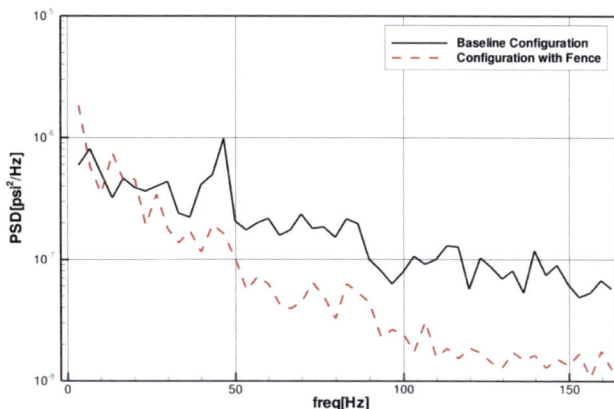

Fig. 8: Simulated PSD average over all telescope pressure sensors with and without a fence

Figure 8 shows the frequency spectrum calculated with DES of all telescope pressure sensors under Baseline conditions (Mach number = 0.85, altitude = 41kft) with (red dashed line) and without fence (black line). With a fence installed the mitigation of the acoustic energy over 20Hz is significant.

6 Conclusion

We have briefly presented HPC activities at the Institute of Aerodynamics and Gas Dynamics, Universität Stuttgart, towards the simulation of complex large-scale turbulent flows. Since today's computational infrastructure is still not capable of directly simulate these problems, suitable numerical schemes, turbulence models and optimization strategies are being developed. With highly flexible parallel codes at hand, even highly instationary problems with very complex geometries like the natural gas injection nozzle or the SOFIA Boeing 747SP cavity can be simulated.

7 Acknowledgments

The research presented in this paper was supported in parts by Deutsche Forschungsgemeinschaft (DFG), amongst others within the Schwerpunktprogramm 1276: MetStroem, the Bundesministerium für Bildung und Forschung (BMBF, Federal Ministry for Education and Research) in the HPC Software Initiative Projekt "STEDG: Hocheffiziente und skalierbare Software für die Simulation turbulenter Strömungen in komplexen Geometrien". The SOFIA project is funded on behalf of the Deutsches Zentrum für Luft- und Raumfahrt e.V. (DLR, German Aerospace Centre, grant: 50OK0901) by the Federal Ministry of Economics and Technology based on legislation by the German Parliament, the state of Baden-Württemberg and the Universität Stuttgart.

References

[1] G. Gassner, M. Dumbser, F. Hindenlang, and C.-D. Munz. Explicit one-step time discretizations for discontinuous galerkin and finite volume schemes based on local predictors. *Submitted to J. Comput. Phys.*, 2010.

[2] G. Gassner, F. Lörcher, and C.-D. Munz. A discontinuous Galerkin scheme based on a space-time expansion. II. Viscous flow equations in multi dimensions. *J. Sci. Comp.*, 34(3):260–286, 2008.

[3] T. Gerhold. Numerical Flow Simulation for Aircraft Design, chap. Overview of the Hybrid RANS Code TAU. *Springer-Verlag*, pages 81–92, 2005.

[4] H. Kaercher, A. Krabbe, and T. Wegmann. The SOFIA Telescope: Preparing for Early Science. In *SPIE's Conference on Astronomical Instrumentation*, Marseille, France, June 2008.

[5] S. Schmid, T. Lutz, and E. Krämer. Control of the unsteady flow inside the SOFIA telescope cavity by means of a porous fence. In *Third Symposium on Hybrid RANS-LES Methods*, Gdansk, Poland, June 2009.

[6] S. Schmid, T. Lutz, E. Krämer, and T. Kühn. Passive Control of the Flow Around the Stratospheric Observatory For Infrared Astronomy. *AIAA Paper*, pages 2008–6717, 2010.